© KELLY KREGLOW SPITZNAGEL

ERIC SPITZNAGEL writes for magazines such as *Playboy*, *Esquire*, *Vanity Fair*, *Rolling Stone*, *Men's Health*, *Billboard*, *The Believer*, and the *New York Times Magazine*, among many others. He's the author of six books, one of which was translated into German and features a cat on the cover for no apparent reason. He lives in Chicago with his wife and son, the latter of whom wants to be a "mad scientist" when he grows up. (That's now in print, so the author intends to hold him to it.)

Praise for *Old Records Never Die*

"I can't remember when a book had me get out my black pen and underline so many wonderful things. Maybe never. Loss and laughter and all those denizens of sonic ghost town record stores willing but often unable to make us all whole again. Something on every page to stoke the geek heart with sad recognition and hope."

—Marc Spitz, author of *Poseur: A Memoir of Downtown New York City in the '90s*

"Spitznagel's quest for the actual records of his youth could have been a gimmick. Instead it's a touching exploration of loss: of opportunities, of loved ones, of the ability to even remotely discern what's hip. Hilarious and heartfelt, this is a book for anyone who has ever spent entire years of their lives haunting record stores, dissecting the merits of *Doolittle*, and studying liner notes with the intense focus of a Talmudic scholar."

—Jancee Dunn, author of *But Enough About Me*

"A funny and heartfelt memoir about music collecting that gives birth to a new branch of social science: Gen-X archaeology."

—Neal Pollack, author of *Alternadad*

"Eric Spitznagel is the only music nerd in the world who's not entirely insufferable. *Old Records Never Die* will make you wish you were his roommate."

—Martha Plimpton, actress

"To say *Old Records Never Die* is a book about music is to say *On the Road* is a book about cars. Really, Eric Spitznagel's energetic and endlessly engaging memoir is a book about the ways we seek to discover and recover our essential selves. Music lovers will love this book; unrepentant nostalgics, like myself, can expect to be absolutely riveted."

—Davy Rothbart, creator of *FOUND* magazine
and author of *My Heart Is an Idiot*

"Eric Spitznagel is just like Captain Ahab, if Ahab were chasing Billy Joel albums instead of a white whale. As he recounts in this very funny book, Spitznagel found way more than he bargained for. And just like Ahab, he dies in the end. (Spoiler alert.)"

—Rob Tannenbaum, coauthor of *I Want My MTV: The Uncensored Story of the Music Video Revolution*

Old Records Never Die

One Man's Quest for His Vinyl and His Past

Eric Spitznagel

A PLUME BOOK

PLUME
An imprint of Penguin Random House LLC
375 Hudson Street
New York, New York 10014

P REGISTERED TRADEMARK—MARCA REGISTRADA

All photos courtesy of the author.

LIBRARY OF CONGRESS CATALOGING-IN-PUBLICATION DATA

Names: Spitznagel, Eric, author. | Tweedy, Jeff, 1967– writer of foreword.
Title: Old records never die : one man's quest for his vinyl and his past /
Eric Spitznagel.
Description: New York, New York : Plume, [2016] | 2016
Identifiers: LCCN 2015038989| ISBN 9780142181614 (trade pbk.) |
ISBN 9780698168046 (ebook)
Subjects: LCSH: Spitznagel, Eric. | Collectors and collecting—United
States—Biography. | Sound recordings—Collectors and collecting.
Classification: LCC ML429.S66 A3 2016 | DDC 780.26/6—dc23 LC record available
at http://lccn.loc.gov/2015038989

Printed in the United States of America
10 9 8 7 6 5 4 3 2 1

For Kelly and Charlie,
the beginning and ending of everything

Why the Premise for This Book Might Not Be Entirely Insane

A FOREWORD OF SORTS

by Jeff Tweedy

The first records I remember buying with my own money were forty-fives. It was 1974 or thereabouts, and I was maybe seven at the time. My sister was home from college, and she took me to a Record Bar. I bought "Dream On" by Aerosmith and "Magic" by Pilot, because I'd heard both songs on the radio and I thought they were miraculous.

The first LP I bought with my own money—which, admittedly, is kind of a ridiculous thing to say because I wasn't pulling in an income, and whatever money I had was just what I'd managed to scrape together from allowances or cash stuffed into birthday cards—anyway, I'd gone down to visit my sister in Tucson, Arizona, where she was living at the time. We took a day trip to Mexico, and I bought a Spanish version of *Parallel Lines* by Blondie. The songs were in English, but the sleeve was written entirely in Spanish. And it was a very, very, very cheap pressing. Like a flimsy, fifty-gram vinyl. It was almost see-through. It was the same quality as those cutout records that used to come in cereal boxes.

The forty-fives and the Mexican *Parallel Lines*, they were my vinyl training wheels. My collection really started thanks to my brother, Steve.

I'm the youngest in my family by ten years. Steve came home from college when I was very young, probably around eight or nine. He caught me filling out a Columbia House Record Club mail order form. He snatched it out of my hands and said, "What are you doing? Are you serious with this?"

"What?" I said. "They're offering twelve records for a penny. Where else am I going to get twelve records for that kind of money? Twelve records."

"Fine, you want records?" he said. "You can have my records."

He just gave them to me. An entire crate. And it was the weirdest collection of records. He had very eclectic taste, stuff like Harry Chapin and Aphrodite's Child and Kraftwerk and a bunch of Zappa records.

My sister heard about the Columbia House incident, and she gave me some of her records. Her vinyl hand-me-downs included a lot of the Monkees, Herman's Hermits, and the Beatles—it was an education in pop music.

All of a sudden, I went from having nothing to having this amazing, diverse, wide-ranging collection. I immersed myself in it. There was never a record where I was like, "That looks weird. Let's skip it." Everything seemed worthwhile, because somebody had bothered to cut it onto a piece of vinyl and sell it.

As a naive young kid, I was so trusting of the notion that if somebody had found this music important enough to make a record of it, then obviously it had value. If it exists, it has value.

I still have all of my records. All of them. The forty-fives and the Blondie Mexico import and the records from my brother. I know exactly which ones belonged to my brother, because they still have a little white sticker on the sleeves with his initials, SKT.

Even the records that don't have any physical markings, I could tell you which ones are mine, just from the pops and scratches. I could tell you exactly where they are. On my copy of the Clash's *London Calling*, there's a skip during "Death or Glory." To this day, it sounds weird to me when I hear it without the skip. It's not as good. I don't find it as appealing.

If someone offered me a replacement, something that's been remastered and remixed with a fuller, crisper sound quality, I don't think I'd take it. I'd rather keep my old vinyl. Because I don't need better sound from *London Calling*. What I need is that skip. When I hear it without the skip, it breaks the spell for me. I'm taken out of it.

Also, the record represents something meaningful to me. Not just the songs, but the physical object that contains those songs. It's an album that was hard-won, that has a backstory to it.

Growing up, there was a Target in a nearby town that my mom would shop at occasionally. I'd go with her and just hang out and look at the records while she finished. They had a copy of *London Calling* for sale, and I desperately wanted it. But it had a sticker on the front that read PARENTAL ADVISORY, EXPLICIT CONTENT, STRONG LANGUAGE or something to that effect. This was before Tipper Gore and the Parents Music Resource Center, so I don't know if it was the label or the store that put it on there. Either way, I had to get it off. There was no way my mom was buying me a record with an EXPLICIT CONTENT warning on the front.

I tried scratching off the sticker with my fingernail. It didn't go so well. I got only about a third of it off. And then we had to leave. So I hid the record in a different section and vowed to come back for it.

We returned two weeks later, and *London Calling* was still there. I went to work on it, scratching at the sticker like a cat on a new couch. This time, I got another third of it off before we had to go. Those stickers were surprisingly resilient.

A month or two passed before we returned, and I was convinced the *London Calling* would be gone. But it was still there, and this time I finally got all of the sticker off. I took the record up to my mom and asked her, as casually as I could manage, "Hey, can I get this?"

She glanced at it, shrugged, and said, "Sure, fine."

I threw it in the cart, amazed that I was somehow getting away with the perfect crime.

I still have that record. You can distinctly see my fingernail imprints on the jacket, from where I dug into the shrink-wrap, attacking the EXPLICIT CONTENT sticker. I like that those gouges are still there. It's evidence that this record didn't come easy. I was like Tim Robbins's character in *The Shawshank Redemption*, slowly digging his way to freedom with a rock hammer, chipping away at the wall, hoping the warden didn't notice.

It reminds me of what it felt like to be amazed that I was able to hear the Clash. This wasn't music you bought and listened to a few times and then put back on the shelf and forgot about. It was contraband. Every time I put *London Calling* on a turntable, there was a palpable sense of danger. I was pretty sure a SWAT team would kick down my bedroom door and take it away.

I still have some records from when I worked at Euclid Records in Saint Louis. I know exactly which ones came from Euclid, because they're all marked with a *Z*. When somebody brought in a big pile of records to sell, you had to scope out the ones you wanted. The way it would work, you'd give them fifty dollars for a stack of maybe one hundred records. And then you would put a sticker on each record, that had a code for how much we paid for it, so the owner could go through the records later and price each one.

When you were buying records and there was something in there you wanted, you had to make sure you didn't overpay for anything. There was a code for free, which was *Z*. If you raised the price for every other record by a dime, you could make the ones you wanted be a Z pretty easily.

Any Z record, you could just take. Even if it was out in the bins. But you had to game the system a little bit. I'm not proud of it, but I definitely have a few records in my collection with a Z sticker on them that probably weren't Zs.

Have you heard *The Flowers of Romance* by Public Image Ltd? It came out in 1981, when I was fourteen years old. I put it on a list of records that I wanted for Christmas from my parents. I never expected to get it. But somehow, unbelievably, they actually found it and bought it for me. When I opened it up on Christmas morning, I was gobsmacked. It was like *London Calling* all over again, but this time, it'd been too easy.

And then my dad said, "Why don't you put on one of your new Christmas records and play it for everybody?"

We had a house full of family. Aunts, uncles, grandparents, cousins—they were all there. Even a few neighbors had stopped by. As they waited, I tore the shrink-wrap off my *Flowers of Romance*, brought it over to the family turntable, and dropped the needle onto the first song.

If you're unfamiliar with the album, the first song is called "Four Enclosed Walls." And I played it at full blast in my family's living room on Christmas morning 1981. It's a really spooky song, with decidedly non-Christmasy lyrics like "Doom sits in gloom in his room" and "Destroy the infidel" and "Joan of Arc was a sorcerer."

I still have that record. And there's still a scratch across the first song, from when it was yanked from the family turntable with extreme prejudice. I believe my father's exact words were, "What in the hell is that? Boy, are you trying to kill me? Why would anybody listen to that! What is going on?!"

I have every record that ever meant anything to me. I never sold any of them. When CDs came out, I wasn't that impressed. The sound quality was kind of iffy. Any CDs I bought were more for the convenience than anything else. I liked that they were portable, that I could put them in a Walkman or a boom box and take them places. And when digital music came along, sure, I'm not an idiot. I listen to music on an iPod. But it's never been a replacement for vinyl.

So I feel a little weird writing this introduction to Eric's book. Because the thing he did, which you're going to read about in the following pages, I don't really understand it.

I don't want to spoil this for you, but seriously, something is wrong with this guy.

Eric and I have had a few discussions, trying to figure out what I should write. 'Cause I honestly don't know what to say, other than "Why would you do that? That's such an insane thing to do. Stop doing things that are insane."

I'm not even talking about losing your records. I'm talking about trying to find the records you've lost. Don't get me wrong, I think it's a completely noble effort to try and track down all the records from your youth that you somehow let slip away. But if I was in his shoes, I would probably . . . I don't know . . . not do that thing. I would argue for letting go and moving forward and making new memories.

So he asked me, as a sort of experiment, to put myself in a hypothetical. My house is burning. After I save my wife and kids, what records from my collection do I save? Do I go after *London Calling*, with the "Death or Glory" skip and my prepubescent claw marks across the sleeve? Do I save any of the records covered with *Z*s or *SKT*s? Do I grab *The Flowers of Romance* that still has the skid marks of my father's outrage?

I thought about this. And my first response was, probably none of it. I'm pretty pragmatic about things. I'm sure, in the moment, in the trauma of the situation, it would occur to me that there's something significant being lost that I'll never be able to retrieve. When I think of the rarest records that I own, I'd be sad at the loss. But would they really be irreplaceable?

But then, as I'm trying to imagine this scenario, I think of a Tyrannosaurus Rex record. *A Beard of Stars*. And I'm not sure why. It's one of the records that my brother gave to me. For reasons I couldn't begin to explain, it's important to me.

This record, this one record, has been passed down through several generations. I got it from my brother, and I listened to it incessantly. And now my sons, Spencer and Sam, have become fond of it. From an early age, they were listening to it. I don't know what it is about that record that resonates with Tweedys. It's not like it's an especially important or popular record in Marc Bolan's body of work. But it means something to us.

Maybe it's the songs. Or maybe it's because I can't think about that record without imagining the SKT sticker on the front—proof that it once belonged to my brother and had a history long before I ever discovered it. That sticker, inexplicably, makes it valuable.

Also, why the hell is my house on fire? Why can't I save my guitars? Everything about this is starting to sound fishy.

Old Records
Never Die

Preface

Think about the first song that meant something to you.

I don't mean a song that just had a hummable melody and you knew all the lyrics because it was on the radio incessantly, and you were like "I love this song," but you meant it like people mean "I love ice cream," which is just something people feel about ice cream when they're in the midst of eating it. But ice cream isn't something you stay up late thinking about. You don't argue about ice cream's deeper meanings with your friends. You don't obsess over ice cream because you feel like ice cream understands you in ways you didn't think it was possible to be understood. Nobody says, "This is the ice cream I want eaten at my funeral."

I'm talking about the kind of music that sinks into your pores, that enters your bloodstream and becomes part of your DNA. It's the song that stuck by you when you felt abandoned or misunderstood, and you're pretty convinced it was written specifically for you. When you hear people say "I love that song too," you just smirk. What do they know of love? Their relationship with the song is a one-night stand—a summer fling at best—but you and this song, you're soul mates.

When people challenge you with that hypothetical poser "If you could bring only one album to a desert island, what would it be?" you always mention a certain record, because it's got that song you're pretty sure you could spend the rest of your earthly time listening to on a constant loop, as you collected firewood and hunted for animals with crudely made spears and went slowly insane. That song, that particular arrangement of notes and words, would be all the comfort you needed as you died alone on a beach. But you don't say that. You pretend it's a difficult question, and it's the first time you're considering it, and you're like, "Hmm, let me think about that." You try to be all cool and casual about it, pretending that your feelings about the song aren't a little bit inappropriate, and hearing it doesn't automatically make you feel less alone in the universe, and if it didn't exist, something about you would be different on a molecular level.

Think about that song right now. Close your eyes and let those familiar chords drift through your head.

Is it there? Can you hear it?

What does it smell like?

Now, for some of you, what I just asked will make no sense. You think I'm talking gibberish. And that's okay. You're from a generation that knows about music only as a digital thing. It isn't something that can be touched or held. It's not a physical thing. It's in the ether. It's on a screen and needs to be bitstream compliant. It's all about megabytes and gigabytes and compression algorithms. It has to be downloaded or streamed or kept in a cloud.

Not so long ago, there were two audio formats: "That sounds good" and "Nope, sounds like an Alvin and the Chipmunks record." That was all you needed to know. Now, when you get new music, you have to ask, "Am I going to need a LAME MP3 encoder to hear this?" Or "Does it have enough kilobits? Just 128? I accept nothing less than 640!"

MP3s, or M4As or WMAs or AIFFs or OGGs, whatever your digital format of choice, don't smell like anything. The device that plays your music—your iPod or laptop or whatever—that may smell like something. But it'll smell like that same thing whether you're listening to Foo Fighters or Jay Z. It's not unique to a particular song or album.

Records are something different. They're physical objects. Big, bulky, inconvenient, easily damaged objects. Vinyl is like skin that changes, in good and bad ways, over a lifetime. Skin gets damaged, intentionally or by accident—maybe it gets burned, or tattooed, or scarred—but it always retains some of its original character. It's the same skin—it's just weathered some life.

Some of these records—the good ones anyway—have a distinct smell. They might smell like the beach. Or your dad's cologne. Or when you bought Elton John's *Greatest Hits* for two dollars in 1977 at a Lions Club's garage sale in a recently renovated building that used to be a cherry processing plant, and even a decade after the fact, the record smells like cherries.

Here's another one. Billy Joel's *The Stranger*. I can't even look at the album cover without smelling Calvin Klein's Obsession.

During the mideighties, my grandmother was diagnosed with gallbladder cancer. My parents flew out to New York for the surgery, and my brother and I were sent to stay with family friends. The family that took me in had a daughter, Debbie, who was about two years older than me, and almost unfairly attractive. A woman who looked like her in a Whitesnake video was one thing, but existing in the world, walking past you in the school hallway, a reminder of how your fantasies can be right in front of you but also a million miles away, was just not cool.

I remember being dropped off at her house and her parents taking me to her room, saying, "This is where you'll be sleeping." And

I sat there, in her room, totally mesmerized. Because Jesus Christ, I was in her bedroom. The place where she slept, maybe in her underwear.

I went immediately to her records, because I just had to know—what does a beautiful woman listen to while sitting around her room in sexy underwear? The first record I pulled out was Billy Joel's *The Stranger*. I'd never heard of it before, but the cover was amazing. Joel is sitting on a bed, wearing a full suit and no shoes, gazing down at a white theater mask next to him, with a pair of boxing gloves on the wall. Cringingly pretentious, but for a thirteen-year-old boy who still owned all of his original *Star Wars* action figures, Billy Joel seemed supercomplex and deep.

I made a mental note to wear more suits and buy some boxing gloves.

The record had its own unmistakable scent. I wasn't able to put a name to it until decades later, when I was on a blind date and the girl was wearing Obsession. While we were making out, I took a deep breath of her neck and said, "You smell like Billy Joel's *The Stranger*." (It didn't end well.)

I'm not sure how long I was sitting there, smelling Debbie's *The Stranger*, when the door burst open and Debbie came charging in.

"Hey," she said, beaming. "You're here."

"Yep," I said, staring at her like she was a black bear that'd just wandered into my campsite.

She nodded, inching closer to me. "This is going to be so cool," she said.

I had no idea what she meant by that. I remember thinking, "Cool how? What's so cool about it? And why's she standing so close to me? Is she waiting for me to do something? Maybe kiss her? Oh Jesus, should I kiss her? Of course I should kiss her! There couldn't be a more obvious signal. I'm totally going to kiss her."

I didn't kiss her. And I never really talked to her again during the entire week I was at her house. It's possible I missed my opportunity. It's even more possible that she'd confused me with another boy and was too polite to say anything when she got close enough to realize it.

I eventually bought my own copy of *The Stranger*. But it wasn't the same. The songs sounded generally similar, but something fundamental was missing. It didn't have that hot-girl smell.

There's another record whose unmistakable odor has become a sort of personal mythology for me. The Replacements' *Let It Be*, first released in 1984, first purchased by me in 1986, and my copy eventually sold in 1999. For the vast majority of its existence, the record sleeve was used for more than just a protective envelope for the vinyl. It also served as a sort of safe-deposit box for my stash of marijuana.

It's amazing I ever thought I was getting away with anything. I think my thought process was, if somebody—my parents, DEA agents doing random searches of teenage bedrooms—got the crazy idea that kids were hiding marijuana in record sleeves, they'd look at titles a little more obvious. They'd probably check my Cypress Hill. Or my Grateful Dead. Or my Bob Marley *Legend*, which I kept in my closet in clear sight specifically as a weed red herring. It'd never cross their minds to look elsewhere. They'd be, "Oh, don't bother looking for his stash in any of those 'Mats records. They were into heavy drinking, not weed." Because obviously, both the DEA and my mother would have done extensive research on the intoxicants of choice of my favorite artists.

I was never busted, and not because *Let It Be* was such a clever disguise. Obviously nobody cared that I was smoking marijuana.

I haven't stopped listening to those songs. I've owned the album on several formats. I've had three CDs of *Let It Be*, and numerous MP3s of the songs, which I've synced to too many iPods, iPads, nanos, minis, and shuffles. The notes are the same, the voice sounds familiar, but it doesn't feel like my music anymore. For one thing, the smell is gone. And the scratches, well, there aren't any scratches. Which isn't something you'd think you'd miss. But I miss those scratches more than anything.

The scratches matter. They're not just an imperfection. Something meaningful happens when those scratches are made. Something is etched into the grooves. Something important has become a part of your permanent record. And the song is your witness. It's borne witness to your milestones; it held your proverbial hand when life got shitty, or gave you a danceable beat when there was something to celebrate. The song, yes, but more significantly, the physical object that was with you, that you touched and held on to and watched spin around and around as you listened to it make the music that felt like it might be the only thing keeping you alive. It wasn't just the messenger. It was your companion. It was an accomplice.

If you saw it again—that record, that specific record—would you recognize it?

Would you know it was yours?

If it was one of my records, I'd like to think I'd recognize it. Even if it's been sitting in a damp basement, or stored under a leaky air conditioner. I know where all the scratches are; I put them there myself. I know every pop and hiss. I'd recognize my records like I'd recognize my own flesh and blood.

During the first few months after my dad died in 1999, I had this recurring fantasy that he'd faked his so-called fatal heart attack. Maybe he did it so he could skip town to evade back taxes, or run away with his mistress. Whatever it was, the story was comforting. It was my life raft during his funeral: the thing that kept my head above water so I didn't suffocate on grief. I imagined him somewhere in New Orleans, with a bad dye job and a mustache, living a gypsy lifestyle as he moves from motel to motel with his Brazilian lover.

Sometimes, when I'm daydreaming, I have this vision of myself wandering through a Mardi Gras parade, and I see him in the distance, with a handlebar mustache and a safari hat, sucking back the last of his hurricane before kissing the neck of . . . what's her name? Rosario? Yolanda? And then our eyes meet, and I know that he knows that I know it's him, and he smiles at me in that weak way that says, "I'm sorry, son. I'm sorry that I wasn't there for you over these past fifteen years, and I'm sorry that I missed so much of your life. I love you more than you can begin to imagine, and I wish I didn't have to leave, but *la vida es corta*! You'll understand someday."

And then *poof*, he's gone, disappeared into the crowd. I chase after him, pushing people out of the way, stumbling over revelers in masks and slipping through guys on stilts and knocking drinks out of the hands of tourists and running and running and running, the sound of joyous laughter and music and celebration all around me. I know I'm never going to find him, but somehow it's okay, just knowing he's still out there, and he's still breathing the same humid air that I am, and at least now he realizes that he never fooled me with his silly "he had a heart attack at sixty" ruse.

Just like I'd recognize my father's eyes in a Mardi Gras parade, I'd recognize my copy of the Replacements' *Let It Be*. The one that was with me through puberty and too many girlfriends and years of stomach-clenching loneliness and an ego that sometimes felt like it was held together with Scotch tape and sloppy punk riffs. If I saw it again, I'd know it was mine. And not just because it smells like weed.

Of course I'd recognize it. Assuming I was ever in the same room with it again, it'd be impossible for me not to recognize it. But that's not the hard part. The hard part would be finding it, since I sold the record when I was still in my twenties. A lot has happened in my life since I let it go. I got married, and had my first meaningful employment, and buried my father, and almost got divorced, and became a parent. It would be laughably impossible, but maybe, if you looked long enough, and hard enough, and refused to give up, maybe you do find it again. Maybe you find your dead dad in the Mardi Gras parade. The thing you thought was lost forever, that part of yourself that just disappeared, that vanished when you weren't paying attention, maybe you chased it down and kept running until you cornered it in a back alley and you managed to get it back.

But then what?

One

Can I help you?"

A female employee with blond hair and pink highlights had noticed me loitering near the register, obviously wanting to ask something. She looked exactly like you'd want a woman who works at a record store to look: punk but not so punk you think she might cut you, a Cramps T-shirt and lip ring, eating grapes.

She'd asked a pretty innocuous question—one I've been asked thousands of times by a thousand different store employees—and it's not a complicated question. It's not like a troll is asking you to answer a riddle before you can cross his bridge. It usually requires nothing more than a "No, thanks, I'm fine." But my mouth muscles weren't cooperating. She smiled at me, waiting for me to get my bearings. This was obviously not unfamiliar territory for her.

I was at Reckless Records, in Chicago's Lakeview neighborhood—just a few blocks from my first apartment. I hadn't been inside this store in almost two decades. And it felt, well, pretty much the same as the last time I was here. The store's soundtrack, as always, was something obscure and amazing, designed to make you feel musically illiterate. (All I know is that there were trumpets, and the vocalist sounded like Iggy Pop trying to do a Bono-circa-*Rattle-and-Hum* impression.) Sullen, unshaven men guarded their sections as they flipped through records like old-timey accountants tapping calculators.

Every other record store I'd frequented during the eighties and nineties was, as far as I could tell, extinct. The legendary Rose Records in the Loop, with an escalator to the second floor where they kept all the on-sale stuff (and an elevator to get out), is now a barber school. The church-like Evil Clown on Halsted, once located on the same block as an S&M leather shop and a hole-in-the-wall coffee place owned by a sweet old man whose son was eaten by Jeffrey Dahmer, is gone too. It's been replaced with something called Batteries Not Included, a "bachelorette party store." The place at Clark and Belmont, whose name I don't remember anymore, is now a Dandy Dollar.

Reckless was it. And it had moved across the street from its original location. Which was weirdly upsetting. It was like coming home from college and finding that your parents had moved your bedroom into the dining room. You still had a place to sleep, and it might even be an improvement, with more square footage and better access to things like food and TV. But it wasn't what you remembered. All the important stuff that had happened to you, it happened in that other room.

I have only one real memory of Reckless. But it was one of those "this is where I became a man" stories. Not the milestones that seemed pretty awful at the time. Like when you lost your virginity, which involved a lot of fumbling and bad decisions and neither of you enjoyed it very much but thank god that was done. The smaller but no-less-significant milestones. Like the first time a girl started flirting with you hard at a high school party, and you were like,

"Whoa, what's happening here?" And at some point, when nobody's looking, she leans in close and whispers in your ear, "I want you inside me." Which is kind of hilarious and adorable when it comes from a sixteen-year-old, because there's no way in hell that's ever happening. She might as well have said, "I want to take a space shuttle to Mars with you and build a colony and our children will build a new human civilization." It has as much a chance of happening as the "being inside her" idea. But you both like the way it sounds—it feels like the most erotic thing that has ever happened to anybody in the history of human beings with genitals. You go home with the electric crackle of being desired, and you don't sleep a wink that night, you just stay up, thinking about the bizarre idea that somebody in the world wants to see you naked.

My main memory from Reckless happened in 1993. I was flipping through the bins and happened to be near a group of guys who were all several years older than me. They had rumpled T-shirts with the names of bands I'd never heard of, complicated tattoos on their forearms, and one guy had a spiderweb covering his neck.

They were talking about Nirvana, and how Cobain had so obviously stolen his best ideas from the Pixies, and how even though Cobain had admitted as much, it was still musical robbery, and Nirvana was still the biggest band in the universe and the mainstream still ignored the Pixies, which just goes to prove that the vast majority of the music-listening public are idiots.

"It's like they've got Mozart conducting right across the street, but they'd rather listen to Salieri," one of them sneered. He was the obvious leader of the group. He had a shaved head, stretched-out earlobes pierced with plates the size of mayonnaise jar lids, and smelled like Marlboro Reds. I let out a muffled laugh, just to let them know that I was listening and agreed.

"Yeah," another guy guffawed. "It's like somebody who thinks

Stone Temple Pilots is an amazing band, and you're like, 'Dude, have you not heard of Pearl Jam?' "

The cool bald guy with the jar lids didn't laugh. He narrowed his eyes and scowled at him.

Without looking up from the records, I did a growling parody of Eddie Vedder's baritone. The tune was "Daughter" but I invented my own lyrics. "Don't call me music," I belted. "Not meant to!"

But the cool bald guy smiled. He chuckled even. And then he summoned me over. "Hey, kid," he said. "I got something you should check out."

I swear, it felt like my balls crawled up inside my body cavity. I was elated and scared shitless all at once.

He brought me over to the checkout table and reached over to a box of new arrivals. He pulled out a Pixies import called *Into the White*. It was a collection of BBC recordings, nothing I'd ever heard of, or would ever consider buying. Certainly not with a $50 price tag. But the cool bald guy with the trash can earlobes had deemed me worthy. What was I gonna say: "My grandma just loaned me $50 to help pay my rent; I really shouldn't be spending it on Pixies songs I already own that have just been rerecorded for a British radio show"?

I'm not sure what I was expecting to happen after this transaction. Actually, no, that's not true. I knew what I hoped would happen. I hoped he'd invite me back to his apartment, where all the cool kids would be hanging out, doing drugs from elaborate contraptions that looked like hookahs, having friendly debates about their favorite *Ben Is Dead* issues or *Simpsons* episodes or Hal Hartley movies. And then we'd listen to the Pixies, and he'd blare "Debaser" from big black speakers hung from ceiling chains, and I'd nod with a wry smile, because I appreciated the song's subversiveness, and it didn't in any way scare the living bejesus out of me and make me want to drive home to my parents' house in the suburbs and hide in my old bedroom and listen to Billy Joel's "Keeping the Faith" over and over.

None of that happened. After I bought the Pixies import, I went back to the Chicago apartment I shared with four roommates, slipped it into the wood crate with all the other overpriced imports and bootlegs I didn't listen to, and immediately called my grandma to ask for another fifty dollars.

Here I was, twenty years later, just as insecure and hungry for approval. The girl with the Cramps shirt kept popping grapes into her mouth.

It was hard for me not to stare. I missed this as much as my record collection. I missed the experience of being in a place like this, a place that sold objects containing music, which provided reasons—perfectly justifiable reasons—for you to talk with hot women, their hair streaked with pink highlights and their mouths brandishing lip rings, who know fascinating minutiae about music I never knew existed but that would soon change my life.

"Are you looking for anything in particular?" she asked.

I guess the answer is I want the old thrill back, the adrenaline rush of hunting for music the way it's supposed to be hunted for.

I'm an iTunes customer, and it's great. It makes everything easier. When I find out that one of my favorite bands is putting out a new album, I just give iTunes my credit card information, and on the release date they automatically download it onto my iPod, like a spouse surprising you with breakfast in bed on your birthday. Except it's not a surprise at all, because it's your birthday, and you kinda knew it was coming, and later that night you'll be having sex that's mildly dirty, not because it's spontaneous and creative but because that's the mutual understanding that comes with an enduring relationship, whether it's between two mostly loveless life companions or a customer and his or her iTunes account. The seduction is gone, but you'll get what you want if you just wait long enough.

Music shouldn't feel like date-night sex. It should be dangerous. Legitimately dangerous. And it used to be. There was a time when the mere act of owning a record could put you in physical peril.

When I was a teenager, I was thrilled by rumors that if you played "Stairway to Heaven" backward, you could hear satanic messages. I never tried it, but I had friends who knew guys who knew guys who had purportedly figured out a way to play a record backward, and they swore you could hear a voice muttering, "Here's to my sweet Satan," or "I sing because I live with Satan," or some variation on how Satan is his roommate and they have hootenannies.

This knowledge made the record even more valuable to me. Because it wasn't just the song. The song was fine, but when I heard it on the radio, it didn't seem especially frightening or dangerous. But the record, well, that was like owning an Aleister Crowley book. That actual document, the physical object more than the song, was the terrifying thing. Because you could only unlock the Satan shout-out by manipulating the record in a certain way. It didn't exist without the record. I was scared of the record for the same reason I was scared of turning out the lights in a bathroom and saying "Bloody Mary, Bloody Mary" three times while spinning around. I kinda knew it was bullshit, but I wasn't taking any chances.

Twenty years later, I downloaded a Robert Plant solo album. I don't remember the name. The one with Alison Krauss. I didn't really even want to hear it, but the reviews were good, and I was bored and I found it on a BitTorrent site and I was like, "Eh, whatever." I made it through only the first song before it crashed my iPod. When I took it to an Apple store, Karl the tech guy asked me if I'd been "messing around" with LimeWire.

"Nope," I said. And I wasn't lying. I'd already figured out that anything you downloaded from LimeWire was likely to be just audio of Bill Clinton. Like a responsible Internet thief, I stole my music from Pirate Bay.

Karl the tech guy explained that my stolen files were probably a viral Trojan horse. And it didn't help matters that my iPod was a "classic." Which is a polite way of saying "old."

I've reached an age when most of the things I love are becoming "classic" at an alarming rate. This is especially true when it comes to music. A good 85 percent of my music collection has crossed or is on the verge of crossing over into classic-rock territory. I've only recently (and still begrudgingly) accepted that U2's *The Joshua Tree* is classic rock now. And despite having heard it categorized as "classic" repeatedly, I refuse to admit that Neutral Milk Hotel's *In the Aeroplane over the Sea* shares any DNA with music created by old hippies with comb-overs and grandchildren. But okay, fine, I'm a realist; I know that time marches on, and when fifteen or more years have passed, it's unrealistic to think that the things that seemed so fresh and current yesterday aren't showing a little rust today.

But not in this case. Not with a music-playing device that I bought shortly after a black man was elected US president. Just by the numbers, that's not nearly enough time to give anything nostalgic street cred.

"Can you fix it?" I asked Karl the tech guy.

"Well, no," he said matter-of-factly. "I can sell you a new iPod, and you can stop stealing music."

"A new iPod?" I asked. This was patently absurd to me. "You can't just take the bad songs off of it?"

"No, sorry, it doesn't work like that."

I was just annoyed enough to start complaining like an old man, telling him how things were different in my day. I remember when music was only ever victimized by easily manageable danger. If the sound got too smudgy—your favorite song was smeared with thumbprints—you could scrub it down with a little isopropyl alcohol and it'd be as good as new. Or maybe your needle was the problem. I could replace a turntable needle with one hand and roll a joint with the other. But that all changed with MP3s. You couldn't slather an MP3 with isopropyl alcohol and fix it. You had to call a guy, a smart-ass college kid in a cobalt-blue T-shirt to lecture you about how your iPod is too "classic."

In my day, if you listened to music under the right circumstances, it might fill your head with satanic messages, ensuring the eternal damnation of your rock-horn-saluting soul. But under no goddamn circumstances did playing the bad music require you to pay three hundred fucking dollars for a replacement stereo system.

As I browsed Reckless, there were albums that were entirely foreign to me, and albums that were instantly familiar. But the old friends, they'd all been given an upgrade. Fugazi's *Repeater*? A reissue. The Smiths' *The Queen Is Dead*? Another reissue. Anything by the Replacements? Only one *Tim* and two *Pleased to Meet Me*s, both reissues. Even the crown jewel of my collection, the record I bought solely because a guy with Elvis Costello glasses and a nose ring behind the counter at Record Swap recommended it, Screeching Weasel's *How to Make Enemies and Irritate People*, was only available as a reissue.

Everything was a deluxe edition, remastered on 180-gram vinyl, now with original artwork. The stickers that used to read FEATURING THE RADIO HIT . . . now promised things like INCLUDES A DOWNLOAD CODE AND HIGH-RES DIGITAL AUDIO EDITIONS IN 2.8 MHZ, 12 KHZ / 24-BIT, AND 96 KHZ / 24-BIT! I recognized the covers, but the albums felt different. It's not just that they were new; there was something too slick in the design, too high-definition in the packaging.

The girl with the Cramps T-shirt was almost finished with her grapes. I would have to say something soon.

"Could you, uh . . . ," I attempted. "Tell me where you . . . heh . . . Just curious if you . . . you know . . . the used records?"

She smiled warmly at me, like it was a question she got all the time from old guys with gray in their beards.

"It's right behind you, sweetie," she said, gesturing toward the middle aisle.

I thanked her and drifted toward the used section, which was actually labeled LAST-CHANCE SALOON.

This was more promising. Here were the records that might've come from my personal library. Not the titles, necessarily, but the general poor condition. They smelled like something that'd been left in the basement during a Chicago winter. If you grabbed them with too much force, the sleeves folded back. I spent almost a full minute cradling albums like Bryan Adams's *Cuts Like a Knife* and the Greg Kihn Band's *Kihnspiracy*, not because they were records I particularly cherished, but because they had the physical battle scars of music from my era. Also, it didn't hurt that the average price for a bargain bin record—fifty-nine cents on the high end—meant I could probably buy back my entire collection for about a hundred dollars.

I'm all for superior sound quality, but vinyl made after 2000 is fundamentally different from vinyl made in the twentieth century. It smells different, it feels different. The vinyl copy of the Pixies' *Doolittle* I purchased at Reckless in 1990 is only tangentially related to the reissue vinyl copy, ticket price $19.99, currently for sale at Reckless. I don't give a shit about rare test pressings. Or when new albums come with free download coupons. Or colored vinyl. Or goddamn picture discs. I want the records I recognize. The records that feel like a part of my double helix.

I spent an hour combing through the Last-Chance Saloon.

And then I brought the Pixies' *Doolittle* reissue for $19.99 to the counter. Because I am weak and everything in the Last-Chance Saloon was shit.

I gave the hot girl in the Cramps T-shirt a credit card.

"Did you find everything you needed?" she asked.

"Sure," I said. But that was a lie. I hadn't even come close to finding everything I needed. But I couldn't answer her honestly without getting into a whole thing about music and memories and authenticity. I'd have to tell her about feelings that would probably sound crazy to someone like her—what are they calling people in their twenties now? Postmillennials? Have we rolled around to Generation A yet? I'd have to tell her about memory and reconnecting with your past and how to reconcile that with growing up and how shitty and wonderful but mostly shitty it is to be an adult with a head full of preadolescent emotions, and she'd probably just nod politely as I was telling her all this, while she was inching her fingers toward that silent alarm button under the desk. And of course I'd have to mention Questlove, the drummer from the Roots, and how this all traces back to him. He's where it all started. And that would take us into a whole rabbit hole of explanations and backstories and justifications, none of which would make all that much sense to her.

But nobody wants to hear that old-man yammering, do they? Oh, what the hell.

I'm going to back up.

I'm a journalist. An "entertainment" journalist, if you want to get all specific about it.

This wasn't my choice.

When I was coming out of college, my first intention was to be a playwright. I would move to Chicago and write hilariously profane and poignant plays for the Steppenwolf Theatre Company. I'd be like a modern-day Christopher Durang but without the religious hang-ups, or an August Strindberg who watched too much porn and too many Woody Allen movies. I stumbled into journalism by accident. The father of my writing partner was a columnist for *Playboy*, and after meeting several silver-fox editors at social functions, my friend and I were paid way too much money to write funny stories for the magazine about *Baywatch* and lesbians.

For lack of any other options, I stayed with the money, and within a few decades, I was writing regularly for publications like *Vanity Fair*, *Esquire*, and the *New York Times Magazine*, mostly interviewing celebrities like Tina Fey, Sir Ian McKellen, Willie Nelson, Stephen Colbert, Sarah Silverman, and (as of this writing) approximately 213 other people you've probably heard of.

When you talk to famous people for a living, it all starts to blend together after a while. You remember meeting people like Buzz Aldrin and John Cusack and Isabella Rossellini, but you have only a vague recollection of what you discussed with them. But that wasn't the case with Questlove, the coolest neo-soul drummer in the universe. I can remember everything about our phone conversation. It was an assignment for MTV Hive, a website offshoot of MTV. Quest had a new memoir out, and I was tasked with getting a few ridiculous yarns out of him. For the first twenty minutes or so of our conversation, it was more or less as expected. We talked about the time he roller-skated with Prince, and ran out of a Tracy Morgan toe-licking party. But then the topic turned to the Sugarhill Gang's "Rapper's Delight."

We both laughed as we recounted the brilliantly weird lyrics. "I said a hip, hop, the hippy to the hippy / To the hip hip hop, you don't stop. . . ." If you were alive in the early eighties and didn't identify as a grown-up, you can probably remember where you were when you first heard "Rapper's Delight."

For Quest, it was while washing dishes with his sister and listening to a local soul station in Philadelphia. He immediately went out and bought the song on a twelve-inch. It was the first record he ever purchased with his own money. He found his copy at the Listening Booth on Chestnut Street in Philly, and it cost $2.99 plus tax. $3.17 total.

It was the first piece in what grew to be his seventy-thousand-plus record collection.

"Seventy thousand?" I asked, dumbfounded. "You have seventy thousand records?"

"Something like that," he said. "I'm rounding down."

Instead of buying a home with his new income as the *Tonight Show* bandleader, he invested in a vinyl library "with a cherrywood floor and a sliding ladder. It was necessary, because it was getting to a point where the records were taking over. You had to have some sort of Indiana Jones skill level to navigate my house, just to jump over stuff without cracking a record."

"Is there anything in your collection that's indispensable?" I asked. "Anything you'd never sell?"

"Well, I'd never sell my 'Rapper's Delight,'" he said.

"You still have it?"

"Oh yeah."

"You have the original? The one you bought for $3.17?"

"The original." He laughed. "I've never given it up. Never even occurred to me."

He had held on to a tiny piece of plastic for more than three decades?

"I've always taken meticulous care of that stuff," he told me. "I've always had some sort of library system for my records, so nothing just disappeared without me knowing about it. Not just 'Rapper's Delight,' but all my records. They've never been in any danger. You're probably the same way about your records."

I was silent for a second.

"I don't have records anymore," I told him. "I sold them all long ago."

Now there was silence on the other end of the phone.

"Oh, man, I'm sorry," Quest finally said, his voice a whisper. He seemed sincerely shaken by my admission, like I'd just casually confessed that I'd put a pillow over my dad's face while he slept and held it there until he stopped breathing.

"Well, you know, I could always get them back," I said, backpedaling.

"Sure, yeah, absolutely," Quest said. But he didn't believe it, I could tell. It was like when a clearly crazy person says, "I'm not crazy," and you're like "Oh, yeah, totally, you're not crazy at all," but you absolutely think that motherfucker is crazy.

We moved on to another topic, but in my head, I was still thinking about it. It's not like I just threw out all my records one day, made a bonfire, and watched the vinyl burn. It happened over time, as these things usually do.

It started because of CDs. Right? That's why we all gave up on vinyl. Because the technology changed. You don't want to be the one who's like, "Enjoy your jetpacks. I'll stick with my Volvo."

My first CD was the Traveling Wilburys Vol. 1 album. It was 1988. Late December. I'd gotten a CD boom box for Christmas from my parents, and I needed to christen it. I visited the mall and picked the Wilburys' CD only because that goddamn video for "Handle with Care" had been hammered into my subconscious by MTV. Listening to the compact disc was breathtaking. I'd never heard music with so much clarity. And so fucking loud. This was clearly the future.

Over the coming months, I began selling off my records. I was like the guy who gets kissed by a hot girl and decides he has to get rid of his porn collection immediately because "I won't be needing this anymore." I'd been that guy—several times, in fact, back when getting rid of porn meant filling a pillowcase full of VHS tapes and taking them to the nearest inconspicuous Dumpster—but my vinyl wasn't as easy to cast off.

At first, I sold off just the nonessentials. Nothing that would be missed. A few dozen greatest-hits albums, and artists who seemed like a good idea at the time but had outgrown their usefulness (the Dream Academy, Blind Melon, Porno for Pyros, 4 Non Blondes). Entire chunks of certain artists' canons were easy to let go— early-period Tom Waits, late-period Genesis, Christian-period Bob Dylan. If I were on a helicopter filled with all my records and it started going down and the pilot screamed, "We need to lose some weight," those would have been the records I threw over- board first.

I never had remorse or worries that I might never see this music again. Selling my copy of the Police's *Synchronicity* or the Pixies' *Doolittle* was just a means to an end, not an irrevocable act. If I ever had a change of heart, I could always buy another copy—hell, I could go back to the same Discount Record and Tapes at Lincoln Mall in the south suburbs of Chicago, the exact place where I'd bought both of those records, and find copies in the cutout bin for a fraction of what I sold them for. Selling records in the late twentieth century was a victimless crime.

And the money was good. My Clash records alone—I had all six studio albums and the "Hitsville U.K." 7-inch—paid for an entire week of groceries from the liquor store down the block. Even when the profits were middling—I got ten cents for John Cougar Mellen- camp's *Scarecrow*—it still felt like a victory. Being able to hear "Small

Town" whenever I wanted was not inherently valuable, but you never knew when you might need an extra dime.

It never occurred to me that I might ever run out of records. The last time I counted, somewhere around 1987, I had in the ballpark of two thousand. The first purge of three hundred barely left a dent. And from there, it was just a few records here, a few dozen there, as I needed them. I never made the conscious decision to deep-six my vinyl. It was always just, "Shit, I need beer money for the weekend. Oh wait, I still have that copy of the Stooges' *Raw Power!*" It was like a low-interest-bearing savings account with guilt-free withdrawals. I was never going to get rich on a bunch of old Elvis Costello records held together with Scotch tape, or a *Purple Rain* that was so warped it sounded like the doves were crying because Prince was having a stroke. These weren't investments, they were just antiques from my past that had small yet immediate monetary value.

Most of my records disappeared in a blur. But I remember the last one. It was the Replacements' *Let It Be*. I sold it in 1999, the year I got married and my dad died. I was still embarrassingly poor, and needed money fast. During a visit to my parents, I found it in my old bedroom closet—the one record I'd always managed to talk myself out of selling. But at this point, it seemed silly to hold on to it. I already had the CD, which was vastly superior (or so I thought at the time). The ragged and well-worn vinyl had long outlasted its usefulness, even as its secondary purpose, as a brilliant hiding spot for my weed.

That was my one concern when I visited the Record Swap in suburban Homewood—ironically, the very same record store where I bought my original copy of *Let It Be* back in 1986. Would they actually buy a record that smelled so pungently of marijuana? As it turned out, yes they would.

Driving back to Chicago from the Record Swap, I felt lighter, like I'd unburdened myself of some great worry. There was no value in these physical relics, which (I'd told myself) symbolized only lonely nights in my teenage bedroom. I was a snake shedding its skin; if somebody wanted to give me cash for that discarded rind, well, my gas tank thanks you, sucker. I blasted "I Will Dare" from my car stereo as I sped down Lake Shore Drive, all the windows open, and believed I hadn't actually lost anything.

And that's what I kept telling myself, and kept believing. Until Questlove came along and fucked everything up.

"Those skates looked like something out of *Xanadu*," Questlove said, trying to describe Prince's roller skates. "That's the only way I could describe them. They glowed and sparkled. It was so magical, I had to pinch myself."

I laughed at all the right spots, like I would do in any interview, but I was barely listening. I was still stuck on his records, and how he'd held on to the things I let slip away without a second thought.

"So listen, quick follow up about 'Rapper's Delight,'" I said.

"Um, yeah?" Quest said.

"Not saying that you would, but if you had sold it . . ."

"I'd never sell it."

"No, of course not. But if you lost it. Or if you lent it to somebody and they never gave it back."

"I'd just go ask them—"

"But they lent it to another friend, who took it on a backpacking trip to Europe, and he's not a hundred percent sure where he left it, but maybe at a youth hostel in Amsterdam."

Questlove said nothing, but I could hear him swallowing hard.

"Or your wife had a garage sale without telling you, not because you needed the money but just to get all this crap out of the house. 'Rapper's Delight' is gone, and she doesn't have a clue who bought it."

More silence.

"Okay," he finally managed. "I guess anything's possible."

"Would you go looking for it?"

"The record?"

"Yes," I said. "Would you try to find it, despite the ridiculous odds against you ever seeing it again?"

He didn't hesitate. "I would, yeah."

Two

"Are you okay?"

This was a question that Kelly, my wife, had been asking me a lot lately. Not in the rhetorical way she might ask if I'd had too much to drink the night before, or if I'd been spending too much time on Facebook. A gentle nudge that maybe I hadn't been making the best of decisions. No, this time she asked with a worried lilt to her voice. Like she was legitimately concerned about my emotional well-being.

"I'm great," I told her.

She stood next to the door of my office, looking at me with a fixed gaze, all but daring me to stick with that story.

She didn't need to explain what was making her uneasy. It was painfully obvious. I was sitting alone in my office at noon, the computer turned off, doing no discernible work, just staring at my copy of *Doolittle*, the vinyl record I'd bought from Reckless a few days ago. Which of course I hadn't played, because we didn't own a record player. But I carried it around like a widower might carry around a photo of his dead wife.

I knew I was sad, but I couldn't put my finger on why. I hoped it wasn't the obvious stuff. The fact that I was in my midforties, and life wasn't as uncomplicated and self-indulgent as it was when I was twenty-two. The world didn't revolve around me anymore. But who doesn't realize that eventually? You get married and have a kid—or many kids—and your days suddenly have more structure. You can't say things to your significant other like, "Let's spend the day in bed, watching all of the *Godfather* movies." Certainly not on a Tuesday, when it's the most irresponsible (and therefore the most fun) to binge-watch movies you've seen a thousand times already.

I didn't want it to be that. Because that would mean I was the worst kind of cliché. A midlife crisis? Was I really that one-dimensional? Had growing older made me that predictably melancholy? I was like a fucking Jackson Browne song. Why not just buy a sports car and find a mistress? But it wasn't that simple. I wasn't upset about growing older. I kinda liked being older. It meant fewer expectations. Nobody gets upset when a forty-five-year-old guy with a kid leaves the party at ten because he's tired. Nobody scoffs at the forty-five-year-old who wears a rash guard at the pool because he doesn't feel like sucking in his gut. Nobody blinks at the forty-five-year-old guy who wears polyester bowling shirts and knee-length wallet chains that haven't been cool since *Swingers*. The bar is low for the middle-aged guy, and that's just where I liked it.

But something was missing that I couldn't get past. And it wasn't my youth.

I met Kelly in the midnineties, in Chicago. We were both employees at the Second City comedy theater, the place where comedy legends like John Belushi, Bill Murray, and Stephen Colbert got their start. I worked in the box office, and she was a host—which basically involved making sure everybody in the audience had a chair. We both made minimum wage and had no health insurance, but we stayed up all night drinking with enormously talented people, many of whom would go on to become household names. Sometimes we just slept in the theater, spooning under huge black-and-white photos of Gilda Radner and Chris Farley.

Four years into dating, I asked her to marry me. The engagement ring was a grape-flavored lollipop ring, because it was all I could afford, but it was still enough to make her happy-cry. We decided to leave Chicago and try a new city, because that's what all our friends did. Nobody stayed in Chicago forever. It was like college— the place you learned everything you needed, to go someplace else and become an adult.

Over the next few decades, we lived in every time zone in the country—in LA as we both tried and failed to be screenwriters; in Salt Lake City, Utah, while she worked for the Sundance Film Festival and I was a househusband; in various cities in Florida, when we decided being warm all the time was enough; in Sonoma, California, when we decided being drunk on expensive wine was enough. We kept moving, looking for whatever was next, staying just long enough to decide this wasn't what we wanted.

And now we were back in Chicago, renting a tiny twelve-hundred-square-foot second-floor apartment on the North Side, with a three-year-old son named Charlie with boundless energy and beautiful blond locks. Our days moved at a dizzying pace, and there just never seemed to be enough time to do everything that needed doing. There were playdates to be hosted, and groceries to be put away, and laundry to be folded, and preschool applications to be filled out, and savings accounts to be emptied because we totally forgot that our car payment was overdue, and a son to be reminded, "No, no, you can't put Sharpie on turkey meat" or "You are absolutely not running outside naked, covered in lotion! I don't care if you're an alien now!"

When I heard myself complain, I wanted to punch myself in my own whiny face. It wasn't like I was juggling three jobs to make ends meet, or was ever one missed mortgage payment away from being homeless, or argued with the insurance company because my kid has cancer and he wasn't getting the right treatment. I was angry because my time wasn't my own anymore, and my days were filled with making sure we had enough batteries, and we remembered to pay the electric bill, and my son hadn't been watching too much TV, and my wife felt like I was actually paying attention to her and not just nodding while I checked my e-mail. I found the perfect balance between my family and my work, even though that meant I didn't get a moment to myself until 10:00 p.m. usually, and at that point I just wanted to crawl into bed and fall asleep watching *Seinfeld* reruns.

My life was fine. Blessed, even.

I was acutely reminded of this when the wife of an old friend was diagnosed with breast cancer. It spread to her brain, and eventually the rest of her body. The asshole cancer finally got the better of her, and her doctors sent her home, saying there was nothing else they could do. She had just a few months to live, maybe less. So we drove out to say our good-byes. Standing by her deathbed—her literal deathbed, as in the bed in which she'd be dying, possibly while we were standing there, holding her hand and wondering what to say—was surreal. I'd visited sick people, but never someone who'd been told to stop fighting, that all they can do now is wait for the end. Especially when that person is right around your age, and your last memory of them is from the previous summer, when you had her and her husband over for dinner, and you all got drunk on too many bottles of red wine and talked about trying to get pregnant (she and Kelly were fertility buddies), and joked about the past and how quickly it vanished and was replaced by adult responsibilities and isn't that unfair, but oh well, let's crank up the music and open another bottle. Now here she was, her eyes red and swollen shut, her mouth agape, like she was doing an impression of Edvard Munch's *The Scream*, so close to the end that just watching her chest rise and fall seemed like a miracle.

We left after an hour, and Kelly and I didn't say much during the drive home. We were too shaken. If we needed a reminder that life is precious and fleeting, and you should be thankful for every minute, this was it. We promised ourselves never to forget how lucky we were, and how much we had to be grateful for.

It only took a few days for that to wear off, and for us to start grumbling again. Yes, yes, our friend with cancer. Life is precious; we get it. But it's garbage night, and I still haven't put out the recycling, and Charlie needs a bath and somehow Kelly got it into her head that it's my turn, which is fucking bullshit, and I have three stories due by tomorrow morning, and a couple dozen e-mails to respond to, and our credit score has plummeted again because somebody (I'm not pointing any fingers) forgot to pay the cable bill, and I haven't checked Facebook in hours, and Jesus Christ, I can't even get a moment to hear myself think!

When I looked at old photos of Kelly and me, back in our twenties, I was amazed. Not by how young we were, or how effortlessly thin, but how carefree we seemed. How uncomplicated our lives were, even if we didn't realize it at the time. We used to be so unburdened by . . . everything, really. In those pictures, we have the relaxed expressions of people who don't have demanding careers or obligations or commitments (other than to each other). Being poor isn't fun, but being poor when you're twenty-three and you know you can probably call your parents and beg them into sending you a rent check if you run out of options, well, there are worse things in this world.

If we wanted to, we could have just disappeared. We could have gone off the grid for weeks, dropping what little responsibilities we had, on the grounds that we had to "find ourselves" or, just as important, take the weekend to listen to the new Beck record—I mean really listen to it, until we knew all the songs by heart and could sing along without thinking about it.

Kelly and I got married at thirty—by my father, who was a pastor—and carried on living pretty much like we had before. There'd be time enough for buying houses, or jobs we'd stay at for longer than a year, or cities we wouldn't abandon when they got too familiar. And kids. We wanted kids, sure, but kids someday. It was always someday, in the vaguely-near-but-definitely-distant future. And when we had a kid, oh boy, it would be spectacular. We wouldn't be like those parents content with raising tiny pink versions of themselves. Ours would be different. They would be cool and uncomplicated and happy, because we'd be old enough not to fall into the same parenting traps that we saw the people in their twenties fall into. We'd watch the *Star Wars* movies with them (which they'd love even more than we did) and we'd introduce them to all the cool music and pop culture, and they'd be so grateful. But we'd also be the disciplinarians. When they'd ask to get a tattoo of the Neutral Milk Hotel aeroplane phonograph, we'd say absolutely not, until you're at least eighteen. Sorry to be the bad guys, but that's what parents do.

We didn't get around to having a kid until we were both forty. It felt like that part in action movies when the hero skids under a metal or stone wall as it's closing, just barely making it through before the wall comes crashing down on his legs. We'd tried on our own, and then tried fertility treatments, and were on the verge of giving up when, after a night fueled by too much vodka, we got pregnant the old-fashioned way.

After Charlie was born, our life changed fast. And it kept changing, usually in inches, until one day I woke up and looked at myself in the mirror and couldn't believe how tired I looked. Not old, just tired.

Which led me to where I was that day, sitting listlessly in my office, feeling brain-dead and sad for no particular reason, holding on to an overpriced Pixies remaster like a life raft.

I wasn't really paying attention when Charlie wandered into the room and slipped the *Doolittle* out of my hands. He sat on the floor and examined it more closely. He emptied the record out of its sleeve and brushed a finger against the black vinyl, like he was trying to wake up a tablet computer.

"How does this work?" he asked.

"It doesn't play by itself," I explained. "It needs something called a record player."

He looked at me. "What's that?"

"It's a big machine with a plate on top that spins around and around, and you put the record on the spinning plate, and then there's a little robot arm with a tiny needle that you put on the record as it's spinning, and that makes music."

He grimaced. Actually grimaced. A three-year-old boy rarely grimaces, unless he's being forced to eat vegetables or take a bath when he's perfectly happy being muddy. But my explanation of how a record player works was enough to make him grimace.

He turned his attention to the *Doolittle* album cover. "Who's the monkey?" he asked earnestly.

"I don't know, just some monkey. He's not in the band or anything."

"Who's in the band?"

"Black Francis. Kim Deal. And two other guys. They're a band called the Pixies. Daddy used to love them."

"You don't love them anymore?" Charlie asked.

Well, my young Charlie, that's a whole can of worms you're opening up. Of course I still loved them. I used to listen to their records like it was my job, like I was being paid to sit in a dark apartment, headphones strapped to my head, and absorb the songs until they felt indistinguishable from my own memories. I would jump into cars with guys I hardly knew, based only on vague promises that they knew a guy who knew a guy who knew a guy who could get us tickets to a Pixies show.

But I'd reached an age when my enthusiasm for rock shows wasn't what it used to be. Just a few weeks before this conversation with my son, an old friend—a guy I'd seen more than a few Pixies shows with in my youth—offered me tickets to a Pixies reunion in Chicago. I'd seen my last Pixies show with him just a few years earlier, in Detroit. And the experience was underwhelming. A Pixies concert in the twenty-first century is a strange juxtaposition. On the one hand, you have the inherent badassness of the music. But then you look around and realize that the audience is a sea of forty-something dudes like you, with Black Francis man-nipples and nowhere to go but down. The wave of mutilation has been replaced by a wave of "I'm going to sit down during the slow songs."

Even so, I didn't want to turn down another chance to see them live. If I said no this time, it'd mean something significant. Like realizing it'd been a few months since you'd made love with your wife and you were okay with that. But I had to say no to the ticket anyway, for a myriad of reasons. There were work obligations—several interviews that at least had to be transcribed before the next day—and Kelly had already made plans with her mommy friends, and it was her night to go out, and I could always get a babysitter, but that would require calls to friends who were only sorta friends who had teenage girls old enough to babysit, and it all seemed too complicated and annoying.

As I put Charlie to sleep later that night, he was still holding on to the Pixies album. Maybe he knew how much it meant to me, and he was determined to find out why. He'd been the same way about other riddles we'd declined to explain satisfactorily. Like where his Grandpa Spitz was, and what exactly it meant when somebody dies.

I didn't mention that while I was tucking him in, reading him books about hopping on Pop and the Night Kitchen, I could have been at a Pixies show. I didn't want him to feel bad. It wasn't a tragedy. It was a good thing, a lucky thing. Between the two options, I'd made the only choice worth making. But you still feel the loss.

When he wouldn't stop asking, I told him about the Pixies show that was most vivid in my memory. I remember it in Technicolor, like an especially vibrant dream. It was December 1991, at the Riviera Theatre in Chicago. I came to the show with a head full of drugs (I left this part out), two dollars in my bank account, and no idea how (or if) I was going to make it home. I couldn't tell you the exact setlist—I'm pretty sure they played everything I loved, but I wasn't exactly taking notes—but I do know that I've rarely felt so alive and excited and grateful.

Charlie yawned during my story, and then asked, "Were there robots?"

"Yeah," I conceded. "There were robots."

"Did they have lasers coming out of their hands?"

"Absolutely," I said, because in my memory, they kinda did.

Then I kissed him on the head and went out to the living room, where my wife and I polished off a bottle of white wine while watching *Love It or List It* reruns. Because I'm a goddamn grown-up.

The next day, I drove down Lake Shore Drive in our Honda CR-V. It's a tricked-out gangsta ride with gold trim, tinted windows, crushed velour seats, thirty-inch chrome rims, and a custom chain steering wheel. Actually, no, none of that. It's just a standard Honda CR-V with enough trunk room for a stroller. But it did come with something that Kelly and I, during our twenty-plus years as a sporadically employed couple, have never been able to afford until recently: satellite radio.

"Coming up in the next hour, we've got Def Leppard, Corey Hart, and we'll round it out with everybody's favorite, Hall and Oates."

Like it always was when Kelly was the last one to use the car, it was tuned to the eighties station. This particular hour of nostalgia was hosted by Alan Hunter, one of the original MTV VJs. But of course, anyone listening to an eighties-themed satellite radio station did not need to be reminded who Alan Hunter is. This was a man who (at least for me) had been in the room—albeit in TV form—for the vast majority of the sexual activity I experienced during the eighties. And he was narrating! He was always in the background, blandly announcing a Spandau Ballet video and totally not judging your futile attempts to find your girlfriend's clitoris over a pair of acid-washed jeans.

"We've got some Bon Jovi coming up," he said. "Boy, that brings me back."

It was "Livin' on a Prayer." I didn't immediately turn the channel, as I usually do when anything by Bon Jovi comes on the radio.

I let it play out. And I listened to it, actually listened, taking in every earnest cliché about working-class kids and their shitty jobs. Even in the eighties, when I first heard it, the song seemed so heavy-handed and self-serious. I believed in Tommy and Gina's plight about as much as I believed that Lionel Richie was capable of dancing on a ceiling.

So why did I ever care? Why do I know "Livin' on a Prayer" inside and out, when I could have just . . .

Oh yeah, that's right, Heather G.

Heather was my first girlfriend. But before that, she was the one

I watched a little too intently from across the band room in high school. She played clarinet, and I played trombone. For that reason alone, she was hopelessly out of my league. (Trombonists do not, historically, get the girl.) To make matters worse, she was also a cheerleader, and showed up for band practices wearing those little cheerleader dresses. My first attempt to impress her musically—which was the only way I was able to impress a girl in my teens, lacking anything like athletic ability or a desirable jawline—was an unmitigated disaster. I'd offered to give her a ride to school, in a maroon Plymouth Valiant whose only redeeming feature was its cassette deck. I popped in *Sticky Fingers*, which I assumed would demonstrate that I was indeed a little sexually dangerous, despite the trombone case in my backseat. I knew all the lyrics to "Bitch" and was capable of singing them with a snarl, which as far as I knew made a pretty convincing case for my bad boy–ness.

But during this unfortunately brief journey, the cassette had been cued to "Dead Flowers," which didn't have the same menace.

"You like country music?" she asked with a bemused smile.

"This isn't country," I protested. "It's the Stones."

She listened for a few more seconds. Jagger's twangy drawl was hard to argue with.

"No, that's definitely country," she concluded.

For a teenage girl in south suburban Chicago in 1985, nothing was less sexy than country music. For her, it was all about Duran Duran and the Police and Bon Jovi. Especially Bon Jovi. Every person in the vicinity of her social circle was well aware that her favorite artist, the rock performer who truly understood her aching heart, and her personal fantasy paramour, was Jon Bon Jovi.

I had to prove to her that we had something musical in common. I couldn't stand Bon Jovi and his unconvincing "I'm a cowboy" posturing. But if it meant I might have a chance with Heather, I would have air-guitared along with Gregorian chants. So I bought a copy of *Slippery When Wet*. I didn't get it from my usual record sources. I went to a place that nobody went anymore in the mall where they found that dead girl in the bushes.

I bought the album and brought it to school, and left it casually in my open trombone case during band practice, waiting for Heather to discover it. Which, of course, she did.

"Isn't it so great," she said, holding the record sleeve like she was gripping a lover's hip bones before climbing on top of him. "What's your favorite song?"

"'Social Disease,'" I said. I picked this song because it was the non-hit. If I'd learned anything from hanging out in record stores, it's that true fans always prefer the non-hits, the songs not yet devoured by fair-weather fans.

She seemed duly impressed. Or maybe it just seemed that way because she was making eye contact with me.

We made plans to get together later, to play some tunes and talk about all things JBJ. She gave me her phone number, and I wrote it on the album cover. This, I hoped, communicated to her the seriousness of my intentions. I hadn't just written her number on a piece of paper I might throw away or lose. I had tattooed her digits onto my favorite album, made her a permanent fixture on the record sleeve I stared at every night as I fell asleep, humming the lyrics to "Never Say Goodbye" or whatever. I'd look at her number and think, "Oh yeah, there's another lost soul out there who loves the Jov as much as I love the Jov."

I kept that record when we started dating, and I kept it when she ended it and broke my heart. I took that record with me to college, and to my first few Chicago apartments. I don't know why. God knows I didn't listen to it. But it had her phone number scrawled into it, which made it feel too personal to throw away or sell. I guess

I did cast it off eventually, like I did with all my records. But god, I'd give anything just to . . .

. . . see it . . . one more . . .

There in the car, driving down Lake Shore and listening to "Livin' on a Prayer," I had a moment of intense clarity. It was suddenly so obvious what I had to do. I needed to find that record. Not just any record. *The* record. The one with Heather's phone number written on it. The exact copy I once owned, that represented something hugely important to me, some rite of passage into adulthood.

I came just short of bringing the car to a skidding halt, turning into oncoming traffic as I changed course.

I headed toward the south suburbs. To the Record Swap. A store I hadn't visited in fifteen years. I didn't know if Heather's record was there, but that seemed like the most logical place to start.

And why stop with one record? Why not get all of them? Not duplicates. Not those reissues that smell like nothing I recognize. Like the *Doolittle* reissue, which was in the seat next to me. It looked like something that used to be meaningful to me, but it was just a carbon copy. Just because it sounded better—with crisper highs and knee-rattling lows—didn't mean it was better.

I wanted my records. My exact records. My literal exact records. I wanted them back.

All of them. Or at least as many as I could find.

It's what Questlove would've done.

Three

I can tell you many things about the Record Swap, but almost none of it will be accurate.

Here are things that I'm pretty sure are true:

The Record Swap is a record store in Homewood, Illinois, about an hour's drive south of Chicago. It's on Dixie Highway, though I couldn't give you the exact address, even when I was going there regularly. It's next to a Chinese restaurant, across the street from the Melody Mart where I bought my first trombone, long before I discovered how the right music could change everything. What else? There's a Tweety and Clifford the Big Red Dog painted on the alley wall next to the back door, which led up to the all-ages live music club behind the record store that smelled like clove cigarettes.

The sign out front is a terrible drawing of a man in profile, with a weirdly geometric haircut, a business suit, and thick glasses. He's clutching a record in one arm, and running. It's not just a brisk walk; he's definitely running.

That's what I can definitively tell you about the Record Swap.

After that, it begins to get fuzzy. I have this vision of walking into the store for the first time, and I'm pretty sure the Replacements' "Bastards of Young" was playing. But that can't be, can it? It's too perfect, too cinematic. I'm some teenager with a bad haircut and clothes that Rivers Cuomo couldn't make ironic. And I'm carrying a handful of Billy Joel records. That much I know actually was true. I had too many copies of *Glass Houses*, thanks to overenthusiastic grandparents with no other gift-giving ideas. I thought I could make a trade, get some quick cash, and buy something new, something Billy Joel–esque.

I went over to the counter and I gave them my Billy Joel records. The staff—who were all pierced and tattooed, but also had kind faces, and talked in reassuring tones, like you'd want from a nurse or a doctor as they're preparing you for major surgery—they took my records and they put them into a pizza-style brick oven, shoving them into the flames with one of those wooden pizza-loading peels. I tried to object, but they put a finger over my lips, and then took me by the hand and led me deeper into the store.

They picked out records at random for me, records that would change me, that would give me the confidence to realize that I was fundamentally better than everybody at my high school, with their unapologetic lack of originality or musical adventurousness, who would listen to Phil Collins and think, "That'll do." It wouldn't do for us, goddammit! Because we were different! We felt things! We knew the world in ways they were incapable of knowing the world, even though we'd all seen pretty much the same amount of the world, which didn't extend beyond the Chess King at the mall or the mostly abandoned parking lot near JCPenney, where everybody went to get hand jobs.

But I owned Camper Van Beethoven's *Telephone Free Landslide Victory*. And the Cramps' *Bad Music for Bad People*. And the Dead

Kennedys' *Frankenchrist*. And Tom Waits's *Swordfishtrombones*. How could I have these records and not know more about the world? Other people had based their knowledge of the outside world on things like Bryan Adams's *Reckless*. And Lisa Lisa and Cult Jam's *Spanish Fly*. And that fucking *Miami Vice* soundtrack. And that "We Are the World" record. And Wham!'s *Make It Big*, a band that added an exclamation point to their name, just because they were so excited about their blow-dried hair and white pants. I didn't need to travel anywhere to know that they were wrong. So very, very wrong. I had the evidence in these records.

I went into Record Swap an insecure kid. And I came out just as insecure. But now I was a Lou Reed type of insecure, where your insecurity just makes you cooler.

I know my hindsight isn't to be trusted. It's all overromanticized. A few things are true. I did discover the Dead Kennedys because of a particularly generous sales clerk willing to take Billy Joel off my hands. But I think the ovens were in my imagination.

It was beautiful though. It's what high school was for some people. I didn't discover anything about myself at my actual high school. But in the Record Swap, digging through those bins, building a record collection that was like a never-ending scavenger hunt, getting into afternoon-long conversations about the minutiae of Dinosaur Jr. with twenty-three-year-old guys who look exactly like J Mascis, this is where I felt the most normal, and the most like myself.

I never expected to walk back into it and have everything be exactly the same. There'd be different people working there, obviously. The Jesus Lizard and Sonic Youth posters would likely have been taken down, replaced with, I don't know, Animal Collective and the Black Keys maybe? Or something more obscure and confusing to forty-year-old guys? It'd have a fresh coat of paint, it wouldn't smell as much like clove cigarettes, the jazz section would be where they used to keep the country stuff, and god only knows what they did with R&B. I was prepared for all of that.

I wasn't prepared for it to be gone.

"Can I give you a tour?" the nice guy in the unnecessarily tight karate gi asked me.

I'd just been standing there in the lobby for I don't know how long. I finally found the courage to walk in, after passing the entrance several times. This couldn't be right. It couldn't be the same place. Although the Melody Mart across the street was still there, as was the Chinese restaurant next door. Everything looked right. Except in the spot where the Record Swap should've been, it had been replaced with something called the Draco Academy.

The lobby made no sense. If this was indeed the same building, the walls were in the wrong places. It used to be open, like a loft space, with a curve to the right where the counter was, and rows of records running vertically from the door. This was . . . I don't know what this was. There was a lobby about the size of the bathroom in my first apartment. And a fountain. A fucking fountain.

I just stood there disbelievingly, trying to remember if this was where they kept the new releases or the soundtracks.

The nice man in the unnecessarily tight karate gi—I think his name was Richard—came over and introduced himself. He offered to answer any questions I might have. Did I have a son or daughter who was interested in karate?

I lied.

Well, only partly. I did have a son. But he wasn't between the ages of five and ten, which would qualify him for their junior dragons class. He offered a tour when he noticed me peering over his shoulder, straining to see the rooms down the hall, obstructed by walls that DIDN'T USED TO BE THERE. There were kids back there—I could hear them, grunting as they kicked at the air. The heavy thud of bodies being thrown against mats.

He walked me back, through a narrow hallway and into a larger room, covered in mats and prepubescents. Parents loitered near the walls and eyed me suspiciously. I felt awkward and conspicuous, very much out of place in my Replacements T-shirt and trench coat. Richard in the unnecessarily tight karate gi was giving me the sales pitch. I pretended to listen, while running a finger across the grooves of a white wall, like I was tracing lines on a map, looking for something specific.

I still remember everything about the first time I heard the New York Dolls' eponymous debut. It was in 1989, in the apartment of a girl I'd just met. What was her name? Abby? Abigail? Abrianna? Something like that. She had purple dreadlocks. I don't remember if she worked for the Record Swap or if she was just a customer, or why in the hell she was talking to me at all.

She made the first move. She made every move. She coaxed me into a conversation about Henry Rollins, because I happened to be holding a Black Flag record at the time. She invited me out to coffee, which was soon aborted when neither of us could think of a coffee place in Homewood, and we both laughed at our obvious lie.

Abby or Abigail, whoever she was, she took me back to her apartment. Which wasn't far from here. It was like visiting a foreign planet. I wanted very badly to sleep with her, which may explain why I agreed to lie on her futon with her and listen to a band fronted by a guy who, to the best of my knowledge, hit his artistic peak with the single "Hot Hot Hot." I was caught off guard by "Personality Crisis," recorded almost two decades earlier, which was admittedly catchy as hell. But I couldn't shake the mental image of Poindexter's pompadour, or that album cover of him in a tuxedo, sipping a martini, with an expression of "you caught me" delight.

You don't get to pick a new identity unless you're David Bowie.

He can be Ziggy Stardust one day and then the Thin White Duke the next, because both of those stage personas are fucking awesome. But he's the exception that makes the rule. Everybody else is subject to the rock 'n' roll law of diminishing returns. It's why Mike Nesmith had such a hard time. You start your career as a Monkee, you've made your bed.

"You know what Morrissey said," the purple-dreadlocked girl told me somewhere around the middle of side one. "Mick Jagger stole all his dance moves from David Johansen."

As much as I wanted to see her naked, those beautiful lavender locks cascading over my chest, I just couldn't let that ridiculous logic go unanswered.

"How can you say that?" I asked. "It's like saying Muddy Waters learned how to play the blues from George Thorogood."

We argued through the rest of the record, and by the final crashing notes of "Jet Boy," it had become painfully obvious that we weren't in any way musically compatible.

"I guess there's no point in asking if you're a fan of Johnny Thunders and the Heartbreakers," she said with an eye roll.

"Tom Petty's band?" I asked, incredulous. "Well, I guess that explains the Traveling Wilburys. Poor bastard can't keep a band."

I did not get laid that night.

I love that moment. I love it like I love home videos of my son trying to walk, and falling hard on his face, and then trying to make it seem like that's what he intended all along, that he'd really been reaching for that toy, and walking is—*pfft*—whatever. That's the warm feeling I get when I think about missing my chance with the hot girl with the purple dreadlocks whose name might have started with an *A*.

I was trying so hard to be cool, and failing so spectacularly.

"Are you okay?" I heard Richard with the unnecessarily tight karate gi asking me.

"You know," I finally told him. "This used to be a record store."

"Is that so?" he asked. Somewhere behind him, a boy was taking a punch in the stomach. He made a sound that came out like a BLEEERT.

"So," I said awkwardly. "I guess it, uh . . . I guess it closed."

He looked around the room, at the kids dressed like Ralph Macchio in *The Karate Kid*, giving each other karate chops. "It looks like it," he agreed.

He might have wondered why I was smelling his walls, which didn't make much sense to me even as I was doing it.

I could explain it if I had to. It was like when I got my dad's ashes and I immediately took a whiff of the urn. I didn't open it or anything, I just sat on the stairs with it and put my nose just close enough to see if it smelled like anything I recognized. It was totally nonsensical. But I did it anyway.

Or here's what else it's like. When your child is born and the first thing you do is smell his or her head. A newborn's head is just amazing. It's magical, like a Florida orange fresh off the tree. For at least the first year of my son's life, I smelled his head at least twenty times a day. But then that wonderful smell just suddenly stops. You don't know why, it's just gone. But you smell his or her head anyway, looking for some hint of what you lost, hoping it might come back if you breathe in hard enough.

I can't explain it better than that. I smelled the walls of a martial arts school for the same reasons I smelled the head of my non-infant son. Because I was sad about what it used to be.

Richard with the unnecessarily tight karate gi and I made some small talk, about what classes were coming up that might be appropriate for my son that Richard now seemed pretty convinced didn't exist. I took some brochures, and I almost gave him my credit card, if only to prove that I hadn't just been wasting his time all along. And then, with one more lingering stroke of a freshly painted wall, I got the hell out of there.

I sat in a booth at the Eat Rice Chinese restaurant, next door to what used to be the Record Swap, and made notes on a cocktail napkin, listing every record from my former collection that I was reasonably certain I could identify by sight. Or in some cases, smell.

Exile in Guyville, **Liz Phair.** With a store sticker still on the front sleeve, priced in UK pounds, bought during a summer backpacking trip to London and northern England. My intention was to purchase a Smiths record in Manchester, which I felt was significant, like buying a Beatles record in Liverpool or a Nirvana record in Seattle. And I came very close. I had *Louder Than Bombs* in my hands, and I was en route to the register at Piccadilly Records on Oldham Street. But then I talked to some guys with thick British accents who were really, really into Liz Phair, and they made a convincing case that Liz Phair was the most important artist in our lifetime, certainly the most important artist making songs about being a blow job queen. So I bought *Exile in Guyville* instead. I essentially traveled thirty-eight hundred miles to pay three times the amount for an album that was recorded in a Chicago studio located six miles from my apartment.

Let It Bleed, **the Rolling Stones.** The cover sleeve contains the radio station call letters WBCR written in big black Sharpie. Also, a muddy boot print. Doc Martens, I'm pretty sure. The boot print was not accidental, but a very earnest attempt by a college radio station manager to destroy the record. It was unsuccessful.

Alive II, **KISS**. In ballpoint pen, written across the band's name, it reads: "HANDS OFF!!!" A warning from Mark, my younger brother by two years—when he was approximately seven and I was nine—that any further attempts to lay claim to his vinyl property would result in swift and merciless vengeance. I remember very explicitly that there were three exclamation points. Because one would not be enough to convey the full force of his threat. This was no joke.

I don't know if my brother even remembers this—not just writing a cryptic warning on a KISS record, but owning a KISS record at all. He's a very different person than he was when we were kids. For one thing, he's filthy rich.

Mark wasn't born rich. If he was, I'd be rich too. He got that way because he's very good at making bad bets. He's what some people have called a "doomsday investor." He bets on market calamity, the financial disasters that nobody expects to happen. Every time you turn on the news and the stock market has taken another hit and the federal debt ceiling is on the verge of caving in, Mark just made another million.

Mark and I aren't just in different tax brackets—we're in different universes.

When I tell people that my brother is rich, their first question is usually: "So you guys probably don't get along anymore, right?" Which is a weird thing to assume, especially the "anymore" part.

If I'm being honest, okay sure, my brother and I aren't as close as we were when we were kids. But that's inevitable. You'll never be as emotionally connected to somebody as you were when you lived across the hall from them, and his unfairly bogarting the KISS record seemed like the only thing in the universe that mattered. He wasn't just my brother, he was my nemesis, somebody I thought about constantly, mostly about how he was a dick and was always hogging the cool records.

The last time I visited my brother, I had dinner with him in his gigantic backyard, and we stayed up far too late drinking Scotch that cost more than my electricity bill for a year. We talked about the recent happenings in our life, and pretended our lives weren't different in every fundamental way.

KISS *Alive II* isn't a good record. It's a pretty shitty one, if memory serves. You realize that almost immediately, before the first song even begins, when a tour crew member opens the record by screaming at the audience, like a toddler having a meltdown: "You wanted the best and you got the best! The hottest band in the world! KIIIIIISS!!" But I remember weekends spent just staring at the cover, listening to every song in chronological order, and being utterly hypnotized. I'm not sure if I ever made the conscious decision "This is music that aesthetically appeals to me." But it felt important somehow. The same way it felt important to stare at the hot girl in chemistry class in high school, the one with the amazing black hair that she'd twirl around her pinkie finger in an absentminded sort of way that felt weirdly intimate, like I was witnessing something I wasn't supposed to. That's what listening to KISS's *Alive II* while looking at a grainy photo of Gene Simmons gurgling blood in the rain felt like.

But more than any of that, I wanted my old copy of KISS *Alive II* for the threatening graffiti on the front sleeve—irrefutable proof that my brother and I used to be the most important people in each other's lives.

Band on the Run, Paul McCartney and Wings. Contains a large sticker on the front sleeve that reads PROPERTY OF RICHTON PARK PUBLIC LIBRARY. The last person to have listened to this record, before I stole it from the library, was a guy named Steve, who went to my high school.

I knew this because I'd tried to check it out from the Richton Park library, but the librarian told me that Steve had it. And then he returned it, and the librarian called to tell me it was back. And then I heard that Steve killed his mom.

The details were pretty grim. He shot her during an argument at their home, and then dragged her body into the trunk of his car, intending to bury it in a nearby forest preserve. He almost made it, but a cop pulled him over for having a busted taillight and noticed the stench of death. Whenever I get together with my friends from back in the day we still talk about it. "Remember that guy who killed his mom?" one of us will say. And then we'll all solemnly nod our heads, like matricide was just a normal part of our day-to-day lives.

In the months after Steve was caught, I listened to *Band on the Run* a lot. I became obsessed with it. I wondered, was this what did it? Is this what drove him to murder his own mom? And when it came time to return the record to the library, I hid it. First in my closet, and then in the basement, tucked into the bottom of a box filled with blankets. I couldn't take the chance that it might be discovered and returned to the nonprofit lending institution that couldn't possibly understand the value of what they had. I had no interest in Paul McCartney, and even less in *Band on the Run*. But this particular record, which was probably still smeared with Steve's fingerprints, was like owning one of John Wayne Gacy's paintings. It was like owning a document of madness. I paid the fine, made some excuse about having lost it, and it was mine.

Rain Dogs, **Tom Waits.** With red lipstick smeared on the cover, over the lips of who I thought at the time was Tom Waits but apparently is just a really old photo of a sailor being comforted by a prostitute. I don't remember whose lipstick it was. Probably somebody I was dating, or just sleeping with. Was it her record or mine? I don't have any recall of those details.

Since then, I've lived with many roommates, and a few girl-friends, and every time we parted ways, and it came time to divvy up our respective record collections, I could say, "My *Rain Dogs* is the one with the lipstick on it."

New York Dolls—but with Prince's *Sign o' the Times* inside (or maybe vice versa). I never really got over making a monumental ass of myself with Abby or Abigail—the girl with the purple dreadlocks who assumed I had any idea who the New York Dolls were, because she confused me with somebody she might feasibly have sex with. That's not something you just forget. It's not a "learn from my mistakes" moment. It's an "I need to buy and study the New York Dolls immediately just in case lightning strikes twice" moment. But there was a problem, in that I was concurrently in a pretty heavy Prince period. I was much more interested in listening to *Sign o' the Times* than an androgynous junkie glam punk band that'd broken up when I was six years old. But a guy hoping to have sex with girls with a punk sensibility can't be openly expressing a Prince fandom and hope to reap sexual rewards. So I hid my *Sign o' the Times* in the New York Dolls record, and the Dolls record ended up in the *Sign o' the Times* sleeve. I'm almost positive both records were sold or given away before the records were reunited with their correct packaging.

Let It Be, **The Replacements.** Of all my old records, this is the one I'm most confident I'll be able to find again. It was the last record from my collection that I gave up, so the law of averages is on my side. It's only been in wide circulation for sixteen or so years. How long do they wait before giving up on a missing child? At least twenty, right? Maybe never.

If it's still out there, if it's findable, I'll smell it before I see it. I don't care if it's buried underground like a cemetery under the *Poltergeist* house, those pot resin fumes will come bubbling to the surface like angry ghosts.

I wasn't just doodling. This was a battle plan. A declaration of intent.

I wasn't about to give up because the record store where I'd sold the majority of my records was gone, out of business and with no forwarding address. My records were still out there. They had to be. Unless they'd been melted down to ash in a warehouse fire, they at least still existed. Somebody owned them. Maybe the people who had them didn't even know they had them. Maybe they were in a basement, shoved into the bottom of a water-damaged Meijer's wine box, or in a friend's attic, in a stack of high school yearbooks and letters from dead relatives that nobody remembers were left up there. They were gathering dust in some dark corner, waiting to be rediscovered.

Was I just being stupidly nostalgic? I'd considered that. But it's not like I wanted my floppy disks back. I wasn't on a mission to find old AOL sign-up CDs, or those Nintendo cartridges that could be "fixed" by blowing in them. If I could find these records again, it'd rewire my brain somehow. I was sure of it. It'd be like hitting the reset button.

It was raining when I left the restaurant. I let it drench me as I walked too slowly back to my car.

A good Chicago rain reminds me of that John Cusack movie *Say Anything*, when he's in the backseat of a car with his girlfriend, or the girl he wants to be his girlfriend, and they've just had sex for the first time, and they're listening to Peter Gabriel and shivering. I always thought that he was as much in love with the music as he was with the girl. Because the music captured his emotions at that exact moment he was feeling them, and reflected them back to him perfectly. That kind of connection happens so rarely, almost never between two human beings, and only occasionally between a person and a song. You can't really wrap your head around what you're feeling, but then a song comes on and you're like, "That's it!"

Cusack's character in *Say Anything* is going to remember that moment for the rest of his life. He may not remember the girl; he probably lost touch with her, or he's Facebook friends with her. He may not even remember her name anymore. But he remembers that night in the rainstorm, listening to Peter Gabriel in the backseat of a car, holding on to a girl and shivering because he was so overcome with feelings that Peter Gabriel helped him feel a little more beautifully.

That's everything I've ever wanted from any song. I just want it to make me tremble while I'm falling in love in a car during a rainstorm. But not every song can be that perfect.

I climbed into the Honda and flipped on the radio, hoping for something goose bumps–inducing, something that would make me want to just sit there with the car off, clutching the steering wheel, watching the rain beat out a gentle rhythm on the front windshield as I thought about life in some profound new way.

It was Bon Jovi's "Livin' on a Prayer."

Again.

For the second time that day.

I know it was my own fault, for leaving it on the eighties station, but it felt like the universe was making fun of me.

Four

When Charlie, my baby boy, was just a week old, he was perched like an inchworm on my stomach, as I softly sang to him what I hoped was becoming his favorite lullaby.

Normalize the signal and you're banging on freon
Paleolithic eon

For the nine months leading up to Charlie's birth, friends and family members—both with kids and otherwise—told me repeatedly about all the terrible children's music I'd be forced to endure in the coming years. And they always said it with a smirk, like they could barely suppress their schadenfreude at the inevitability of my musical suffering. They'd tell me about Thomas, the anthropomorphic and underachieving British train engine; and *VeggieTales*, with their not-in-any-way subtle proselytizing; and *Yo Gabba Gabba!*, whose name sounds like the frightened last words of somebody having a stroke. Well you know what? Fuck them.

Long before I had unprotected sex with my wife, I was determined to never, ever learn the lyrics to songs like "Toot Toot, Chugga Chugga, Big Red Car," unless it's performed by Iggy Pop and the "big red car" is a metaphor for Iggy's penis.

I don't believe in children's music. It's unnecessary. Because every artist has at least one baby-appropriate song. Take the Pixies. Obviously you shouldn't play "Wave of Mutilation" or "You Fucking Die" for a newborn. But what about "Where Is My Mind?" It's only creepy because you associate it with *Fight Club*. Or that time you bought hash from that albino guy in Bucktown and got way higher than you should have. But in the right context, the lyrics are innocuous and sweetly poetic, like something from a Shel Silverstein book. "I was swimming in the Caribbean / Animals were hiding behind the rocks." Adorable!

About five minutes into listening to Soul Coughing's *Ruby Vroom* for the first time, in a Chicago apartment across the street from the bar that blows up in *The Untouchables*, and I'd made up my mind about "Sugar Free Jazz." I knew instantly that I'd be singing it to my child someday. There's just something about the melody that sounds like a children's song. I may've been stoned, and almost two decades away from reproducing. But I could see it all so clearly. This was the song.

I announced this to everybody. Which always made people uncomfortable. Usually because when you're listening to music in your early twenties, you're not also having a discussion about babies. Girls, unsurprisingly, never responded positively to this unsolicited piece of information.

My future wife—who, in the late nineties, was just a girlfriend who stuck around longer than the others—was more tolerant when I made these proclamations, although she also wasn't afraid of making fun of me.

I remember one night in particular—I was smoking cigarettes

out the window of her studio apartment, while wearing a single rubber, yellow dishwashing glove because it was frigid outside. As I smoked, I told her how I'd be singing "Sugar Free Jazz" to my infant child someday—boy or girl, it didn't matter.

"So you're going to show off for your baby?" she asked.

"What? No. It's a sweet song."

"You're like the delusional old guy in that Randy Newman song," she said.

I knew what she meant. All Randy Newman songs are essentially about delusional old guys. But she was referring specifically to the delusional old guy in "Memo to My Son," with the narrator who chastises an infant for not being more impressed with his father's knowledge.

> *Wait'll you learn how to talk, baby*
> *I'll show you how smart I am.*

It was just accurate enough to shut me the hell up.

At the time, it seemed inconceivable that my future son or daughter wouldn't share my musical obsessions. I didn't care if they looked nothing like me, if their physical features made us look like strangers. But obviously, my child and I would cry at the same records. Why would you even have a kid if this wasn't something that happened? Sure, I never had that connection with my dad. But that was his fault. He just listened to the wrong music. If his record collection had been a little more eclectic than Willie Nelson and Cat Stevens and Jim Croce, we might've had a chance.

Age brings at least a little wisdom. As I held my son and at last sang the gibberish lyrics from "Sugar Free Jazz" to him, as I always knew I would, I could feel in my gut that the gesture was fleeting. By the time he's old enough to have a musical point of view, our personal tastes will be so incompatible that I'll start to doubt whether we actually share DNA. I could fill his baby head with as many of my songs as I wanted, but it won't make a damn bit of difference in the long run. When he's sixteen, he'll be listening to acid robot hip-hop, or whatever the fuck is popular among teens in the future, and he'll roll his eyes when I remind him of the songs I used to sing to him as a baby.

It doesn't matter. The lullabies are for me.

When Charlie was born, I felt love like I've never experienced before in my life. But by day two, I was in free-fall panic mode. What chance did I have of raising this tiny, fragile human being without fucking him up? Some people are born to be parents. They can change a diaper with the precision of a sushi chef, or carry the numerous baby apparatuses on their backs like Sherpas. I still think getting day drunk on a weekday and waiting for a "final notice" bill from the electric company sound like good ideas.

When the baby anxiety gripped me, I would sing to him. I don't know if it calmed him, but it definitely calmed me. It was the same reason why I sang along to the Replacements' "Unsatisfied" as a teenager until I got hoarse. Because it made me feel, at least temporarily, that I had life in any way figured out.

It's also the reason why Kelly and I put so much thought into the labor soundtrack for our son's delivery. We spent weeks arguing about it, bouncing song ideas back and forth. We devoted more time to creating and fine-tuning playlists than reading baby books. We once wasted an entire evening debating whether Ani DiFranco's "Dilate" should be included, despite having nothing to do with cervixes, and ended up missing a birthing class. The only song we actually agreed on was the Foo Fighters' "Razor," which was lyrically perfect without being too explicit. "Wake up it's time / We need to find a better place to hide." Maybe Dave Grohl wasn't talking about a stubborn womb-squatting baby, but he might as well have been.

A few verses and my son was gurgling happily.

Fossilize apostle and I comb it with a rake
You can't escape

And I swear to you, right around the lyric about bombing schools, little, innocent, pink-faced Charlie smiled up at me. I know it was probably just a fart, but to me, it felt like a victory.

I was at the Chicagoland Record Collectors Show in Hillside, a western suburb of Chicago. The gathering of record sellers, held every other month at a Best Western hotel off the Eisenhower Expressway, has been called the "largest vinyl show in the Midwest." I don't know if that's in any way impressive. It could be like saying, "We've got the best shrimp in Michigan!"

Within a few minutes of walking inside, I'd uncovered treasure. In a booth near the front entrance, I'd found a copy of the Soul Coughing "Sugar Free Jazz" twelve-inch—with the four useless remixes and no actual album art, other than the bloody Slash Records logo. I was practically trembling. It had to be mine, I told myself. Everything about it looked exactly the same. It had the FOR PROMOTIONAL USE ONLY—NOT FOR RESALE sticker. The sleeve looked a little warped, suggesting that its previous owner took a lackadaisical approach to caring for it. Bingo! Guilty as charged!

But then I slipped the record out of its packaging, and my heart sank. It was in pristine shape. The grooves were so clean and shimmery, they almost reflected the light like a disco ball. It had clearly only ever been held correctly, on the outer edges, to prevent thumbprints and fingernail scratches.

The guy behind the card table—lined with dozens of boxes of

vinyl records—caught my eye and gravitated toward me from his stool. He had long hair, white as a department store Santa's, pulled back into a ponytail, and he wore a Rush T-shirt that looked like it'd been ironed. He smelled like Pert Plus and peppermint gum.

"Never been played," he told me, snapping his gum. "That's a mint-condition item right there."

I slipped it back into the sleeve. "Thanks," I said, handing it back to him. "Not what I'm looking for."

White Ponytail narrowed his eyes, sizing me up. "Okay, I'll tell you what I'm gonna do." He lowered his voice to a whisper. "I'll give it to you for ten." He looked over my shoulder, like he half expected the crowd to come lunging toward us, cash in hand, when they overheard that he was discounting records.

"I appreciate that," I told him. "But I'm not interested."

"You're not going to find a better copy of that record anywhere," he said. "These are really rare, especially in this condition."

"I believe you," I said. "I'm just looking for something else."

"There was only one pressing of this single," he said, growing impatient. "If you're looking for a different catalog number, I don't think—"

"I'm looking for a copy with scratches."

He paused, midchew.

"A very specific scratch, actually," I continued. "Somewhere on the 'Molasses Dub.' Which, you know . . ." I forced a laugh. "No big loss, right?"

White Ponytail said nothing, just watched me.

"You want me to scratch it for you?" he finally said. "I'll scratch it for you. Or scratch it yourself, I don't care."

"No, thanks. I was kinda hoping for a scratch from 1998."

He waited silently, perhaps hoping that this was just some joke he didn't understand, a preamble to finally pulling out my wallet and paying for the damn record already. And then, satisfied that I was a lost cause, he drifted away, moving on to the next customer down the line.

No matter, there were plenty of other dealers here. I gazed out at the sea of heads, all faced downward, their thumbs busy flipping records, filling the room with a faint drone not unlike chirping crickets. But these insects weren't looking for mates so much as Beatles forty-fives.

These records I'm trying to find, it's reasonable to assume they were still in the state. If not within the city limits, at least a morning's drive away. I could go from store to store, thrift shop to yard sale, hoping I'd be able to piecemeal together my collection. Or I find their ground zero—a record fair that all the dealers and sellers and serious addicts attend, their vans filled with records, ready to unload their stock in a hotel banquet hall that smells like cheap wedding cake.

But what if some of my records had crossed state lines? I'd thought about that possibility. But the guys selling records at this Best Western weren't just locals. They came from Michigan, Indiana, Missouri, Iowa, Wisconsin, Colorado. These weren't people making their first trip to Chicago. They'd been here many times—maybe they make a pilgrimage to the Record Collectors Show every year. They could've bought one of my records a decade ago, brought it home, listened to it a few times, then decided, "I paid too much for this piece of shit. It's got Sharpie all over it, it skips at all the best songs, I'm going to see if I can get another sucker to buy it." So they brought it right back to where they found it.

I knew a guy once, a former federal marshal, who said that when you want to find an escaped con, check out the bars in the next town over. They're not on a plane bound for Mexico. They're at the next exit off 94, drinking with Schmitty.

When I walked into the main hall and saw the endless rows of records, which seemed to stretch on for miles, it was exhilarating. I felt lightheaded and giddy, and I had this weird urge to just run through the tiny rows between tables, knocking crates over like Sting did to candles in that video for "Wrapped Around Your Finger." But my enthusiasm was premature. I'm not sure what I was thinking. Did I assume all the sellers had gotten together before the doors opened and said, "Okay, fellas, let's make sure everything here is alphabetical. You got any R's, put them on that side of the room."

Many tables seemed purposively designed to be as confusing as possible. Some dealers separated their stock into categories that were either laughably broad ("twentieth-century pop") or needlessly amphibological ("popcorn titty shakers," which even after searching its stacks, I still couldn't tell you what genre it was jokingly trying to define). When they did have a category that offered something approaching clarity—good old-fashioned "rock"—the contents were usually nothing of the kind. In a single "rock"-labeled crate, I found George Burns's *I Wish I Was Eighteen Again*, Sheila E's *The Glamorous Life*, Elvis Presley's *Let's Be Friends*, *Champagne Jam* by the Atlanta Rhythm Section, Betty Wright's *Danger High Voltage*, Gary Marshal's *Show Stopper!!*, the Eagles' *Greatest Hits*, something just called *Funny Bone Favorites*, *Best of the Beach Boys*, *The Secret Value of Daydreaming* by Julian Lennon, and a forty-five of Jim Foster's "X-Ray Eyes" (edited version).

I don't know if it would've made a difference, but I was kicking myself for not coming for the early-bird hours, starting at 6:00 a.m. That's when the professionals were here, the lifelong crate diggers who are like gold prospectors but for vinyl. The guys who showed up with their own bags, who may've forgotten their IDs but never leave home without a carbon fiber brush. They've met new people, made new friends, but haven't yet made eye contact with anybody. I'd heard that Sonic Youth guitarist Thurston Moore came to a few of these shows. He was probably one of the early-birders. He found what he wanted, cherry-picked the good stuff, and then got the hell out.

I guess it helped that the records I was looking for didn't count in any conventional sense as "the good stuff."

I was singularly focused, looking for my records. But every so often, I'd happen upon something that caught my eye. I paused at something called *Signs of Life* by the Penguin Cafe Orchestra. I'd never heard of the band or the record. But the front cover was a painting of totally naked people with penguin heads. I just stared at it for several minutes, wondering what I was looking at. There was also a monkey with a penguin head riding a minibicycle and waving a gun. I mean, what was I supposed to feel about that?

And then you get something like Queensrÿche's *Hear in the Now Frontier*. While flipping through records, I ignored hundreds of albums and artists I knew I didn't like. But I stopped on this one. I've never been a fan of Queensrÿche. But something about this cover gave me pause. It was a desert scene, with five disembodied, pickled ears in mason jars. I stared at it, contemplated it, even pulled it out of the crate for a better look. I knew what Queensrÿche sounded like. I knew that buying this record—even at four dollars—was a mistake. I'd take it home, give it a listen, and somewhere around the first song think, "Well, this is ear rape." And then I'd put it away and never touch it again. But holding the record, without any of that information— inevitable though it might be—I was too transfixed by the ears in jars to think of anything else. I was fooled by possibility, which is exactly what a great record cover should do.

That was how it used to be, back when you couldn't listen to music before buying it. You sometimes had to make decisions based solely on cover art. Imagine having to look at the cover of the Dead Kennedys' *Frankenchrist* and decide whether this was music you needed to hear when the only criteria you had was that image of a

Shriners parade. You had to ask some tough questions—is this album cover being ironic or sincere? Is this a random art choice, or does it have some thematic parallel to the music? You have to trust your gut, and sometimes your gut can be very, very wrong.

My gut was right when it came to Jane's Addiction's *Nothing's Shocking*—turns out naked twins with fire hair is a good indication that you're about to have your musical mind blown—and sometimes it's very, very wrong: never trust an Assyrian lion, even when it's on a late-period Rolling Stones album.

"Do you have the Band's first record?" the albino man next to me asked, looking agitated.

Maybe he wasn't albino, but he was very, very white. Like translucent white. If his eyes had pupils, I didn't see them. He had long, stringy hair and a jean jacket, and he looked like Johnny Winter if the guitarist had been really, really into mac and cheese.

The guy behind the table frowned deeply, thinking. "You mean as the Hawks, or with Dylan, or what?"

The albino man snorted, like an angry bull. "The one with 'The Weight.'"

"*Big Pink*," the dealer said, smiling, and then paused to consider this. "No, I haven't seen that one for a while."

The albino man groaned. The exaggerated, melodramatic groan of somebody who'd been told no too many times.

I'd been eavesdropping on his plight. He was just ahead of me in the current, the assembly line of bodies, lurching slowly forward from table to table, box to box, flipping and moving on, flipping and moving on. I'd heard him ask this question to at least a half dozen sellers. And every time, they just shook their heads. He seemed resigned the first six or seven times, but he was becoming increasingly irritable. This, his pupilless eyes screamed, should be easier.

He was right. And the crazy thing is, there was an easier way.

There were literally hundreds of less time-consuming ways to find a copy of the Band's *Music from Big Pink*. He could go on eBay and find many copies for sale, on various formats—vinyl, cassette, CD, even eight-track, if that was his thing—selling for far less than anything he'd find here. Or, if he wanted to hear the album quicker, there were numerous places on the Internet where he could download it in seconds, at a cost of exactly nothing.

Surely he knew this, right? He wasn't unfamiliar with how the world worked. He knew he didn't have to drive out to a suburban Best Western off the Eisenhower Expressway to find an album he could buy at home, on his computer, without even putting on pants. This wasn't just the hard way; it was the stupid hard way. It's a harrowing moment when you realize that the only thing separating you and a Civil War reenactor is better underwear.

And that's when I saw him, out of the corner of my eye, rounding a corner and weaving through skinny-jeaned legs. My son, Charlie, was dressed in an ironic cardigan smeared with chocolate thumbprints and doughnut crumbs. He'd been given a perilous dosage of sugar—which, full disclosure, was probably mostly my fault. I wanted him to be as excited about this adventure as I was. And sugar seemed like the fastest and least complicated way to get to the same mental space. It's roughly the same reason I did coke—my first and only time—before a Garth Brooks concert. I didn't want to be there, but I thought, hey, maybe some cocaine will help.

It worked with Garth Brooks. I was a cowboy-loving, honky-tonking dance machine. I think I even cried a little at "The River." But coke to me was not sugar to Charlie. He was just bored and wired, a dangerous combination.

"Charlie, no," I said calmly, without looking up from a Bob Mould record in my hands. He scurried past, narrowly avoiding puncturing his head on a crate with sharp metal corners.

Kelly was right behind him. But just barely.

"Are you going to be much longer?" she asked.

I gave her my best "Are you kidding me?" look. But she never saw it. She continued in the foxhunt for our son, pushing past bearded men in Pavement T-shirts and muttering apologies, trying to remind herself why being a single parent would somehow be less annoying than this.

I hadn't meant to bring them. I mean, that wasn't the original plan. The original plan was to come alone. Or, barring that, come out with some guy friends, some other dudes who didn't see the social awkwardness of driving an hour out to the suburbs only to ignore one another and look at records for six hours. They all backed out at the last minute, claiming they had "a thing" that they'd completely forgotten about, or their respective wives had surprised them with weekend obligations that couldn't be wiggled out of.

I was resigned to going by myself, until Kelly decided that this would be a great chance for a family outing. It wasn't, of course. This was immediately apparent to me, but she'd made up her mind. It only became clear to her during the long drive out to the suburbs that this wouldn't be like one of those quick trips to the Gap or the Apple store. This wasn't an "I'll just be a second" type of shopping venture.

"How many records are you planning on buying?" she asked, with the nervous dread of somebody on the slow climb upward on a roller coaster.

"I don't know," I said, shrugging. "Whatever it takes."

We both watched the road, and I could almost feel the air change as her shoulders tightened.

"Where would we even put them?" she asked. "We don't have that much room in our apartment as it is. Are you just going to start piling things in a corner?"

"No."

"It just doesn't make sense to me. You're going to buy a bunch of records that we don't have space for. And we don't have a record player. You're just going to look at them?"

"I'll get a record player," I said.

"And where are you putting that? Our bedroom? Tell me where this magic record player is going."

She was in full panic mode. An emotion I rarely saw in her. Even Charlie, distracted by his little portable DVD player in the backseat, could tell that something was wrong. Mommy was upset, and it was Daddy's fault.

She launched into a familiar routine—telling me why I didn't need to worry about music, or losing music, or whatever it was that was compelling me to fill our small city apartment with more objects, bulky disks with too much cardboard from another era that took up space in her home and meant there was less room for other things. Also—and this was the point that made the veins on her neck start to throb—having things when you didn't need those things was madness. We already had music. We had all the music we'd ever need—everything we'd ever owned or listened to—and it didn't require having enough room in a closet. It was in a cloud.

This is where she lost me.

I don't understand clouds. "It protects all of your music," she told me, not for the first time. Not by a long shot. "You don't have to worry about crashing and losing everything."

Crashing. I was never what you'd call a technophile when it came to record players—I don't know a damn thing about frequency extension or tonal correctness or the best way to reduce relative distortion during playback—but I know that a record player, any record player, would never do something as apocalyptic as "crashing." Nothing could happen to a record player that would cause everything you owned, every piece of music, to just be . . . gone.

Which is kind of ironic, if you think about it. Because all those records that couldn't be destroyed, that I could play forever on even the shittiest of record players, which were virtually indestructible, all of those records were now just . . . gone.

When I was briefly, unwisely, considering handing over all evidence of my music to an ethereal, intangible lockbox that exists only in theory, I called Glenn, an old friend who knows his way around computers. I just needed some guidance, or maybe some reassurance.

"So all my old music just disappears?" I asked him, my voice hitting a panicky treble.

"No, no, no," Glenn assured me. "They just store an identical version in iCloud, but it's got a better sound quality."

"What about album art?" I asked.

"All your metadata is transferred to the new audio files. Everything."

"What if, say, my cover art for Tom Waits's *Swordfishtrombones* is the Japanese import with a record-store sticker on the front written in kanji symbols? Will that be transferred too?"

This gave him pause. "Is that important to you?"

It most certainly was.

"And what about genres?" I asked. "Are my files going to revert back to those boring iTunes genres, or do I get to keep my own grouping system?"

I'd put a lot of effort into coming up with more descriptive genres than iTunes provides. "Alternative & punk" and "rock" doesn't tell me anything meaningful about my music. So I've organized my MP3s into categories like "androgynous pop-rock" and "mildly annoying baby boomers" and "indie rock that I'm marginally interested in" and "alt-country songs about booze, sad sex, and Jesus."

"I'm pretty sure you could keep that stuff," Glenn told me unconvincingly.

"So if iTunes classifies a song as 'folk,' they'll let me change it to 'nasally musicians I adore unconditionally'?"

"I suppose so, sure."

"And even if they want something to be 'blues,' I can insist on calling it 'white guys playing the blues that seemed more interesting when I was smoking pot in high school'?"

"I really don't know for sure. Why do you even care about this stuff? As long as the music sounds good, who cares how it's labeled?"

I cared. I'd spent days—literally twenty-four-hour days—obsessing over this stuff, scouring the Internet for the perfect cover art, a reproduction of a water-damaged vinyl sleeve with the Tower Records price tag still in the upper corner, or trying to decide if the Gaslight Anthem qualifies as "unironic working-class anthems" or "Springsteeny." If iTunes Match erased all that useless minutiae, then it would confirm that it was really just useless minutiae after all.

There was a time not so long ago, in the latter half of the twentieth century (and maybe before that, I don't know), when you had to be careful about who you invited to your house. Even the most sane-looking person could have dark impulses, an inexplicable and insatiable need to fuck with the CD collections of strangers. If you left them unattended for even a few minutes, you might come back to discover that your music had been unhelpfully realphabetized. Or worse, separated by genre or time period, or arranged in aesthetically ornate piles. They were always so pleased with themselves, like they were providing a valuable service. "I noticed that some of your CDs were in the wrong jewel cases," they'd say. "*Daydream Nation* was in the case for *Doolittle*. I mean, how ridiculous is that, right? You never would've found it." The only thing to do was smile tersely and make a mental note never to let meddling idiots near your music again.

My music isn't on any clouds, and it probably never will be. Because I want my music to be flawed. I like the hisses and pops of my old records and CDs. And I like that if somebody picked up my iPod, they'd probably be confused and angry by the asinine way that the songs are organized. But I'd rather risk losing it all in a hard-drive crash than have my music library become just another homogenized collection of songs.

"Just don't spend too much money on records you can't listen to and we don't have room for," Kelly said.

Two hours later, I don't know where either of them are, and I'm holding a copy of *Bona Drag*, transfixed by the faded Crayola-blue cover. Pulling it out was like turning a corner and running into an ex-girlfriend, somebody whose old letters you still kept in a shoe box.

"Charlie, no!"

Kelly's voice jolted me out of daydreaming. I couldn't see her, but I could hear him, somewhere behind me, his little feet scurrying like a rat in a tenement, giggling as he ducked through legs and evaded capture. I could see the eyes widen in the adults who noticed him, alarmed not so much about a three-year-old running so fast through a maze fraught with so many dangers, but those outstretched chocolate fingers, aimed like swords at their precious vinyl.

"Elvis Costello!"

Charlie was crouched under a table, pulling records out of boxes and roughly examining them. He'd pretend to read each title before yelling "Elvis Costello!" and then he'd slam each delicate little disk onto the floor, with such force it was a miracle they didn't shatter under his fist.

The night before, we'd listened to some Elvis Costello—his favorite artist of the moment—and he asked if Costello had records. I told him yes, many, many records, some better than others, and if he searched really hard tomorrow, looked in every box and on every table, he might find some.

A man with bushy gray eyebrows and Frank Zappa facial hair

was zeroing in on Charlie. "Sir, sir, please be careful with those," he blustered, looking panicky and uncertain. This was obviously new terrain for him, as he called a three-year-old "sir."

"Elvis Costello go BAM!"

My forehead tightened. I loosened my grip on *Bona Drag*, let it fall back into the box. I had to restrain my child before he destroyed enough records to decimate my entire record-buying budget.

"That your kid?" I heard a voice ask, as I wrestled an already battered copy of *Spike* out of Charlie's lobster claws. I looked up and saw two guys, roughly my own age, with the compulsory rock T-shirts—one sported a Dinosaur Jr. album illustration, the other was Guns N' Roses. They had bodies like Russian nesting dolls, neckless and smooth. They were, thus far, the only people in this building who had looked at Charlie with anything besides fearful derision. As I held tightly on to Charlie, the one in the Dinosaur Jr. T-shirt told me, unsolicited, everything about his history with recorded music.

"I got my first record player when I was about his age," he said, nodding to my son. "I used to sit on the floor and watch the records go around and around and around. I was a psycho." He burst into loud laughter.

"You're still a fucking psycho," his friend in the Guns N' Roses shirt offered.

"Fuck your ass," Dinosaur Jr. countered.

I covered Charlie's ears. They both continued talking, telling me how their childhood fascination had grown into a lifelong hobby that sounded just slightly less depressing than a tax accountant's.

"I've got over fifty thousand albums," said Guns N' Roses. "That includes about ten thousand in my core collection, which are the ones I won't sell. They're my babies. I also have about seven thousand forty-fives that are also my babies. The others are hobos. Those are the ones that travel."

"And you'll sell the hobos?" I asked.

"Hobos can always go. One way or another, they'll come back to you. But the babies, you have to protect them. Keep them in the house, away from the world . . ."

Dinosaur Jr. was laughing. "You're so queer."

Guns N' Roses just shrugged. "You know what the thing is though? I'm finally starting to lose interest."

"Liar."

"No, it's happening. I'm always looking for new stuff, but then you get the new stuff, and you play it a few times, and then file it away in a box. I've got responsibilities now. I have to cut the grass."

Kelly emerged from the crowd, and without even breaking stride, lifted Charlie from my arms. "I've got him," she said, still moving.

"Wait, are you—?" I called after her.

"Do what you need to do," she said. "Just please be fast about it, okay?"

"Can we help you find something?" Guns N' Roses asked.

I glanced down at the dozen or so boxes of records, which now seemed like a hopelessly time-consuming job.

"You have the Replacements' *Let It Be*?" I asked.

They both laughed. "Setting the bar a little high, aren't you?" Dinosaur Jr. asked.

"So . . . no?"

"I've seen a *Don't Tell a Soul* every once in a while," he said. "And a few months ago I had a copy of *Tim* in my store for almost exactly thirty minutes before it sold. But I have never, in my forty years of doing this professionally, seen an original *Let It Be*. Like ever. That includes in the eighties."

"So it's like looking for Bigfoot?" I asked, trying to be funny.

"No," Dinosaur Jr. said matter-of-factly. "I've seen Bigfoot before."

"Yeah, I've seen Bigfoot," said Guns N' Roses. "That's no big deal."

I don't know why *Let It Be* was so important to me. There are a million reasons why it shouldn't be. There is almost nothing about it that is or has ever been directly relatable to me or my life. I've had no experience with androgyny—other than wearing pseudo-drag to a *Rocky Horror Picture Show* screening during my freshman year of college—and have never had any friends with androgynous tendencies, other than the aforementioned *Rocky Horror Picture Show* outings and the occasional David Bowie Halloween costume. I've never been an alcoholic who's had a moment of sad self-realization at his favorite dive bar, and I've never been in a band bemused by a more popular band's video on MTV. I've never been in a long-distance relationship with somebody and tried to call her at night and left a series of answering-machine messages that made me feel emotionally alienated. I've never even had my tonsils taken out. I've had boners, of course, but nothing on "Gary's Got a Boner" spoke to my experience with erections, especially the "gonna stick it to her" part.

Probably the only song that I felt even slightly connected to a personal level was "Unsatisfied." I'm not sure what was unsatisfying to Paul Westerberg, but it probably didn't involve sneaking into a mall movie theater to see *Hardbodies 2* and not being all that impressed with the naked boobs, which you'd been led to believe would be in greater numbers.

As a teenager, nothing about me was punk. I didn't have any piercings, my body was utterly untattooed, and when I first started listening to the 'Mats, I hadn't smoked so much as a joint. But I still loved *Let It Be*. Probably because it was the complete opposite of who I was at the time. I was the awkward teenager who played trombone, was terrible at sports, and listened to too much Billy Joel. Maybe the Billy Joel part wasn't so bad, but from my experience, teenagers who say things like "I can sing the lyrics to 'You May Be Right' from memory" don't also say things like "I'm exhausted from getting all these hand jobs!"

When I listened to *Let It Be*, it made me feel instantly like one of the cool kids, who were losers by choice, and whose disaffection was at least partly a pose, because they were almost certainly getting laid. My *Let It Be* album was a security blanket, a secret that I carried with me every time I went to school, or had any interaction with my suburban peers. I knew something that they didn't. These fucking assholes, who thought Duran Duran and Corey fucking Hart were music. They thought they had it all figured out. But it was like they were looking for nourishment in Coke commercials when I'd found Salinger novels. And they didn't even realize that Salinger existed! They were starving to death, and they didn't even realize it.

After another humiliating and unfulfilling day, I'd come home and go to my bedroom and put on *Let It Be*, and cling to the record sleeve and stare at the front cover photo of those four wasted Midwestern punks sitting on a rooftop. It was like gamma rays going into Bruce Banner. It turned me into the Hulk. Maybe not on the outside. But a Hulk heart was beating in my chest, even if nobody else noticed it.

As a teen, I somehow ended up in possession of a tattered copy of the Replacements' bootleg *The Shit Hits the Fans*. To hear me talk about it now, it was my musical bible, a lifeline to sanity in a suburban Scheol. But really, I probably listened to it only once or twice, and then only halfheartedly. Hindsight, as least when it comes to music, is never twenty-twenty. You downplay your fist-pumping devotion to Def Leppard and Poison and hyperbolize your unconditional love for the Pixies and the Meat Puppets.

But I don't think I've given too much credit to *Let It Be*. Because my biggest, most visceral memory of that record is not having it when I really needed it the most.

I can remember everything and nothing about the day my father died. Everything about the shape of the day is a blur. But the details that stick in my head are inanely specific. I remember that Kelly and I were drinking Australian wine in the afternoon. We'd recently moved to Burbank and were so oppressively poor that getting a buzz on inexpensive booze in the afternoon was one of the few pleasures we could afford. I remember that the married couple across the street were blaring that Sugar Ray song—"every morning" bah-bah-bah-bah "my girlfriend's four-post bed"—it was the same song they always played whenever they were fighting because they thought it drowned out the noise, but it really didn't. We could still hear them, although only in bursts, just enough to create a tapestry of marital misery. A little "your goddamn mother" here and "you never touch me" there, and we got the general idea.

I remember when my mom called, and we talked for several minutes about nothing in particular. She told me about the weather in Michigan—it had snowed recently, and though it was only a few inches, there were apparently more snowplows on the streets than cars—and she asked innocuous questions about our new apartment and the smog in Los Angeles and if there was a grocery store near us that didn't require getting on a freeway. And then, just as I thought we'd covered the necessary chitchat topics and I was preparing to hang up, she dropped the bomb.

She told me where she'd found him, facedown on the kitchen floor, a half-eaten egg salad sandwich on the table, and how she'd immediately called 911, although she could tell from his lack of a pulse and the coldness of his skin that it was a lost cause.

"I should come home," I told her.

"No, no," she said. "You're busy."

"Mom."

"It's too expensive. Have you seen the cost of plane tickets lately? It's outrageous! I can't do that to you."

"I can afford it," I insisted.

"You can barely afford your phone bill, how can you afford a flight from California to Michigan?"

"Do we have to do this now?"

"I'm just saying, I'm worried about you. You don't need another unexpected expense. I don't want to be a burden. Especially now, with your father gone. We're all going through a lot."

I wondered why she wasn't crying. And then I wondered why I wasn't crying. Was none of this real? It didn't seem real. It seemed like that moment in a dream when you realize it's a dream and you think, "Oh man, this is crazy. I gotta pay attention so I remember this when I wake up."

"If you need to come out," she finally relented, "let me pay for it."

"No."

"I insist. Hold on, just let me find the credit card."

I heard a rustling sound, like an arm plunged into an overflowing garbage can.

"You don't have to do this," I pleaded with her.

"I want to do it," she assured me. "Just don't book your flight with Southwest again."

"What's wrong with Southwest?"

"Do you know what it cost us to fly you out for Thanksgiving?"

"That wasn't my idea."

"I can't even talk about it. It makes me sick."

"They'll try and charge you an arm and a leg because it's last-minute," she warned me. "Maybe you should wait to come out until next weekend."

"Mom, stop it!"

"I'm just saying, those big airlines know how to take advantage. Don't let them overcharge you. Have you thought about Spirit Airlines? They're always very reasonable."

"I don't think they have flights from California."

"No? That's surprising. They have wonderful rates for flights between Michigan and Florida. The last time I visited your great-aunt, I booked the entire trip for less than eighty-nine dollars. Isn't that remarkable?"

"It is, yes."

"You just have to know who to call."

"I'll see what I can do, Mom."

My mother paused. "I'm sorry, sweetie," she said. "I'll get you that MasterCard number as soon as I can. It's in your father's front pocket, and I just haven't been able to roll him over yet."

The reality of what had happened—what was still happening—came crashing into my brain. I could see it all so clearly now—my mom on the floor in a dark kitchen, kneeling next to my father's body, right where she had found him, or maybe sitting Indian-style because one of her legs had started to fall asleep, a finger nervously winding and unwinding the phone cord because she didn't know what to do with her hands. All this time, she'd probably been trying to slide the wallet out of his pocket, trying to do it without moving him, without touching him too much, because touching him would just confirm that, yes, she was really sitting in a dark kitchen with her dead husband, talking to her son in California, a million miles away.

She finally retrieved the credit card, and we didn't speak of wallets or dead bodies again. We bickered over airline connections and why my brother was so difficult to track down because he's been so busy lately.

We were an aurora borealis.

And then I heard footsteps in the kitchen and she told me that the paramedics had arrived and she had to go but she'd call me later.

I dropped the phone like it had suddenly gotten very hot, and I looked at Kelly and told her, "My dad's dead." And then I just tuned everything out. She was crying and I wondered why I still wasn't and my body went numb. At some point I wandered into the living room and collapsed onto the couch, trying not to think, unwilling or unable to make sense of what had just happened, and listening as Kelly made the necessary calls, telling the people who needed to know, and yelling at whatever poor sap happened to be working the late shift at the airline reservations hotline.

The pain was closing in fast. I could see it surrounding me. I could smell it in the air. It was circling me like a shark, searching for a way in. If I just sat there, it'd find a way to burrow into my chest sooner or later. I had to do something, find a way to keep my brain occupied and distracted. So I went looking for my *Let It Be* record. It wasn't in the usual spots, so I widened the search. I went through our shelves, pulled out boxes, dug through every closet, practically tore the house apart trying to find it.

Kelly watched me, looking worried, but she didn't ask any questions. I couldn't make another move before sitting and listening to at least a few songs from that album. Not any album, it had to be that one. And it had to be something loud. None of the emotional shit like "Answering Machine" or "Unsatisfied." I needed something I could scream along to, like "Tommy Gets His Tonsils Out." Or "Seen Your Video," so I could belt out "Your phony rock and rooooolll" over and over.

I never found it. Because it was gone. I'd sold it months earlier—the last of my record collection—for utility money. Or maybe something else, I don't even remember. Maybe I spent it on tacos and Trader Joe's wine.

My record player was gone too. I'd thrown it away not long after I'd sold my *Let It Be*. Which seemed like an obvious choice at the time. Why did I need a record player without records? And why was I looking for a record now, when I knew, even if I found it, I didn't possess a device capable of playing it?

I was not thinking clearly.

Getting rid of my records and record player was something I'd done without hesitation. But on that night, as I wandered through my Burbank apartment in a haze, knocking things off shelves like a thief looking for jewels, I would have given anything to get my *Let It Be* back.

I didn't even really need to hear it. I just needed to hold the sleeve, and stare at that photo, and feel that security again, that illusion of being stronger than I actually was. That's what the album gave me as a teenager, and that kind of power doesn't just evaporate with the years. I knew if I could just be alone with that record again, for a few gloriously inconsequential minutes, I'd be able to make it through whatever was going to happen next.

But it was gone. So I listened to the CD instead. It wasn't the same. The album cover—if you could call it that—was like the delivery menu from a local Chinese place, shoved under an apartment door. The music had been digitized, and by all accounts was vastly superior. It was 44.1 kHz! That's, well . . . a lot more kHz! And the dynamic range was sixteen bits. That's so many more bits than whatever I was getting from the vinyl. At least a dozen, right? So why wasn't it as satisfying? I recognized the notes, the lyrics—everything about it was the same, maybe even more vibrant and cleaner. But sitting next to my computer, listening to songs come out of tiny speakers no bigger than my pinkie nail, it was like hearing an echo from very, very far away.

My dad was dead, and the music wouldn't be able to save me this time.

There's something humbling about being underneath a table, butt sticking out like a raccoon in a trash can, scouring old boxes for elusive treasure. The only difference between me and a homeless guy was that the homeless guy is driven by a survival instinct. He needs food or shelter so he won't die. My driving force wasn't so noble. I was down there because everything was listed at under a dollar, and the guy selling them said he'd pulled everything from his shed, and he wasn't 100 percent sure what was in there.

The guy with the shed yammered on about his collection, and how none of it really mattered to him. "I was watching the Bears game, and I just started pricing 'em," I heard him say. "Didn't even pay attention to what I have. It's all been in the shed for as long as I can remember. It took me about six hours to drag out everything."

Most of the sellers here were like him; just everyday guys with too many records that had been gathering dust in their sheds/attics/mothers' houses for too many years. They weren't expecting big profits, just getting rid of all the junk they'd accumulated. The bartering had probably been more dramatic earlier in the day. But at 4:00 p.m., it was like a Moroccan street market, with vendors in wool caps shouting at anybody with even the most remote interest in their wares, "You've got a nice face. Everything's half price!"

"I have so many boxes in my house," the faceless voice above me continued, as I flipped through his records. "I just buy and buy and buy. And then it just gets stored and stored and stored. When Suzie went down to the basement and saw what I'd taken out, she got so excited. She was like, 'What happened down there? I love you.'"

He may have said more, but I stopped paying attention. I pulled something out of one of his fifty-cent boxes that made my heart stop. It was like a vision from a dream, where you're visited by people who you used to know a long, long time ago, and they're still as young and beautiful and perfect as you remember them, but there's something a little off about them—they've got gills, or their eyes are nothing but pupils, because it's a dream and dreams are all about fucking with your head.

It was a Bon Jovi record. *The* Bon Jovi record. *Slippery When Wet*. And I was pretty sure it was mine.

There was no way to hold it without feeling like it might crumble in my hands. The sleeve was dry but mushy, like the flesh of a dried apple. It had obviously been submerged in water at some point, and then left out to dry somewhere too hot, like the top of a radiator. It wasn't just warped and wrinkled; its entire chemical structure had been altered. It curved at geometrically improbable angles. It was a record cover reimagined as Dadaist art.

It was the first time I'd held this record, the first time I'd even seen the cover image, since the eighties. And I still had the same visceral reaction: that is an absolutely terrible attempt at sexiness. I mean, just really, really awful. Slippery is a Michigan road in February, not the correct adjective for describing aroused lady parts. I imagine Charlie Chaplin trying to run away but repeatedly slipping on vagina juices. "My god, this floor is slippery when wet!"

I stayed under the table a little longer, just put the Bon Jovi to the side and kept flipping through records, trying to look casual. No big deal. But inside, I was a mess. My head was buzzing, my heart was pounding like a Tito Puente mambo beat. My poker face was shit, and I knew it. The more I tried to look relaxed and breezy, the more I looked like an amateur art collector who'd just found a Rembrandt at a garage sale.

It couldn't be this easy, could it? How could I have found The One when my search had barely gotten started? I knew the math; I was well aware that the odds were against me. According to the Recording Industry Association of America, the entire net shipments of vinyl LPs and EPs between the years 1983 and 1985—the time frame in which I purchased at least one hundred records that are truly important to me—are 581.2 million units. That's how many records are out there, produced and distributed during my vinyl golden years. Of those hundred records I want back, I'm pretty sure I could identify five of them from that period, assuming I'm ever in the same room with them.

So, let's break down those odds. I'm looking for five records among 581.2 million. But that number is for the entire country. The number of records shipped to the Midwest is probably more like 200 million. And specifically to Chicago and its surrounding suburbs? That's got to be, what, half a million at most? So that narrows down my numbers. Now I'm looking for five records out of a pool of potentially 500,000. That's . . . okay, pretty daunting. But it's doable. For every record I want back, I just need to sift through about 100,000 records. Not that the record I want will be number 99,999. But, you know, you have to be ready for a little crate-digging carpal tunnel.

At this record show, I've maybe looked through . . . I don't know, a thousand? That might be generous. But after four hours, with my finger in almost constant motion, sure, it's possible. I expected some close calls. I expected a record or two that required closer scrutiny. But I didn't expect to find one of the Holy Grails with 99,000 records still waiting in the wings.

How did I know it was mine?

1) My copy of Bon Jovi's *Slippery When Wet* narrowly survived a car accident—the worst and (as of this writing) only major car accident I've ever been involved in. It was the summer of 1990, and I was on a highway in Michigan, driving from my family's cottage up in the Leelanau Peninsula—near the

pinkie finger of the Michigan mitten—back to our home in the Chicago suburbs. Somewhere around the middle of the trip, my car went off the road. It's difficult to tell you where exactly without using Michigan hand-based cartography.

The accident happened right around here:

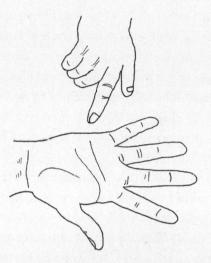

I was driving too fast, and my car was too overloaded. I'd bought a chair from a flea market, and somehow jammed it into the passenger seat. One of the chair's legs was jutting at an angle dangerously near to my temple, and all it took was a small overcorrection on the steering wheel. I was knocked unconscious. The car flipped, according to the police report, head over end seven times before landing in a swamp.

I woke up in the hospital, just as I was being wheeled into a CAT scan. I was fine. Walked away with a few scratches. Not even a broken bone. My car, however, was totaled.

When I came to claim the car, it still had swamp water on it. It looked like something from a murder mystery.

Everything inside was ruined. My clothes, my books, that fucking chair that coldcocked me. All of it was waterlogged and ripped to shreds. The only thing I pulled from the car that wasn't destroyed was *Slippery When Wet*. I hadn't even remembered it was in there. It was shoved under the driver's seat, wrapped in a blanket. God knows how long I'd been driving around with Bon Jovi hiding under my butt.

Why would this, of all things, have come out of a dramatic car accident mostly unscathed? Yes, the sleeve was coated in mud, and the vinyl itself was so warped that any hope of playing it was futile, but it had survived! It hadn't been snapped in two, crushed into a million pieces. The chair was now a pile of jagged wood shards. But you could still look at *Slippery When Wet* and recognize what it was.

And it still had Heather G.'s phone number on the front! Somehow, magically, the numbers hadn't been washed away. It was a goddamn miracle! I was convinced of it. It was a sign, divine intervention, or something. I didn't know, but I was sure there was significance. Was I supposed to call Heather? Or reevaluate my relationship with hair metal? Some higher force had obviously intervened and protected that record when everything around it was being thrashed brutally.

I'm not sure why it didn't occur to me that maybe the divine intervention was that I was still alive and still walking upright and breathing from uncollapsed lungs. Maybe *Slippery When Wet* just having some water damage wasn't nearly as remarkable as the fact that the driver of the car, which he'd flipped seven times into a swamp, was still brain active enough postaccident to be pondering cosmic conspiracy theories about Bon Jovi records and not, well . . . dead.

And now, this gnarled and pudding-skinned copy of *Slippery When Wet*, for sale for just a half dollar, was either an amazing coincidence—the second Midwestern-born Bon Jovi record with a phone number on the front submerged in swamp water—or it was exactly what I thought it was.

And speaking of that phone number . . .

2) It had a 708 phone number written on the front album sleeve! Which, come on, how is that not indisputable evidence?

Unless it's not Heather's phone number. Of course it's possible. She's not the only woman in the Chicago suburban 708 area code to enjoy the faux-cowboy pop rock stylings of Jon Bon Jovi and have access to a pen. It looked like my handwriting, but I couldn't be sure. It's like listening to your voice on a recorder. It never sounds like what you'd expect your voice to sound like. And my handwriting—if it actually was my handwriting—looked ridiculous, like it'd been written by somebody acutely aware that his penmanship was being watched and judged, even if it probably wasn't—which, if I recall correctly, is exactly how I was feeling when I wrote down her number.

The only way to know for sure would be to call the number. And I'd left my cell phone in the car. I could always crawl out from under the table, run out to the parking lot, and take the chance that somebody else wouldn't snatch up the record while I was gone. But for that to be a legitimate concern, you'd need to imagine that there was a person who would willingly crawl on his hands and knees under a table, and upon discovering an unplayable Bon Jovi record in a fifty-cent bargain bin, enthusiastically exclaim "At last! That inexplicably popular Bon Jovi record from the eighties that seems to have been left in muddy water for the last several decades and won't ever again produce music without a truly heroic needle, and probably not even then. And oh, look, a phone number. That's not something I should ignore. How could that number belong to anybody but a girl who wore cheerleader outfits during band practice in high school, and who possessed breathtaking thighs that could be stared at for an entire weekend without losing their ability to captivate? Fifty cents? SOLD!"

I crawled out from under the table with a handful of records.

"This it?" the portly guy asked, sifting through my records and punching numbers into a calculator.

"Yep, that'll do me," I said, doing a terrible job at seeming relaxed.

He paused on the *Slippery When Wet*. "You sure you want this, bud?" he asked. "I got one in better shape."

"Nope, this one is fine," I said, a little insistently.

"I don't even think this will play," he said, pulling out the vinyl and examining it. He was probably right. It looked like it'd served double duty as a cat scratching post and dive bar ashtray.

"I don't mind."

This gave him pause.

"You can have that one for free," he said. "I'm not a monster. You saved me a trip to recycling."

I laughed a little too hard, not because it was funny but out of relief. It was dumb luck that I found it before he did. If I hadn't crawled under this specific card table in this specific suburban hotel banquet hall on this specific weekend, it's entirely plausible that it would've been gone. The portly guy would have noticed it, wondered why he was hanging on to something so useless, and gotten rid of it at the first opportunity. My *Slippery When Wet*, and the last remains of Heather G.'s phone number, would have become compost.

"You got a store?" I asked, making polite conversation as I scanned the crowd for any sign of my wife or kid.

He shrugged without looking up. "Naw, there's no money in it," he said.

I nodded. Having just paid him $1.25, I couldn't really argue his point.

"I'm still in shock that Record Swap went under."

The portly guy's gaze drifted up. "Which one?" he asked.

"The one in the suburbs," I said. "Homewood?"

"Oh yeah, that's been gone for a while. I thought you were talking about the Record Swap down in Champaign."

I waited for him to say more, to volunteer some information on what the actual fuck he was talking about, but he just sat there on his teetering stool.

"They just, um, took the name?" I finally asked.

"No. It's owned by the other brother. Bob Diener, I think. When Ted closed up shop in Homewood, Bob kept going. They've changed locations a few times, but it's still owned by the same guy."

Somewhere behind me, I heard a crash. A table had collapsed— or maybe it was pushed—and a small landslide of vinyl had come barreling to the floor. Several people were shouting, and one of them distinctly said, "Who brought the fucking kid?"

I didn't even need to look. I was pretty sure I knew who was responsible. But I wasn't all that interested in being a parent at the moment. In my head, I was a steel-jawed detective in an old black-and-white crime thriller, and I'd just gotten some toady to spill the exact missing clue I needed. I got it out of him without him even realizing he was giving everything away. In the plot of this ham-fisted tale, the guy I'd suspected of committing all those grisly crimes was dead, but I'd just discovered that he had a twin brother, who had an equally voracious appetite for terror and mayhem.

"You want me to write down the address?" the portly record guy offered. "You should check out the place; Bob's got some great stuff."

I took a drag of an imaginary cigarette. "I just might have to pay him a visit," I said.

Five

The first thing I did upon learning that a second Record Swap existed was google it. And sure enough, it had its own website, which looked like it'd been created in the late nineties and then quickly forgotten about. It's exactly the sort of online presence that a music store selling eight-tracks as a viable audio format should have.

I sent an e-mail to Bob, requesting an interview. I mentioned MTV, which I doubt would've impressed him all that much, and made up something about a story I was working on, about record stores and their continued vitality and cultural significance, or something. Would he be interested in talking to me about the colorful history of the Record Swap, and how his store prevailed when so many others, including his own brother's store, had crumbled to the ground like ancient civilizations? Also, speaking of his brother . . .

No, no, I'd get to that part later. I wasn't sure how or when, but it felt like a secret I had to protect, at least at first. Tip my hand, and I could easily have this door slammed in my face.

I also reached out to John Laurie, the former manager at Record Swap. Not the one in Champaign, the real one—in Homewood. I wasn't sure if he knew Bob at all, but he was (or had been) an integral part of the Record Swap empire. My memories of him are in no way reliable. I don't think I ever talked to him. Even eye contact seemed risky. If he was working the register, I'd leave the store empty-handed and come back later. Because he terrified me. Coolness oozed from his pores. He wasn't like the other Swap employees, or the people trying to impress the Swap employees—who talked passionately and loudly, with lots of hand gestures. I remember him being mostly silent, arms folded, with a half smirk, like he knew more than he was letting on. He had an effortless Jimmy Page swagger about him, if Jimmy Page had had a ponytail and worked for minimum wage at a record store.

I had to swallow my teenage fears and finally talk to him. Because he could potentially be the key. It'd been years since the Swap closed, but Laurie had been among the last, if not the last, to have any responsibility for their inventory. Maybe he had some old accounting ledger—something with a dilapidated leather cover and delicate, yellowing pages—and inside were detailed audits on the whereabouts of every single record, cassette, or eight-track that had come in or out of the Swap.

Laurie could be one of those people, those meticulous detail freaks, who collects records because he's obsessed with order, and has a picture-perfect memory of every record he'd ever so much as touched. I imagined him wearing one of those accounting visors, and a Sonic Youth / Nirvana 1991 tour T-shirt (still as pristine as the day he'd bought it), pausing just for a moment to consider my question before saying, "Tom Waits's *Rain Dogs* with lipstick on the cover? Oh yeah, I remember that one. Serial number 90299-1, right? We sold it in May 1999. I still have the credit card receipt. He lives in Chicago, on Roscoe Street right between Halsted and Broadway. I'll get you his address. Nice guy."

It could happen!

"You want to talk about Record Swap?" Laurie responded in an e-mail. "You know I was merely an employee? Are you talking to any other employees, or the actual owners? There is still a Swap in Champaign, I believe. Anyway, sure, I would be down for a brief interview. I'm here Saturday from noon to six, and could carve out ten minutes or so. Let me know."

In the days following that e-mail, I started preparing for my big reunion with Laurie in ways that were only loosely based on reality. I bought hair gel and spent entire afternoons trying to make my hair look aesthetically messy. I started growing a soul patch, then saw what I looked like in the mirror and shaved it, and then tried growing a Lemmy, and shaved that nonsense as well. I visited countless online retailers that specialized in vintage concert tees, looking for something that would instantly announce to Laurie: "You and me, we are blood brothers." A Ramones T-shirt was way too obvious and cliché. What about something new and hip, like LCD Soundsystem or Deerhunter? But that could backfire, like if he asked me to name my favorite LCD Soundsystem album, or anything at all about Deerhunter, including how it's different from the Robert De Niro movie. Maybe an ironic tee? A Twisted Sister tour shirt, to show him that I didn't take myself too seriously. Or something earnest, like a Smiths *Meat Is Murder*.

And then, a few days later, came this e-mail from Laurie:

Good luck with it, Eric, but I'm not interested in participating.

I was crestfallen. Where had that come from? I wondered if he'd caught wind of my real reasons for wanting to interview him, which had nothing to do with compiling an oral history of his record store. But even if that was true, how could he, of all people, be so dismissive? His entire career had been devoted to helping people find old records. That was literally his life's work. It was all he did. Sure, a little larger in scale. But right in his wheelhouse!

I fantasized about driving straight over to his new shop, Laurie's Planet of Sound, catching him by surprise and begging him to reconsider. I'd do a full-on *Say Anything*—just stand outside his store and hold a boom box over my head, blaring something significant and heart-wrenching. Not Peter Gabriel, obviously. You don't initiate a musical debate with a lifetime record store employee with Top 40. It had to be something he'd respect. Like Bob Mould. A little "If I Can't Change Your Mind" would have the right emotional punch. "I hope you see I'm dedicated / Look how long that I have waited." How could he argue with that?

The only problem, of course, is that I didn't actually own a boom box. I haven't since at least 1988. Which is weird, because my closet is still filled with every computer I've ever owned. If I'm gonna hoard electronics, why not at least one boom box? Well, probably because boom boxes aren't used as porn storage, and you could throw them into a Dumpster without worrying that a tech nerd would find it and go digging around the hard drive and think, "Holy lord, this guy was into some sick shit."

I did still have a Walkman. A Sony WM-DD9. I pulled it out not long ago, just to see if the old girl had some juice left in her. A few fresh double-As and it was good as new. Well . . . newish. The gears made a high-pitched grinding sound, and the whole thing was held together with electrical tape and Soul Coughing stickers. But otherwise, it was in perfect working condition. It's noticeably heavy, which was weirdly refreshing. The iPod touch weighs four ounces, but the Walkman is a meaty twelve ounces. It's the difference between carrying around a credit card and a hoagie. I preferred the girth. It made you feel like you were carrying something significant.

Are there special features? You're fucking right there are. You've got your volume control and your gold-plated headphone jack and your auto-motherfucking-reverse. That's right, bitch, I ain't flipping my tape manually. I let technology do it for me. Oh, are you familiar with something called mega bass? Flick that shit from "norm" to "max" and get ready to melt your brain.

I was fully prepared to make an ass of myself with Laurie, to show up with all the props I needed to get his attention and make him change his mind. But then, something amazing and entirely unexpected happened.

Bob Diener wrote back.

Yes, he said in an e-mail, he'd be happy to meet me at the Swap. "I work alone, so we might be interrupted a bit and there is no telling how busy or not it will be. I could do it after 5:00 p.m. too, if that works out better. Saturday is usually busier and I have a load of LPs coming in the morning, but later in the day would work."

Waiting for the weekend felt like an eternity.

"I have people coming in all the time, going, 'I wonder if this is my album.' And I'm like, 'You sold it twenty years ago? Of course it's not your album, you buffoon!' You know what I mean?"

I had driven two hours through rural Illinois to get to Champaign, just to be in this store—a place I hadn't known existed until a week ago—and talk to the one man who may know where all my records had disappeared. I wasn't about to contradict him.

"Totally," I said.

"I mean come on, it's a Journey album. We've had hundreds of those come through. What are the odds you're going to find that exact one again? Come on, don't be ludicrous. It's not your Journey album. Get over it."

Bob Diener laughed, and I laughed right along with him, even though everything he was saying made me want to cry, or worse, get into a heated argument with him about exactly why he was wrong, including a thorough statistical breakdown of used vinyl record sales in the Midwest between 1998 and that day. But I didn't, because I'm a product of record stores, and as such I've been conditioned to believe that the guy on his side of the counter is always right and deserving of your undivided attention. The guy with full access to the $400 imports and bootlegs mounted on the wall next to the cash register has the floor, and always will.

This was the first time I'd met Bob, but something about him seemed familiar. Maybe I recognized something of his brother in his eyes or the shape of his face. Which is odd, because I don't think I could identify the elder Diener, the one who ran the Homewood store, in a lineup. But the moment I walked in and set eyes on Bob, I knew it was him. Which I guess was obvious, given that he was the only one in the store. But there was something about him, where even outside of this context, you'd take one look and think, "Oh yeah, he has a record store."

Bob had longish, dirty-blond rumpled hair. A plaid flannel button-up that'd seen better days, with a rock T-shirt peeking out, and jeans that had been washed so many times they were almost white. So . . . yeah, pretty much what you'd expect from a record guy.

"But you do get attached to your vinyl," Bob continued, absentmindedly flipping through a stack of new arrivals. "And there's an addiction. I used to say, 'I'm going to run this record store for a certain amount of time, and then I'll open up a clinic to help people get over their addictions. I'll get them both ways, coming and going.'"

I was listening, but I wasn't really listening. There was a lot of chatter but nothing that actually told me anything. He had stories—lots of stories—that bobbed and weaved into other stories, but none of it answered the question that admittedly I never came out and explicitly asked. But if it's necessary, okay fine, WHERE THE FUCK ARE MY RECORDS?

"I don't know the new music," Bob continued. "I know some of it. We'll get a fair amount of it used coming in, and I'll play it. And I'm like, really? Really? People like this? I forget her name, but she sings a lot like Janis Joplin."

"Pink?" I said, making a wild guess.

"Whatever, I don't know. I listen to her and I'm like, why? She's doing Janis Joplin covers! Why do you want that if you can just listen to Janis Joplin?"

"I guess they want somebody who's more modern," I offered. "And not dead."

"See, that's the problem. America has gotten so much more conservative. It's ridiculous. The corporations are taking over. It's almost like we're being programmed to like Lady Gaga."

"Programmed?"

"They're in our brains. That's what the Internet does to you. It changes the way you process music."

My feet were starting to ache. I wasn't sure how long we'd been standing there. It must have been at least an hour, maybe more. I kept waiting for him to invite me to a back office or something, anywhere with chairs that felt more conducive to a long conversation. Everything about this seemed weird. Two guys standing on either side of a counter—him hovering near a cash register, me holding records like I intended to pay for them—suspended in poses of commerce. Everything about the store felt both intimately familiar and completely foreign. The walls were covered with posters I could've sworn had originated from the Homewood location, in the exact same configuration. There was Nirvana coexisting with Tom Waits circa *Small Change*. Tupac standing shoulder to shoulder with Springsteen, Dylan hilariously juxtaposed with the Ramones. These were posters you might see in any record store in any city in the world, and the placement felt comforting and familiar, like the stained-glass windows at the church you went to growing up. You'd seen the same colors and designs a thousand times before, but somehow the windows in your church seemed unique and inimitable.

"I hate hype," Bob said. "And that's all the record industry is, to a certain extent. And I hate it. I don't advertise anymore. I don't need a lot of money. I've got my records, and I'm getting more records. I'm not going to advertise, 'Hey, we're the greatest record store in the world.' I don't care about that. People have to discover us. If they don't discover us, tough."

"It probably helps being in a college town," I offered.

He sniffed. "In the old days, when a kid came to college here, they'd scope all the record stores in the first week. And then CDs got popular, and the digital stuff, and people would come in and say, 'Why are you carrying records, man? They're gone!' They'd laugh at us. We were kind of a joke. From 1999 to 2006, it was really rough. It wasn't until we moved here, to the new location, that things started picking up."

I glanced around the store. It was totally empty. Nobody had even peeked in the windows since I arrived almost two hours ago. Aside from the Carla Thomas playing softly on the store record player, it was eerily quiet.

"A lot of the new thing with records becoming popular again, it's just a hipster thing," he said. "And I'm fairly tired of hipsters. They have terrible taste in music. These kids come in and say, 'You don't have anything that was released this year?' That makes me crazy. We don't need anything from this year!"

He pulled out a record by Thomas Mapfumo & the Blacks Unlimited. I had never heard of them, and know nothing of their music. Zimbabwe is mentioned in the album title, so I gather they're from . . . Africa? Gotta be Africa. I know as much about Africa as any American who got the majority of his African geographical cues from pop music. I know that, according to Toto, Africa is a place where it rains a lot and where you can distinctly hear the drums echoing tonight. I know that the temperatures are pretty hot, making it impossible for them to remember when it's Christmas. I know that Sun City is a bad place, because of apartheid or something, and nobody wants to play there, even Joey Ramone and Hall & Oates. Which is kind of crazy, because that's two extremes of the musical spectrum. People who love Hall & Oates and hearing "Kiss on My List" instantly puts them in an amazing mood, they're not necessarily gonna be disappointed when the Ramones don't come to town. And the Ramones fan, who couldn't have stuck around for so long with his racist parents if it wasn't for "Teenage Lobotomy" and "I Wanna Be Sedated," couldn't really care less that Hall & Oates won't be bringing their world tour to Sun City.

I knew something of racist parents. Not my own, but other people's. The first time I heard Bob Marley's name was from a friend's racist mom. Growing up in a suburb was like getting a tutorial in remedial racism. Many of our neighbors only moved to the burbs because it was "safer" (i.e., there weren't as many black people), but with safety came mediocrity, and that pissed them off. They had a chip on their collective shoulders because the black people had access to all the culture and the best drugs, and they were stuck with strip malls and whippets.

When I got my driver's license, I decided that my first big trip would be up to Chicago. But my best friend's mother announced that doing so would be tantamount to suicide. The city was teeming with dark-skinned criminals, she said, just waiting for their chance to lure some innocent white kid into an alley. She told elaborate stories about black gangs—though I think she was just repeating names she'd heard on *60 Minutes*—who would fillet their victims. Not just murder them, but fillet them. Like a fish. "It's true," my friend's mom lectured us. "It's all that African voodoo they're teaching at inner-city schools. They pump them full of Bob Marley reggae music and it makes them crazy. They hear that 'Electric Avenue' song and they just want to kill white people."

Even with my limited musical knowledge, I knew she didn't mean Eddy Grant. The video for "Electric Avenue" might've inspired a seizure, but definitely not racial violence. But I couldn't vouch for Bob Marley, whose videos weren't on heavy rotation on MTV and was therefore a mystery to me. If this Marley guy was making songs powerful enough to turn otherwise rational people into murderous zombies, it must be fucking awesome. I needed to hear reggae music immediately!

I bought a copy of *Legend*, just in time to bring it with me to college. And then, somewhere around my sophomore year, there was the crushing realization that owning *Legend* makes you a cliché, and you're just one of those frat douche bags who only knows "Stir It Up." So I bought all of Marley's albums—*Exodus, Catch a Fire, Kaya, Natty Dread*—like a frat douche bag pretending to be a hipster.

But soon enough, because I was usually stoned while listening to Marley and didn't always have the motivation or physical strength to hit the skip button, I became exposed to his entire oeuvre. I developed a fondness for the deep cuts and soon favored them to the more recognizable songs that my stoner friends enjoyed. I had become a frat douche bag pretending to be a hipster with illusions of Rastafarian street cred. My favorite Marley song was "Time Will Tell." I especially identified with the lyrics "Jah would never give the power to a baldhead / Run come crucify the dread." I'd nod along like I knew exactly what Bob meant. Fucking baldheads, always fucking our shit up. Fuck them! Jah knows what I'm talkin' 'bout.

But then the Black Crowes, a group of white guys trying to play like black musicians, covered "Time Will Tell" and ruined it for me.

Their version is great, and I actually preferred it to Marley's. And that just made me feel like an asshole. I was a frat douche bag pretending to be a hipster with illusions of Rastafarian street cred who realized he was just another frat douche bag.

I left college the way I entered it, with a copy of *Legend* and a deep-rooted terror that everybody knew I was a fraud.

"In '99, all the record stores were going under," Bob said. "It was just a terrible year."

I nodded like I'd been listening the whole time. "I got divorced," he continued. "Ted closed his store and disappeared. My 2008 recession started in '99. When the real recession came, I was like, that's no problem."

I saw my opening. "If Ted just disappeared, what happened to all those records?"

"He just owed too much money," Bob said. "The bank called in their loan. I never saw the books, but I found out he had doubled his salary for the last four years. We didn't get along. We never got along that well."

"And the records?"

"We were always opposites. He was really good at business in the beginning. I was hopeless, I was just a vinyl addict. That's why we had two stores. He also worked in golf course management. He didn't have the same passion for music that I did. For him, it was just a business. And when they had a dry season . . ."

"Did he just take the records to the dump? Throw them in Lake Michigan? Set fire to the store and then dye his hair in a gas station restroom?"

That made Bob laugh, which came out like a seal bark. "He called me and said, 'The sheriff is coming in, closing down Homewood. Get up here and take whatever vinyl you want.' He owed me some money, so I took a bunch of records."

I leaned in toward him, like he was going to start listing off titles.

"I was able to sell a lot of the CDs," he said. "I just put them in boxes, put them in a safe place, and brought them out slowly when I needed to."

"And the records?" I said.

"Ted had a lot of sealed stuff. Because they sold more new releases than what we did. So I was able to put a lot of that stuff on Amazon and get a good price. And the old stuff that wasn't in good shape, I put some of it in our dollar section, just to get rid of it. College kids will come in, spend ten bucks on records they don't care about, that are in terrible shape but they have a kitsch value."

In my head, I was crunching the numbers. This wasn't going to be hard at all, just time-consuming. All I had to do was ask for all his sales receipts from the past fifteen years, figure out which album titles matched up to the records I was looking for, and then get somebody in the school's alumni affairs to give me the current addresses of ten thousand or so former students, so I could drive to their homes and ask to rummage through their attics. Assuming most of these kids hadn't moved outside the system or at least stayed in the Midwest, I could have this whole thing wrapped up by spring.

"But I probably have most of them," Bob said.

Wait, what?

"I took something like thirty thousand records from him, and I probably sold less than one percent of those," he said. "When Ted unloaded them on me in '99, records were pretty much worthless. You definitely couldn't get any money for used records that were all scratched up and in shoddy shape."

"Why didn't you throw them out?" I asked.

He shrugged. "I don't know. Doesn't make sense to me either. But these were thousands and thousands of records. I couldn't just get rid of them. So I put 'em in boxes and just forgot about them."

"In a storage locker or something?"

"No, in my basement. At my house. It's about a mile from here. It's pretty dry down there, so it's a good spot for them. I honestly haven't looked at them in at least a decade. Last time I cracked open any of those boxes, it was right before the millennium New Year."

"You know, it's funny," I said, trying to sound casual, even though I was practically trembling from excitement. "I sold most of my original record collection at Ted's store in 1999. I wonder if some of those records are down in your basement."

Bob laughed again. "Yeah, wouldn't that be something, huh?"

I said nothing and he said nothing, and it felt like we stood there for a very, very long time, not saying anything. But it probably was just a few seconds. It felt long in my head, because I was staring at the vinyl copy of the Allman Brothers' *The 1971 Fillmore East Recordings* lying on the counter and wondering if it was heavy enough to knock Bob unconscious.

I didn't want to hurt Bob. I just wanted him to go to sleep for a little while, so I could reach into his pants, find his wallet and keys, and then drive to his house and go through all his records.

Almost immediately, I knew that wouldn't work. I needed a more sensible plan.

Maybe I'd follow him home, park a half block away, sleep in my car, and wait until he went to work the next day, then break into his house—I'd throw a brick through his window or something—and take an entire, nonviolent day inventorying his records. Unless he had a wife or girlfriend. Or kids. Then I'd have to tie them up, and that's just not my thing.

I considered the obvious, less-crazy plan: I could just come right out and ask Bob. "Hey, would you mind if I went to your house and looked at some of those records in your basement?" But that was way too risky. What if he said no? Why would he be okay with a total stranger, somebody he had literally met a few hours earlier, entering his home, his private sanctuary, to rummage through his personal belongings? All because this guy thought maybe his old records were down there. Everything about that sounded insane. If he asked me the same thing, I wouldn't think twice about it. I'd tell him no, make up some story about selling all the records to Goodwill, and then stop returning his e-mails. Why should I trust me? I could be a violent criminal! A sociopath! A guy who seems friendly and harmless enough in conversation, but somewhere in his sick brain he's playing out fantasies of clocking you with an Allman Brothers reissue. You don't want a person like that in your home!

I couldn't take the chance that he'd succumb to common sense. I had one shot at this—one chance to make him believe that I was someone to be trusted, that letting me dig through all those boxes in his basement was not just a good thing but perhaps the most decent thing he'd ever do as a human being. I couldn't ask him until I knew the answer was yes, because no just wasn't an option.

In my daydreaming, I never noticed the other customers walking inside. There were three college kids in the back, loudly exclaiming their delight upon finding a Flaming Lips record. Bob was fingering through two crates of records, brought in by a woman in her midforties with frizzy black hair zigzagged with gray and threadbare jeans from some happier time. She looked heartsick and dazed, like someone who'd just agreed to have a sick pet put to sleep.

"I can't believe I'm doing this," she said with a deep sigh.

I watched Bob for a minute, picking through the records, an almost clinical detachment in his eyes.

"I'm sorry, I've gotta do this," he said, not looking up at me. "Are we good? You need anything else from me?"

I just smiled. There was really nothing I could say without freaking him out.

Six

It was a brisk autumn afternoon in Chicago, and the sidewalk outside our apartment was filled with neighbors: drinking beer, firing up grills to cook endless brats for strangers, and soaking in the last of the summer sun. Traffic was blocked so their kids could run free across the empty street, shrieking with a combination of glee and fury.

It was the last block party of the year in our North-Side Chicago neighborhood, and every able body was outside for one last gasp of warm weather. But I hadn't come for fun. I was there on business.

I walked over to Mike, who was gently rocking his three-month-old baby, and practically shoved the record jacket under his nose.

"Does this smell like weed to you?" I asked.

To his credit, he didn't recoil in horror or demand to know why I was bringing contraband to a neighborhood party with minors present. He took a deep whiff and then crinkled his nose like he was evaluating the bouquet on a glass of wine.

"It reminds me of house cleaners," he said.

I considered this. "Is that a yes?"

"I don't know. I haven't smoked any weed lately. Does weed smell like house cleaners?

"Sorry," he said, handing me back the record before disappearing into the crowd to wrestle a hose away from his son.

I wondered briefly where my kid was. I looked out at the bodies on the street, splashing and stomping and hurling over one another, like a prepubescent mosh pit. I honestly couldn't recall if I'd told Kelly that I'd keep an eye on Charlie or if she had volunteered. I hoped it was her, or the rest of our weekend would be ruined by an Amber Alert.

I'd brought the Replacements album sleeve—a bona fide *Let It Be*—on a hunch. Our circle of friends—the other parents in the neighborhood with children Charlie's age, who liked to drink wine in the afternoon as much as we did—were all roughly our age, and with similarly bohemian pasts. We shared a nostalgia for things like smoking cigarettes, staying up past nine, and listening to music that celebrated bad behavior rather than the virtues of homework and picking up your room. All of our friends were old enough to remember when records were the norm, and at least half of them could, if necessary, create a makeshift pipe out of an apple or a soda can. Even if they weren't specifically Replacements fans, they were at least experienced enough to be a useful think tank.

I handed the album to Ryan, who had just passed off a juice box to his daughter. Ryan was tall and lanky, with a thick beard and an olive-green flattop army cap that never left his head. "Does it smell like what?" he asked, with a quizzical smile.

"Does it smell like maybe a teenager in the south suburbs of Chicago used to hide his weed inside the sleeve from the mideighties to about 1995-ish?" I asked.

"Wow," he said, slowly taking the record, like he was slipping a gun out of my hands. "That's . . . really specific. Was this yours?"

"That's what I'm trying to figure out."

I had my doubts, but I was still hopeful. It'd taken me months to find something that was even a remote possibility. When I started crunching the numbers, doing some hard research on my odds of ever finding my copy of *Let It Be*, it was weirdly encouraging. There were 150,000 CDs manufactured, and 51,000 cassettes. But the sole vinyl pressing of *Let It Be* was a paltry 26,000 units. That's a drop in the bucket compared to most iconic records. I don't know how many vinyl copies of Michael Jackson's *Thriller* were actually made, but I remember reading in Quincy Jones's biography that it'd sold 120 million copies.

The number of *Let It Be* records out there was roughly the population of Caucasian males living in Hoboken, New Jersey. But the copies of *Thriller* equaled the entire population of Mexico. Think of it like that, and my task really wasn't that improbable. I expanded my *Let It Be* search to the Internet, since that seemed to be the only place where old 'Mats records were being sold. The problem, of course, was that most copies were going for around two hundred dollars or vastly more, so I couldn't afford to take any wild chances. Whenever a *Let It Be* would appear on an auction site like eBay or eCRATER, I'd send the seller an e-mail, requesting more details. Specifically about whether it was reminiscent of a college dorm room with a lot of Bob Marley posters.

Most of them ignored me, but occasionally I'd get responses. "Just a normal record smell here," one wrote. "Wow, best-question-ever award!"

"I don't make it a habit of smelling my records," another responded, with what felt like snottiness. "And I don't intend to start now."

"Nice try, narc," yet another remarked before pulling his album off eBay completely.

I didn't even bother with the auctions bragging of albums in mint or perfect condition. I looked instead for descriptions like "pretty beaten-up but mostly playable" and "looks like Bob Stinson used this as his personal ashtray." I wanted the ugly children at the vinyl orphanage, the ones with ruddy skin and bad tempers, coughing wet phlegm into their fists.

I got excited when I found a listing that reminded me of imperfections I'd only half remembered. "Side one has a scratch from the end of 'Tommy Gets His Tonsils Out' to the middle of 'Androgynous.' Are also other scratches that appear to be surface."

I had just such a scratch on my *Let It Be*. I could tell you exactly where it was—cutting off Westerberg as he's warbling "He might be a father, but he sure ain't a—" That's how I first heard "Androgynous," and I sort of got used to it. It wasn't an annoyance; it was just a part of the melody.

I wrote to the seller immediately, asking the question I almost didn't want the answer to. I'd been heartbroken dozens of times by now; I almost preferred the idea of just letting it remain a mystery. But I asked anyway. Did it . . . smell of anything in particular?

"There is a musty smell but I do not think it is weed," said the seller, who went by zdmsales. "But I am not positive. It smells like something."

That was enough for me. I bought it immediately, paying fifty times what it cost me in 1986.

Since it arrived on my doorstep, I'd inhaled its musky fragrance at least a few times every hour. Sometimes it smelled like oregano, and sometimes it smelled like a wet attic. I needed a second opinion. And what better place to get that than at a block party filled with forty-something adults sipping on vodka lemonades in red plastic cups while barely monitoring their preschool children.

While simultaneously rocking his four-month-old baby in a BabyBjörn, Carl stuck his nose inside the album and breathed in deep. "Hmm," he said. "That could definitely be a weed smell. Or it could be something totally unrelated."

"Like what?" I asked.

He took another long whiff and then peered inside the sleeve. "What's that dark stuff? Are those seeds in there?"

I took a look. "I thought that was dirt. It looks like something from the bottom of a pair of cleats."

"I kinda want to rip this album cover apart, just to see what's hiding in there."

"Please don't," I gently suggested.

Other guys started wandering over—including a few who'd already weighed in—taking their turn with the record. They passed it around like a joint in a dorm room.

"Whatever it is, I'm pretty sure it's gonna make my face break out in a rash," Jeff offered.

"I think it smells like old paper," Ryan said. "Like a library. I feel like I'm reading a very, very old book in the library."

"It doesn't smell skunky enough," Brad countered.

"Libraries smell skunky?"

"No, I mean for weed. It's not skunky enough to be weed."

I didn't learn anything, other than that guys in their forties who'd had too many vodka lemonades on a Saturday afternoon can't agree on what old pot smells like.

In the end, I knew it wasn't the one. The skip on "Androgynous" was in the wrong place. I tried to convince myself that I'd just misremembered it, or a new scratch had been added by a subsequent owner, wiping out my scratch with a fresher, deeper cut. But the evidence didn't back up this theory. The vinyl's DNA was irrefutable. It wasn't my record.

Let It Be wasn't my only disappointment. I'd done a lot of traveling over the last few months, covering thousands of miles, and I'd gotten my hopes up with some promising leads.

I'd driven up to my mother's house in Ann Arbor, a short drive from the University of Michigan. Like any respectable college town, it hosts a handful of record stores, but until very recently, I hadn't been inside any of them. Still, it seemed reasonable that a few of my records could be hidden in their crates.

Those records that I didn't sell ended up in my mother's basement, until she finally got around to unloading them. She couldn't recall exactly where she'd taken them, other than "you know, those places that buy old junk." I didn't waste time scouring Goodwills or flea markets, as I couldn't imagine they'd hold on to inventory for fifteen years. But anything worth collecting would likely eventually find its own way to one of these musty old stores.

Encore Records, right in the heart of downtown Ann Arbor, was remarkably busy for a Thursday morning. There were almost thirty people in the store, packed together like calves in a veal farm. You couldn't shift your weight even slightly without having a domino effect on the entire herd. They were either college-aged kids or guys who looked old enough to be tenured college professors, who wore berets and called themselves "audiophiles."

It was magical. The muggy, stale air from too many bodies crammed into too small a space. The way everybody moved together in perfect sync, like the muscles inside your arm, every small tendon having its purpose toward the greater good. How you didn't have to dig too deep into a crate to find a record with an IF YOU PLAY IT, SAY IT sticker, which meant it was originally a promo meant for a radio DJ and not intended for sale, which just made it more special—a vinyl forbidden fruit.

"Brown Eyed Girl" came on over the store's sound system, and

I hate "Brown Eyed Girl." Everything about it is just terrible. And I love Van Morrison. I own almost everything he's recorded. My first dance with Kelly at our wedding was to "Sweet Thing." But "Brown Eyed Girl" is a piece of shit. It was killed for me long ago after hearing it too many times on literally every bar jukebox in the free world. It's on every shitty movie soundtrack and every terrible mix tape curated by friends who only owned "best of" compilations. It's musical pizza—the one thing everybody can agree on when they're too tired or bored to have an opinion.

Hearing it again in this fresh context, blaring from an old record player, the hisses and pops were a reminder that this song existed before Julia Roberts movies, before chain restaurants put it on constant repeat. But nobody in the store was acknowledging it. Nobody was singing along, even during the "sha-la-la-la-la-la-la-la-la-la" part. Nobody was announcing how much they loved this fucking song, or how it reminded them of their father, or saying "Oh, this is my favorite part" and then shout-singing one of the terrible lyrics. The song was just part of the background, part of the building's texture. Singing along would be like pointing at someone's pants and saying "Those are totally red!" That would be weird. It's just there. You don't have to acknowledge it.

It's been a long, long time since "Brown Eyed Girl" was just there. Just a thing that could be ignored and not meant as a big, loud social cue: "IS EVERYBODY HAVING FUUUUN?" I'd forgotten that this song could be quietly beautiful, when it wasn't being cheerleadered by people trying too hard to make you love it.

Feeling something for "Brown Eyed Girl" besides bored contempt made me want to revisit Morrison's catalog, see if there was anything else in there I could hear with fresh ears. They had at least one of everything, including a few bootlegs, and a record straight from my personal mythology: *Beautiful Vision*. As far as I know, I was the only person on the planet, living or dead, to ever own a copy. I'd never heard any of its songs played anywhere, like at a friend's apartment or on satellite radio or Pandora. When stacks of vinyl lived on my shelf, and friends would flip through my collection, not once had one of them paused on the sleeve and said, "Oh yeah, I know that record." Or "I've heard of this record. It's something I totally knew existed before right this second."

I liked that. I liked having a secret. Or maybe it only seemed like a secret to me, and everybody was well aware of *Beautiful Vision* but they'd tried to forget about it, because it was so fucking awful. I'm fine with that too.

There was really only one song on *Beautiful Vision* that mattered. "Dweller on the Threshold." That was the song that was playing when I lost my virginity.

Well, no, not exactly. The song I was playing when I lost my virginity was the Pixies' "Gigantic." (Nothing about that was a pleasant memory.) "Dweller on the Threshold" was playing when I realized that sex could be fun. When I was like, hey, this is something I want to do again. As soon as possible. Her name was Susan S. She was blond and pale-skinned, with a voice colored with a slight smoky rasp, like she'd smoked just the right amount of cigarettes. It wasn't her idea to put on *Beautiful Vision*. That was my doing. But she didn't object. She just went with it. She didn't even seem perturbed when I stopped, mid-lovemaking, and crawled over to the record player—which, like my futon, was on the floor—and moved the needle back to track three, cueing up "Dweller on the Threshold" for a second time.

When you think sexy songs, you think Marvin Gaye cooing about getting it on, or D'Angelo asking you how it feels. Not an old fat Irish guy singing about angels and mighty crystal fires. There is nothing even remotely dirty about that.

Which may've been why I liked it. There was a safety in Van's gentle warbling and muted trumpets. It was like rolling up in a down comforter. And after my first few experiences having sex—which were accompanied by shrieking Pixies songs, perfectly mirroring the mood—I needed something that was soothing and reassuring. Something that said, "It's almost entirely unlikely that this woman is going to bite down so hard on your shoulder blades that you start bleeding all over the sheets." (Which may or may not be a hypothetical.)

At some point during our lovemaking, Susan started laughing. I think it was the fourth time I'd replayed "Dweller on the Threshold," and she was starting to actually pay attention to it.

"Are you okay?" I asked. Laughter really wasn't the reaction I was aiming for.

"I'm sorry, I'm sorry," she said, wiping away tears. "You just have such a serious look on your face. And this song . . ." She laughed again, like a snorting trumpet. "Are you listening to this?"

"What's wrong with it?" I asked, but now I was laughing too.

"'Let me pierce the realm of glamour'?" she said, repeating one of the song's less sexy lines. "Really?"

We fell into each other's arms laughing. And then fucked ourselves silly, peaking somewhere in the "mighty crystal fire consuming his darkness" part.

When I saw that album again in the Ann Arbor store, without actually looking for it, just stumbling upon it by accident—which is the best way to find anything, but especially music—I knew it was mine. There was no question. Right there on the cover, there was a sticker, half ripped off, which read RECKLESS RECORDS. Actually, it read LESS CORDS, but you didn't have to be a crime scene investigator to put those missing pieces together. I'd bought my *Beautiful Vision* from Reckless in 1990. I don't remember where I sold it, but Ann Arbor was on the short list of suspects.

There was no other explanation! Unless there was another human being who went to Reckless Records in Chicago and bought the only Van Morrison record that almost nobody remembers or wants and took it across state lines to sell it to a college-town record store in Michigan, 240 miles away, which just coincidentally happened to be a short drive from my mom's house. I bought it and took it back to Chicago, along with a handful of other records that I'd picked up just out of nostalgia. (Billy Joel's *Glass Houses*, Pearl Jam's *Vs.*, the Violent Femmes' debut.) I was barely in the door before I'd pulled out the vinyl and laid it down on my brand-new record player, which had just arrived from Amazon.

It was a Crosley three-speed turntable, with a built-in CD and cassette player, and constructed from the finest paprika-colored hardwood. It was absolutely nothing like anything I'd ever owned, and I hated it.

I'd owned exactly two record players in my life, and I've romanticized them both entirely out of proportion. The first one, acquired when I was only six, was a piece-of-shit plastic thing, made by Fisher-Price or Tele-tone or some company whose name has never been in any way synonymous with "sound quality." But just like kids who grew up in poor families never remember themselves being poor, I was completely satisfied with my puke-green plastic record player. I had no idea that I was basically listening to all treble and the sound quality was just a notch above CB radios.

I shared that record player with my brother until the mideighties, when I finally got around to buying a proper sound system, with a separate turntable, amplifier/preamp, and speakers as big as steam trunks. The turntable was a Luxman PD272, and it looked like something Flash Gordon would have in his bedroom. It was all silver, thinner than a Sunday newspaper, with a glass dustcover that looked like a spaceman's helmet. It had an integrated tonearm. I don't know what that is, but I remember the sales guy at Audio Consultants in Evanston—who zeroed in on me like shark to chum—mentioning its integrated tonearm, and how the technology was so advanced and unlike anything I could imagine—he made it sound like one of those robotic arms that does heart surgery—and it'd change the way I listened to music forever.

He told me that the Luxman PD272 could reach shimmering highs. He used that exact word, *shimmering*, which really stood out for me. Shimmering sounds like something that happens when angels hover over you, all gangbusters to tell you about the messiah. It also had exceptionally good *wow and flutter*. I had no idea what either of those things were, but they sounded important.

The Crosley was a poor substitute. But it was cheap, and buying one didn't involve getting into bidding wars I didn't have the deep pockets to win. I just wanted something that played records and had relatively decent sound and could be delivered in less than forty-eight hours.

"I've never heard of this one," Kelly said, as she studied the *Beautiful Vision* cover. "Is it a bootleg or something?"

"It's an acquired taste," I said.

She and Charlie had joined me in the office for a listening party. Which was both sweet and very, very awkward. When "Dweller on the Threshold" came on, Charlie started dancing, flailing his arms as he hip-thrusted around the room to his own tempo. Kelly laughed and hummed along with the two-note trumpet part. I smiled with a tight grin and tried to pretend like it wasn't completely unsettling watching my three-year-old son do a silly interpretive dance to a song whose only other association for me was those three months in the early nineties when I was having regular wild-monkey sex with a sexy blonde on a busted-ass futon.

"I mean, Van Morrison has done so many better albums," Kelly went on. "What's so special about this one? It sounds like a lot of new age dreck."

The smart thing to do in this situation would've been to make up some innocuous story about how my grandmother had owned it, and how it always reminded me of winter visits down to Florida, sitting on her front porch and peeling oranges. But I told her the truth. Kelly just nodded. She didn't look upset, just a little rattled. It's one thing to say, "This song reminds me of an ex-girlfriend." It's quite another to say, "This song reminds me of making love to an ex-girlfriend, so of course I have to own the song, so I can hear it again and again, remembering all of those great memories of putting my penis inside a woman who isn't you." (That wasn't exactly how I phrased it, but it might as well have been.)

"Is this the same girl whose phone number is on that Bon Jovi record?" she asked.

"What? Oh, no, no, that's a totally different girl."

I'd forgotten about *Slippery When Wet*. I hadn't tried calling the phone number written on the jacket yet, because I was positive she wouldn't answer, and I'd just end up talking to some old guy who'd swear he had this phone number since the sixties, and there wasn't any chance a teenage girl named Heather might've lived there at some point. The odds were stacked too heavily against me, and I just wanted to hold on to that illusion for a little while longer.

"So this whole experiment in finding your old records," Kelly said, "it sounds like it's really about your ex-girlfriends."

"That is ridiculous!" I protested.

"I'm not jealous; it's just interesting. Do any of these records you want have stories that don't involve women you've slept with?"

It wasn't all about that, I told her. Not by a long shot. What about my *Frampton Comes Alive!*? That wasn't about a girl at all. I was way too young. My most visceral memory about that album involved a dead cat.

I remember my parents telling me it was dead. There was a lot of crying; weirdly, more from them than me. It wasn't because they were particularly fond of the cat—he was overweight and aggressive and as my dad liked to point out, "an asshole"—they were just worried about me. They assumed I'd be devastated. I was the one who'd brought the asshole cat home in the first place, and the only one in our family who spent any time with him. I was sad that he was gone, but not nearly to the extent that my parents had braced themselves for. It wasn't the kind of sad that permeates your bones, or makes you want to sob until you're dry-heaving. It was more like the "Oh my god, I can't believe they canceled *The Six Million Dollar Man*" sad.

When my parents were satisfied that they'd done their best to comfort me, I went upstairs to my bedroom to listen to records. I put on *Frampton Comes Alive!*, which I'd recently borrowed from a friend's older sister. I lay on my bed and stared at the ceiling and tried to convince myself that I was fine. This was the first time that anybody—or anything, I guess—close to me had died, and I wasn't sure how to make sense of it. Not just of death, but of everything. I pictured the earth in my head. And then I watched as it got smaller and smaller, becoming one of many planets, until it was just another speck in the vast canvas of the galaxy. And then even our galaxy began to diminish, swallowed up by bigger solar systems and black holes that seemed to stretch on forever. Soon anything even remotely recognizable was gone and it was all just black and emptiness that went on and on and on and . . .

But then there was Peter Frampton, playing that weird guitar that sounded like a scatting droid from *Star Wars*. At first, I thought there was something wrong with my record player. Or maybe I was hallucinating. What the hell was I hearing? When I focused on that fucked-up guitar, I was able to catch my breath again, and my heart didn't sound so much like bongo drums. I never listened to Frampton again, but for one horrible night, it was a life preserver.

"I thought you hated Peter Frampton," she said.

"Oh god, I can't stand him."

"So you want to hear the album again because . . . you miss your cat?"

"No, it's not about the cat. I don't even remember its name."

"Well forgive me if I'm being cynical, but why would you possibly need to hear music you dislike that you only associate with a cat you barely remember?"

I really didn't know how to answer that. Maybe it was like having a tattoo—which I don't have, so I'm entirely going on conjecture—where even though it's faded and looks more like a bruise and you have only a hazy recollection of why you wanted it in the first place, you'd still never get rid of it. Because it's part of your skin now. It's a scar, and scars mean something.

"This whole conversation is just making me sad," Kelly said. "I'm going to go make dinner."

She and Charlie left the office, leaving me with my Van Morrison. I waited until I could hear her footsteps down the hall before lifting the needle and moving it back to the beginning of "Dweller on the Threshold."

When my mom asked me to accompany her on a trip down to Melbourne, Florida, to visit my ninety-four-year-old grandmother—who lived alone in a rickety house on the verge of collapsing—I immediately said yes.

Not because I had any interest in seeing that house again. Or because I was especially interested in being a part of their plot to convince her to leave Florida and move up to Michigan, where she'd be closer to her children and grandchildren (and great-grandchildren). I was just there for the excavation, to help dig through all the trash in Grandma's house and find what deserved to be saved and what should be hauled away to a dump. I eagerly volunteered. Not out of any sense of altruism or interest in preserving the evidence of my family's history. But because I was pretty sure some of my records were in there somewhere.

Over the past half century, my grandmother's house had evolved into a sort of walk-in safe-deposit box. It's where we left everything we didn't want anymore but weren't ready to throw away, because what if we needed it?

My family has not historically been very good with the concept of throwing things away when they outlive their usefulness. And this includes pretty much everything. Clothes, appliances, furniture, food. Not because we're hoarders. We're just very, very cheap. Every relative in my gene pool is incapable of spending money on themselves without worrying that they might be squandering a financial safety net. Heaven forbid that there isn't cash hidden somewhere, to help cushion the blow of that stroke they're pretty sure is just around the corner, or that car accident that robs them of at least one of their essential limbs, or the ancurysm that hits them like lightning when they're innocently trying to shop for groceries, and the house of cards that is life comes tumbling down around them and they have to somehow find a way to pay off the never-ending ticker tape of medical bills.

My family's personal philosophy—its entire raison d'être—is about steeling themselves for inevitable tragedy.

After a few days of digging in her boxes, I uncovered some gems.

There was the Don McLean album with the big thumb on the front—the one with "American Pie" on it—that my mom's older brother, Bob, had given to me as a Christmas present in 1982, and then told me exactly how "American Pie" was really about his drinking buddies down in Florida. He made a convincing case, especially considering that he drove a Chevy and did indeed enjoy drinking whiskey.

I gave it back to him as a Christmas present in 1992, and he seemed genuinely touched. "Did I ever tell you what this song was really about?" he asked.

Finding these records now, I realized how much of my music knowledge came from him, and how much of it was entirely factually inaccurate. Here was that Queen *Greatest Hits* album, which I held on to for too many years, despite not being an especially big fan of Queen, because Bob had told me that if you played "Another One Bites the Dust" backward, you'd hear Freddie Mercury sing "It's fun to smoke marijuana." I tried—oh, how I tried—but I just couldn't make my turntable go in that direction.

I also pulled out *Let It Bleed*, the Rolling Stones album I'd owned no less than six times. Bob had given it to me in high school, when I'd already overplayed it and moved on to greener pastures. But he told me things that made the record seem more frightening, and therefore more appealing. The backup singer on "Gimme Shelter," the one who sang about it being "just a shot away," was pregnant when she walked into the studio. But while singing those lyrics, she'd had a miscarriage.

"A dead baby just plopped out of her, right on the studio floor," Bob told me. "You could see it clear as day."

The way he talked about it, it seemed like he must've been there, like he saw everything firsthand. Of course that was impossible. But you don't question these things when somebody older than you, ostensibly wiser than you, who's smoking unfiltered Winstons like somebody who has lived life in ways you can't imagine, is telling you something is true.

I can still remember listening to that record with him, sitting in my grandmother's kitchen. I'd watch him smoke, studying his technique. He'd pinch his cigarette at the tip and jerk it toward his face with every puff, like he was holding a gecko by the tail as it tried to slither away. He'd grimace when the backup singer hit the really high notes, like he was feeling things I was way too young to understand.

"That's it right there," he said, punching at the air with a pudgy finger. "That was when it probably happened."

I found his Bob Seger records. Those were entirely his. I had never owned a Bob Seger record in my life. But my uncle Bob, he owned them ferociously. Territorially. He owned Seger albums the way some people raised purebred puppies. He nurtured them, took care of them better than he took care of his own body. I've witnessed him eat sticks of butter like lollipops. I've seen his empty cigarette cartons stacked on tables, piled high like grim pyramids, a testament to his bad decisions. But his Bob Seger records he treated with respect, with reverence. He'd hold them by the edges, clean them with a carbon fiber brush. He's worn the same filthy pair of sweatpants, with likely the same salsa stain on the inner thigh, since the mid-eighties. But his Seger records get cleaned every day.

I remember Mark and I sitting in Bob's room, listening to Seger with him, and watching him cry during "Night Moves." I did not see him cry at the funeral for his father, but I saw him weep openly no less than sixteen times while listening to "Night Moves." It was the first time I saw a grown man cry, and for an eight-year-old boy, it was disconcerting. My brother and I didn't know what to say. Should we be comforting him? Giving him an awkward hug before finding an excuse to get the hell out of there?

He always turned the tables on us. When it got to the part in "Night Moves" about the song's hero "tryin' to make some front-page drive-in news," Bob would look up at us and sneer.

"You don't even know what that is, do you?" he'd ask, incredulous. "You've never even heard of a drive-in."

Mark and I shrugged. We knew exactly what a drive-in theater was. It was those abandoned parking lots where old people used to watch movies before they realized they could do that shit inside.

Bob sneered, contemptuous of our youth and all the pop culture references we were obviously missing. "No idea," he said.

Digging deeper in the box, I pulled out a handful of records that made me gasp, like I'd stumbled upon actual bones from a dead relative. It was my father's country albums. Every goddamn one of them; classics by Waylon Jennings and Hank Williams Jr. and Merle Haggard and, his favorite, Willie Nelson. They were the records he kept in the closet of his study, stacked neatly next to his shoes, ready for some private commiserating. For him, listening to music was never a social activity. It was something you did alone, with the door shut, and it was the only thing standing between you and saying things you couldn't take back.

My dad didn't own a cowboy hat, he never used tobacco products, he was unabashedly liberal in his politics, and he'd never lived south of Chicago. I don't have a single memory of him wearing jeans. Not once. He must have owned them, but when I close my eyes, I can only picture him in slacks, ironed within an inch of their life. But he loved country music. Maybe he just appreciated the lack of irony. A country song says what it means. There's no sarcasm in a Hank Williams song. When he sings about being so lonesome he could cry, or how there's a tear in his beer, he's being entirely literal. His beer contains actual tears. Every lyric is 100 percent sincere. Merle Haggard's "I Think I'll Just Stay Here and Drink" is about exactly that. He's going to remain where he is and continue consuming alcoholic beverages. There's no subtext whatsoever.

Maybe that straightforwardness is what appealed to him. Country music was sad without the air quotes. It wasn't sad in a Morrissey kind of way, where the bitterness was couched in cleverness. Country music wore its sadness on its sleeve.

There were plenty of his Willie Nelson records here. *Phases and Stages*, *The Troublemaker*, *Stardust*, *The Electric Horseman* soundtrack, *Yesterday's Wine*, *Shotgun Willie*. But not *the one*. *Always on My Mind* was missing. The one with the portrait of Willie wearing what seemed to be a silver skiing jacket and disco headband. The one with covers of "Bridge over Troubled Water" and "A Whiter Shade of Pale," and the epic "Always on My Mind." I heard that song through the cracks of my dad's study on more nights than I could begin to tell you. Even now, when I hear that song, I instinctively think, oh yeah, my parents almost got divorced.

I'm still not sure exactly what happened. I just remember my parents arguing, thinking my brother and I were out of earshot. They lobbed threats at each other like grenades, and every so often we'd get hit with shrapnel. Words like *move out* and *divorce* came tumbling at us, scarier because of the lack of context. But they told us nothing. Dad kept his distance, and my mom would only say, "I don't want you to lose all respect for your father."

He slept on the couch in the living room. And spent most of his time in his study, where he claimed to be "working late." Whatever he was actually doing in there, it involved a lot of listening to Willie Nelson. There were very few places where we could go in our house and not hear "Always on My Mind" pleading somewhere in the distance.

And then one day, as abruptly as it began, the fighting stopped and my dad returned to their bedroom, and whatever they'd been fighting about was unceremoniously dropped.

I still don't know what almost caused them to get divorced. I never asked either of them about it. For a long time, my brother thought I was being a masochist. "Just leave it alone," he'd say. "What does it matter? It's in the past. Forget it." But I'm still waiting for my window of opportunity. Maybe it's because my mom is getting older and life is fragile and you can't retrace the footsteps of your past if all the eyewitnesses are gone. I don't want to be the guy shaking the ninety-eight-year-old woman with dementia who thinks I'm Teddy Roosevelt and screaming, "I need answers, damn you! Answers!"

Not long after I moved out of my parents' house, I bought that Willie Nelson record on CD. At the time, my musical tastes were more aligned with the Jesus Lizard and the Jon Spencer Blues Explosion. Lots of punk screaming and penis exposure. Not exactly Willie Nelson territory. But I needed that record. It was like a security blanket. It was the album I could pull out whenever I was feeling rejected or misunderstood by a woman. Which, to be honest, was something that happened quite a bit in my early twenties. Willie Nelson helped soothe that anxiety. Which, well sure, you don't even have to dig that deep to see how it was connected to my dad. I saw him struggling with rejection and using Willie Nelson as an emotional force field, so obviously I started associating Willie Nelson songs with self-righteous self-pity. I could listen to "Always on My Mind" and automatically feel like my hurt feelings were justified. Which, of course, was almost always bullshit. Nothing about that song justifies a guy's hurt feelings. It mocks them.

"Always on My Mind" is a song that basically says, "Yes, I ignored you. I was disrespectful and unsupportive and absent, both physically and otherwise. But come on, baby, I was thinking about you. That's got to count for something, right?"

I didn't originally plan on attending the Replacements reunion show at Chicago's Riot Fest because I thought I might stumble upon one of my records there. I was mostly driven by thoughts of "Holy shit, this is totally happening, holy shit, holy shit, holy shiiiit!"

My band—*my band*—was actually fucking reuniting. With only two of the four founding members, but that didn't matter. The songs would be the same. And two of the scruffy old men who created those songs would be up on a stage singing them together for the first time since I was barely old enough to drink. That was enough. That was everything.

As for whether records would be part of the deal, I'd been given false hope. A few online dealers, amused by my "Does it smell like weed?" questions regarding their copies of *Let It Be*, offered suggestions of where I might have better luck. The consensus was that I'd be a fool not to stake out Riot Fest.

"All the hard-core 'Mats guys will be there," one helpful auctioneer insisted. "It's in Chicago, which is where you unloaded your 'Mats stash, right? If your record is still in the central time zone, somebody at that show is gonna have it."

"Are you sure they sell records at these festivals?" I wrote back. I wasn't a newbie at rock festivals. I was accustomed to booths pushing T-shirts, oily-tasting beer, and overpriced fast food. But not used vinyl.

Unsurprisingly, grown men living in rural Ohio who sell used records out of their moms' basements don't have compelling evidence about what happens in urban punk-rock festivals. But I couldn't take any chances. What if they were right? I loaded my pockets with cash, and drove extra early to Humboldt Park, the sketchy Chicago neighborhood where the concert was happening.

For reasons that made sense at the time, I brought my *Let It Be*. The record. The one I'd purchased online, with the deep scratch and funky smell that had failed to be identified by a jury of my peers. I don't know what I was thinking. It had something to do with being in the presence of so many devoted 'Mats fans, some of whom were sure to be record collectors and possibly scholars in vinyl migration patterns. Maybe they'd take one look at my *Let It Be* and go, "Oh yeah, man, I remember that catalog number. You sold it at the Record Swap in Homewood, right? Round about '98, '99? Scratch right across 'Androgynous.' I'm here with some archeology friends who are big 'Matheads. I'm sure they'd be happy to run some carbon-fourteen dating tests on it."

The last time I saw the Replacements live was in 1991, during their farewell concert at Grant Park, exactly 6.53 miles away from where I would be seeing them today, twenty-two years later. Back then, I came to the show with four other guys, all of us broke and young and thoroughly stoned, crammed into a Chevy Chevette like it was a clown car. For today's show, I went alone, because every guy I know my age couldn't find a babysitter, or just wasn't interested in seeing a show that would require several hours of standing.

I considered driving, but the parking situation in Humboldt was desperate at best, hopeless at worst. The other option, taking public transportation, wasn't much better, as the idea of waiting for a bus at midnight made me nervous. I decided to drive, because not caring about whether there's parking is totally punk rock.

I found a space about a mile south from Humboldt Park, in between two abandoned factories. I stepped out into a river of crushed beer cans and surgical gloves. (No, seriously, surgical gloves. I counted at least six floating along the curb.) I locked my car, waiting for the familiar *beep-beep* that gave me no sense of security. And then I locked it again, just to be sure. I walked two blocks toward the park, and then backtracked to lock my car one more time. I was pissed at myself for leaving the stroller and the portable DVD player in the trunk. Now when the car got stolen, which I was convinced it would be, they were just going to be two more things I had to argue with the insurance company about.

I was at the festival so early, they barely had security at the front gates. I wandered the grounds, looking for any vendors who might be selling anything besides $20 pretzels and T-shirts. Nothing. Not a damn thing. The guy selling Replacements T-shirts seemed honestly perplexed by what I was asking for.

"Are you selling?" he asked, pointing to the record in my arms.

"No, I brought this from home."

"Why, dude?" he asked, scratching his neatly pruned beard. "You know there are no record players here, right?"

"Yeah, yeah, I know. I just thought . . . see if anybody, um . . . Never mind."

I walked the periphery of the festival grounds several times, zigzagged across it like I was making a cat's cradle. I finally gave up and just parked in front of a stage to watch Bob Mould perform. After just a few hours, I was a mess, bobbing and teetering like one of those gas station inflatable air dancers. My feet were throbbing pustules, expressing their disapproval with sternly worded neurons. Rain pelted my face like it had something against me personally. There was nothing to do but stand and wait and pray that death, when it came, would come quickly, and with a chair.

And the record, that goddamn *Let It Be* that I never should have brought, I was feeling so much anger and resentment toward it, like it was somehow personally responsible for tagging along. I wanted to just let it drop, let it disappear into the flurry of stomping Doc Martens. But of course, I couldn't do that. That was unthinkable—monstrous, even. When the rain started, I tried hiding it under my T-shirt. But that made it worse somehow, creating a rain funnel around my neck that made sure both the record and my skin were as drenched as possible. So I just held it out in front of me, hoped the cardboard wouldn't disintegrate in my hands. Just holding it felt so unnatural and weird, like I was standing in a crowd with a toaster. What the hell was I doing with this thing?

And then, as a true test of whether I really want to be here, a guy wearing leather wristbands with half-inch rivet spikes pushed past me, and I felt a prick on my arm. And then I saw the blood, streaking down my forearm a little too thickly for my liking.

"What the hell?" I shouted at the guy with the wrist spikes. "You fucking sliced me, man!"

He turned and saw the blood, and offered an apologetic half smile. "Sorry, dude," he said. "That's never happened to me before."

Really? 'Cause I'd think if you had dozens of tiny metal spikes jutting from your wrists, shiving random people in crowds is something that happens to you with some regularity.

Before I could react, the lights went down and the Replacements took the stage. The actual fucking Replacements! I was stunned, barely able to believe my own eyes. My heartbeat was beating ridiculously fast, but perfectly in time with "Takin a Ride," the first song of their set (as well as their discography), so it all worked out. I was way more emotional than I'd anticipated. I'd joked with friends for months that when I finally saw the Replacements play live again, I'd weep like a baby. As it turns out, that wasn't hyperbole. I cried, and I cried hard. Which is a strange thing to do when you're listening to a punk song from the eighties about driving too fast.

I got it together by the third song, "Favorite Thing." But then I lost it again when Paul sang, "Yeah, dad, you're rocking real bad." Because why? I had no fucking clue. Because I was a dad and I was rocking real bad, and Paul knew it? No, that's stupid. Paul wrote the song in a drunken haze, and he probably rhymed *dad* and *bad* because it was easy, not as an Easter egg for fans who would grow up to become middle-aged fathers listening to the song at a reunion concert, long after when most of us should've died from bad decisions, as we downed too many $10 beers and stood in a muddy field, our outdated hipster shoes sinking like dinosaurs into tar pits, our aching knees threatening to collapse, and we realized, twenty years too late, "Oh yeah, I get it now. He was making fun of the future me. Nice burn!"

They strummed the first familiar chords of "Androgynous," and my body started moving in ways it hasn't since getting my cholesterol checked became an annual necessity. They got to that point in the song where Paul sings, "He might be a father, but he sure ain't a—" And I hesitated. I stopped like I was waiting for the music to do what it always did at that exact moment on the record. It didn't, obviously, but somewhere deep in my muscle memory, I was anticipating it. The neurotransmitters in my brain remembered the skip. It was like that knee-jerk reflex test that a doctor gives you in a checkup.

The next song was "Hey Good Lookin'," and I nearly gasped with music nerd joy. A seemingly off-the-cuff cover, except it just so happened to be from the set list of their so-called "final" Grant Park performance twenty-some years ago. Playing an obscurity like "Hey Good Lookin'" was obviously a nod to the grizzled old fans in the crowd with too many bootlegs clogging their iPods, who had driven to the show while listening to the band's 1986 UK bootleg *Boink*, which includes a live version of "Hey Good Lookin'" from 1983.

I wish I had been paying more attention during that last show. I was twenty-two at the time, just out of college and full of opinions that I felt obligated to share, as loudly and as often as possible. About midway through their set, I was grumbling about how the band was playing the wrong songs. There was too much from the new album and not nearly enough of the old punk barn burners. They hadn't played "I Hate Music," or "Raised in the City," or "Take Me Down to the Hospital," or even a goddamn "Unsatisfied."

We left somewhere around "Within Your Reach." On the ride home, we listened to the rest of the concert on the car radio. We laughed and laughed when the DJs pondered if this would indeed be the 'Mats final performance. Those corporate fuckers just didn't get it, we thought. The 'Mats are yanking their chains. Break up? The Replacements can't fucking break up. They'll break up just as surely as one of them will die young because his liver explodes, or have a stroke like my grandfather did in his eighties. Can you imagine? Oh god, these old men and their conspiracy theories. They just don't get it.

They say life is wasted on the young. That's entirely true. Twenty years later, standing in the mud at Riot Fest, there's nothing I wanted to do more than leave early. But I'm old enough now to realize what I'd be missing. You have to snatch these opportunities while you can. When you're young and stupid, you think it'll all last forever. But it doesn't. So I stayed till the end. Even though my old-man bones were rattling, and there was so much mud that it felt like my socks were filled with mayonnaise, and oh my god I had to pee so badly, why the fuck did I have so much Dos Equis Amber? Dumb, dumb, dumb! Didn't matter. I dug in my heels and drank in every last second.

Somebody behind me screamed, "I can't believe this is fucking happening!" A few people in the crowd laughed, but I wanted to hug the guy who said it. I wanted to shout at him, "I can't fucking believe it either, brother!"

It was somewhere around this time that I remembered, "Hey, wasn't I stabbed earlier? I totally was, wasn't I?" I glanced down at my arm, and it was caked with blood. It had dripped down my forearm, snaked across my wrist and onto the record, splattering it like a crime scene. Seeing my blood everywhere should have been cause for panic. Normally, even a minor cut is enough to make me lightheaded and anxious, doing Google searches for the symptoms of sepsis. But with this . . . well, what options did I have?

Whenever I go anywhere with Kelly and Charlie, we bring a diaper bag loaded for any emergency. Bandages, antiseptic, antibiotic cream, antibacterial wipes, anti-everything, whatever you need. But trapped in the middle of this sweaty throng, I didn't have access to first aid. Not even a child-size Dora the Explorer Band-Aid. Nobody here cared if I bled to death. I could have tried to force my way toward the exit, but even then my medical options were limited. I might as well just lose myself in the hammering bass lines and let it bleed, man, let it bleed.

When your entire existence is about being responsible and vigilant and "No, no, don't touch that" and "Because Daddy said so, that's why," there's a wonderful freedom that comes from just letting it bleed.

I raised my arm with the crowd for synchronized fist pumping, and splattered the guy standing next to me in blood. Whatever. You don't want some stranger's plasma on you, maybe you don't come to a punk-rock show, dude!

The 'Mats played mostly everything I wanted them to play. They did "Left of the Dial," "Alex Chilton," and "Bastards of Young." They skipped a few things. I wish they'd played more obscurities. I wish they'd done *Let It Be* in its entirety. I wish for so much. But that's like being the child of divorced parents and the parents get back together and your first thought is "I wish they were rich now too." Don't be greedy, fuckhead! You dreamed about seeing the 'Mats sing "Bastards of Young" live, right in front of you, and you got that. And unlike that farewell show you half paid attention to in 1991, they didn't do anything off the "new album." So with all due respect, shut your fucking old-man indie-snob complaining hole and enjoy the musical riches you were lucky enough to live long enough to witness.

After the show, I walked back to my car and drove home in silence. The apartment was dark and quiet—everybody was fast asleep. My wife and son purred like kittens, oblivious to the shadow with shaky knees leaving muddy footprints past their beds. I was cold and tired and badly in need of a hot shower. But the music was still humming in my head, and I didn't want to lose it just yet.

I tiptoed into my office and closed the door behind me. I pulled a chair toward the record player and sat down next to it. I was still holding my *Let It Be*. I hadn't let go of it for almost twelve straight hours. In the light, it looked worse than I imagined. The sleeve was warped from the rain, its once-smooth surface now a crusty landscape of rolling hills and mushy cardboard valleys. And my blood, now thoroughly soaked in, had created a strangely beautiful mosaic of viscous fluid. It looked like all four band members had been sliced up by a cleaver-wielding maniac, and left to bleed to death on that Minneapolis roof.

I slipped the black disk out of its case, and it was remarkably undamaged. Maybe a spot of blood here or rain there, but mostly pristine. I placed it carefully onto the turntable, and strapped headphones to my ears. I dropped the needle like I was trying to defuse a bomb, and smiled when I heard the familiar crackle.

It was like listening with fresh ears. Something had changed in the record. It had lived through something with me. We had bonded, as only a round piece of black plastic and a tired old animal still shivering from the rain—an imperfect storage device for thoughts and feelings—could.

I closed my eyes and imagined Charlie in college, sitting in his dorm room, hanging with his roommates and listening to music, on whatever weird futuristic device people will be listening to music in another twenty years. Maybe they all have their own ear chip implants or something, I don't know. But there on Charlie's desk, next to the crushed Coke can that had been converted into a makeshift bong (because some things never changed) is my battered copy of *Let It Be*. His friends will ask him about it, and after explaining what a record is and how it works, he'll say, "It was my dad's."

(I'm not sure why I imagined him referring to me in the past tense. Maybe I just assume I'll be dead by the time he gets to college. I'm forty-five now; what are the odds that I make it that long? I don't want to be cocky. Better to assume the worst and then be pleasantly surprised.)

"Dude," one of them will say. "It's covered in blood. What the hell happened?"

He'll tell them the whole story, about how I took the record to a punk-rock show, and then it rained and I sloshed around in the mud, and at some point somebody stabbed me, and I bled everywhere but I didn't fucking care, and the record was baptized with blood and mud and rainwater and the filthy sweat of strangers as we all danced and laughed and sang along with songs about being drunk and unsatisfied.

"Whoa," his friends will say. "Your dad was badass."

"Yeah," Charlie will say, with a smirk. "He kinda was."

Which of course wasn't in any way true. Even I exaggerated it in hindsight. As I drove home from the show, I looked down at the bloody record and thought, "Wow. I let that happen. I'm exactly like Iggy Pop slicing up his chest with broken glass." But I really wasn't. I didn't bleed because the cut was so deep but because I take a baby aspirin every day because I'm terrified of having a heart attack like my dad, so I'm prone to heavy bleeding anyway. And most important, I bled all over the record because it happened to be there, and I had no choice.

But I overromanticized it, and continued to overromanticize it every time I told it. I am not a punk-rock warrior any more than my dad was a brooding intellectual, smoking his pipe in his office as he listened to Willie Nelson records and pondered deep philosophical questions. He probably just thought "Always on My Mind" was pretty and he needed some alone time.

But who cares? Memory isn't about reality, and neither is music. It's about the comforting reflections we want to hold on to, even if they're mostly bullshit. My bloody Replacements record doesn't actually represent me, just like Bob Dylan's *Blood on the Tracks* doesn't represent what happens when a marriage between two human beings falls apart. But it's so much more romantic and perfect than real life. What sort of asshole would you be if you pointed that out?

As the music played, I held the record up to my face, right up to my nose, and breathed in deep. I don't know what it smelled like. Not old pot resin. Definitely not what it smelled like when it first showed up in the mail, wrapped in brown kraft paper. It smelled like something new but also very old, something foreign but intimately familiar.

Nobody on this earth, no soul alive or dead, could tell me that wasn't my record. Maybe not the record I'd been looking for, but goddammit, I had found my record.

Seven

She looked confused at first. Unbelieving. Like the expression you might give to an ex-lover who showed up at your doorstep unannounced, just to tell you about the kid they forgot to mention a few decades ago was yours. Her mouth opened, but the words weren't coming. She gasped. Then giggled. Then gasped again. Her brain was trying to catch up with the clearly ridiculous information that was being delivered to it.

"Is that . . . ? It can't be . . . Are you kidding me?"

Heather G.—twenty-five years older than the last time I'd laid eyes on her—pulled the Bon Jovi record out of my hands like a purse snatcher. She held it close to her face, studying the numbers, tracing them with a finger.

"Jesus Christ, this is my phone number. It is!"

"No it's not," I said, scoffing. I was pretty sure she was mistaken. How could she have recognized it so quickly? If you showed me a random series of digits and asked if it was my home phone number from 1987, I couldn't have told you with any certainty. But she seemed convinced.

"It's absolutely mine," she insisted.

"It can't be!" I said.

"It totally is. I can't even believe you found this."

She reached into her pocket, pulled out a pair of glasses. Granny glasses! Or at least the type of frames I once associated with grandmothers, with the delicate horn rims. She slid them onto her nose, and then pulled the record closer, giving the faded Sharpie on the sleeve a thorough inspection.

The woman for whom I once would have gladly crawled through a bed of hot coals and broken glass just to touch one of her inner thighs was sitting in front of me, older than our parents were when I first touched her breasts over a varsity cheerleader sweater, wearing granny glasses so she could read the fine print on a Bon Jovi record.

"Why didn't you call the number and find out?" she asked. "You should have called. You would have gotten my brother. He's got the number now."

"Come on! Seriously?"

"I still had that number six years ago. When I moved into my parents' house, I just transferred the service over." She laughed, maybe at me, maybe a little at herself. "Not a lot has changed since you've been gone."

So it really was my record. I poured myself another glass of Michigan red wine. Because what the hell, if we were going to do this, let's do this.

Everything about this was surreal. Not just reuniting with my first girlfriend—the first person to ever do things to my body that I had previously only done to myself—but to be in this house, which seemed so familiar, even though I'd never set foot in it before today. It looked almost identical to the house where Heather lived when we were teenagers—which, weirdly, was located less than five miles away from where we were currently sitting.

South Chicago suburban houses all look the same to me. The architecture is the same, the floor plans are generally laid out the same, they even smell the same: a sort of bland potpourri. I think they soak the aluminum siding in it. I swear, I could wander through this neighborhood after dark, walk into any random door, and find my way around the house, in the pitch-black, without much problem at all.

The last time I was out here, in the suburbs of my youth, my brother and I went to visit our old house and spent almost an hour trying to find it. We knew the street, and generally where it should've been, but we couldn't decide how one lime-green house was all that different from another lime-green house two doors down. When we finally located it, I grabbed a fistful of grass from the front lawn and ripped it from the earth. I told my brother that I needed some token of our time there, something to remember that this used to be our home. He looked at me like I'd lost my goddamn mind.

I brought the grass home and put it inside a mason jar. I took it out the next day, to show to Kelly. We both agreed that the grass smelled almost exactly like a mall Cinnabon. I immediately flushed it down the toilet, and we never spoke of it again.

"Bon Jovi was my first concert," Heather said, holding the record in both hands, like it was something heavy that might fall and break one of her toes. "Did I ever tell you that?"

"Yes," I lied.

"It was at the UIC Pavilion. Where they shot the video for 'Wanted Dead or Alive.' Well, some of it. I think Cinderella was the opening act. I went with three friends, and we spent the whole time in the bathroom before the show, making our hair as big as possible. Because we were sure that Jon Bon Jovi would see us and call us onstage."

"You were in the video?" I asked.

"Well, not that you could see my face. But yeah, I might be in there somewhere, in the crowd. Like a blur."

I was speechless. How was I just hearing about this now? We had dated for, well, I don't know how many months, and we'd watched dozens if not hundreds of Bon Jovi videos together. We listened to this record over and over again. I pretended to sing along and enjoy "Wanted Dead or Alive" more times than I care to remember. And I watched the video with fake rapt attention. And not once had she offered up the tidbit, "You know, I was a little bit in this video."

Maybe I had overplayed my fandom, and she feared that revealing her inclusion in Bon Jovi mythology, or Jov-ology, would make it messier to sever ties with me when the time came.

"Should we play it?" she asked, looking up at me expectantly. "Let's play it."

The needle dropped, and her small, tastefully decorated Midwestern dining room was filled with the teenage-girl panty-soaking power chords of the Jov.

I leaned toward my micro recorder, perched between the plate of fancy stuffed olives and the rapidly disappearing bottle of wine, and whispered, "Let the record show that Heather is currently dancing to a Bon Jovi song I'm hearing for the first time."

This was true. I absolutely didn't know what I was listening to. Whatever the first track on side two is called. Where Jovi rhymes "you're under the gun" with "out on the run." (That doesn't sound specific enough. It may be a recurring lyrical motif in the Jovi canon.) I didn't know, or didn't remember, the specific song, but seeing Heather dance to it, well, that was a different matter. The way she moved—chin up high, a slow hip shuffle that was like stirring pancake batter—was seared into my subconscious.

"I love this song," she said, her smile beaming.

"I fucking hate this," I said.

And we both laughed. Because we both already knew it, but it had taken me twenty-five years to admit it.

I could understand why this whole evening might seem a little suspicious. A married man drives out to the suburbs to see an old flame, brings along a bottle of wine and a bunch of old records they used to listen to, it wouldn't be unfair to wonder if maybe the intentions weren't entirely chaste. But Kelly was well aware of what was happening, and she was fine with it. It may have been because she knew that Heather was happily married . . . to a lovely African-American woman named Amanda.

We listened to the second half in its entirety, even though it was the half without any of the hits. Except I guess that "Never Say Goodbye" song, which I vaguely recall slow-dancing to with her.

"What else do you have in there?" she asked, nudging at the loose mountain of records on her kitchen table.

I had a few things. In the weeks leading up to this visit, I made several record-buying excursions—I went to Dave's Records, in Chicago's Lincoln Park, and the Reckless Records in Wicker Park. I picked up as many of the old records from our youth as I could remember. Not the stuff I brag about when I'm with middle-aged friends and I want to make it seem like I was way more musically sophisticated than I was. "Oh yeah, I only listened to Joy Division and the Smiths in high school." No, I mean the music I actually consumed as a teenager in the 1980s, while dancing awkwardly during junior high dances, or playing spin the bottle during birthday parties. I brought a few Police records, a few Phil Collins records, some U2, and a badly warped Duran Duran forty-five.

And also, the things I would have listened to with a teenage girl, if given the chance. Like the *Barbarella* soundtrack. At some point during my sexually impressionable years, I got it into my head that this album could act as a sort of aphrodisiac. Inspiring . . . I don't know what. A girl to do a striptease in zero gravity? I was never clear on what I was expecting, just that it would subliminally suggest something that a Huey Lewis record couldn't accomplish.

I watched her eyes as she looked through the records, and I felt that old anxiety again, of watching a woman review your musical tastes in real time. When she smiled, that meant I'd done something right, that I'd proved myself worthy somehow. When she gasped, her jaw falling open like she'd momentarily lost motor function, oh, that gave me a special sense of pride, as if I'd somehow personally choreographed the endorphin rush of nostalgia.

"Did he always have a mustache?" Heather asked, gazing at a Lionel Richie record.

"Lionel Richie? You're asking me if Lionel Richie had a mustache?"

"I'm serious."

"So am I," I said. "How do you not know that Lionel Richie has a mustache? That's like asking if Bon Jovi had enormous hair."

She laughed. "I'm sorry, I'm not big on facial hair. I try not to notice things like that."

I didn't imagine that it'd be that easy, that she'd just broach the subject herself, directly address the elephant in the room, without me having to bring it up awkwardly. The Mustache Question, which seemed so important back in 1986, easily the most important question you could ask, or at least just a notch or two below "What happens after we die?" It was so big, so massive in its significance that it stayed with me, lodged in my brain long after it didn't have any significance. But I still wanted to know. I needed to know.

"Was it the mustache?" I asked.

She didn't hear me. She was too focused on trying to remember the lyrics to whatever Lionel Richie song was being blasted through tinny speakers. So I waited, and wondered if I was just asking questions I already knew the answer to.

During one of my recent record-store visits, I'd stumbled upon an old Hüsker Dü EP, the "Eight Miles High / Makes No Sense At All" split side that was my introduction to the band. I loved it instantly, if only because it was so aggressively not the Thompson Twins. I listened to both songs on a constant loop for an entire weekend—flipping and then reflipping the record every three minutes—until I'd committed every wail and clattering guitar riff to memory.

I studied the black-and-white photo of the band on the cover like some teenage boys study pornography. Bob Mould looked like me—pudgy, pale, uncomfortable in his own skin, yet somehow infinitely cooler. And that other guy, Greg Norton, with his unimaginable handlebar mustache. He looked ridiculous, and yet somehow personified everything I wished I could be. It was like two little middle fingers sprouting out of both sides of his upper lip, a preemptive strike against the world.

I stared at that mustache for endless hours, the same songs pounding into my head over and over, and I came out the other side thinking, "Nothing wrong with a mustache. That's punk rock, man. That's how you stick it to the man."

It was around this same time that I was getting deeply immersed in late sixties and seventies white-guy rock. Which was basically an entire era of music devoted to the idea that growing a 'stache was something that made you desirable and fucking awesome. The proof was everywhere, staring back at me from endless record sleeves. Frank Zappa, Duane Allman, Jimi Hendrix, Captain Beefheart, Bryan Ferry, Thin Lizzy's Phil Lynott, the *Sgt. Pepper's*–era Beatles, the Nuge, Jim Croce, John fucking Bonham, everyone in Black Sabbath but Ozzy (especially Tony Iommi, the man who invented the heavy metal riff). And Lemmy! For the love of all that is unholy, Lemmy! The album cover for Motörhead's *Ace of Spades* is the kind of thing a teenage boy looks at with breathless wonder and promises to pledge allegiance to whatever dark lord will help him grow something even a fraction as menacing on his upper lip.

Heather, meanwhile, was very much immersed in popular bands of the day. She was into modern pop like Duran Duran, Bon Jovi, Def Leppard, Mötley Crüe, Van Halen, Journey, the Smiths, Whitesnake, Simple Minds, the Human League. What do all of these bands have in common? Not a single mustache among them. Mustaches in 1986 were very much an African-American face fixture. A little lip hair looked fine on Prince or Luther Vandross or Lionel Richie or Quincy Jones. The only Caucasian singers she saw with flavor savors were John Oates and Freddie Mercury and that guy in Toto.

So when I grew my mustache in 1986, that was her only comparison. She looked at me and thought, "He's trying to be John Oates." But in my head, I was like, "I'm so obviously a cross between Greg Norton and Lemmy." That's what I saw when I considered my reflection in the mirror. I wanted to be Greg Norton! But she'd never heard of Hüsker Dü. They never played their videos on MTV, or at least not during the prime after-school hours.

That was my theory. That's why she broke up with me about a year later, broke my heart into a million pieces. It was because of the mustache. Which was because we were listening to different records. Or more specifically, she was listening to the wrong records.

If she'd just bothered to spend a weekend obsessing over Hüsker Dü's "Eight Miles High," she'd know where I was coming from.

"Seriously," I said, when she'd finally gotten tired of Lionel Richie. "It was the mustache, wasn't it?"

She laughed, finally understanding what I was asking. "A little bit, it was, yeah," she said.

"A little bit? Come on!"

"Okay, a lot. I hated the mustache. I really, really hated it."

I flipped through my stack of records, looking for the Hüsker Dü EP, which I'd brought because . . . I don't know. To prove a point? To show her that she was wrong to dump me in the empty stands of that baseball field next to my house? Because, look, Greg Norton was cool. She'd made a mistake!

Heather, meanwhile, had picked out another selection. She dropped the needle, and I heard the unmistakable piano opening of "Don't Stop Believin'." Which just so happened to be my wedding song. "I guess I never liked the way it felt," she said. "It felt weird."

"Felt weird how?" I asked.

"You know." She was starting to blush. "I have gotten . . . burned. In that area."

"Your lady business," I said matter-of-factly, almost exactly when Steve Perry was telling us to hold on to that feeling.

"It was not one of my favorite sensations, obviously," she said.

"Wow. I was going to try and defend myself, but I guess I owe you an apology."

"We're talking some serious chafing, dude. Doesn't matter how sweet a guy is, that's kind of a deal breaker."

We paused and listened to Journey. There really wasn't much else to say. I'd brought along the Hüsker Dü EP—it was my slam-dunk evidence that she'd been all wrong about mustaches—but it was clearly useless now. I could imagine Greg Norton on the cover, his smile gone, his once-proud mustache wilted, shrugging, saying, "Don't look at me, why are you taking life advice from album covers anyway?"

"Oh my god, speaking of mustaches!"

Heather had pulled out *Attila*, and held it high, like a Baptist minister might brandish a Bible. The album, of course, is Billy Joel's presolo 1970 metal power duo, featuring Joel playing an oppressively loud Hammond B-3 organ. And on the cover, he and his drummer are dressed as Huns, surrounded by slabs of meat. It is an awe-inspiring cover—matched only by the epic loudness of the music—and sure enough, Joel is wearing a mustache that fits the inane tableau perfectly.

"Even Billy Joel knew this was a bad idea," Heather declared.

"Bad idea how?"

"He never had a mustache after this, did he? He shaved it and never looked back."

"He never did another album with a bunch of raw meat on the cover again either. That doesn't make it a bad idea."

"Oh, come on." She picked up *The Stranger* and placed it next to *Attila*. "Which one of these is a better Billy Joel? The one with a mustache in the body armor and kilt, or the one in a suit and no facial hair?"

This wasn't an easy question to answer. Because on one hand, sure, I guess *The Stranger* Billy Joel is conventionally cooler. But I'm drawn—I've always been drawn—to *Attila* Billy Joel. The one who looks like he might be smoking cigarettes behind a 7-Eleven. The other one, *The Stranger* Billy Joel, looks like somebody who dates supermodels and does a lot of cocaine. But the *Attila* Billy Joel, he's the one who goes to ren fairs, had his last sexual experience in the parking lot of a community college, and wouldn't be caught dead singing a song like "She's Always a Woman."

My parents love *The Stranger* Billy Joel. My dad, a pastor, thought "Only the Good Die Young" was hilarious. But they're a little freaked out by the *Attila* Billy Joel. Once, I was playing "Wonder Woman" way too loud in my bedroom, and my dad banged on the door, shouting from the hallway, "I don't know who's melodically raping a cat in there, but please make them stop!" I loved that.

His anger about *Attila* made *The Stranger*–loving part of myself seem a little less conspicuous.

I've spent most of my adult life trying to deny the full extent of my Billy Joel fandom. But it's there. It's always been there. I have, on several occasions, air-pianoed to "Angry Young Man" in front of a mirror. I've attended several Billy Joel concerts, two during the *Innocent Man* tour, and in every case I was disappointed that he didn't play more "deep cuts." And I've carefully evaluated the romantic subtext of almost every song in the Billy Joel canon, determining exactly how much they communicated the complicated emotions I was feeling toward the girls I wanted to have sex with, and then I would record those songs onto cassettes, along with other songs that shared similarly sexual or romantic themes, and then deliver those cassettes to the aforementioned girls who I hoped would listen to these mix tapes and decide, based on the airtight arguments contained within the songs, to have sex with me—including one girl who grew up to become a woman who would marry another woman and with whom I'm currently eating fancy cheese and drinking Michigan wine.

"I want you to know, I thought you were really cool for liking him," Heather said, somewhere around the middle of "Scenes from an Italian Restaurant."

I smirked at this, and poured myself more wine. "You're being kind."

She picked up another Joel record, *52nd Street*. "Look at him," she said, pointing at the cover. "He's so New York cool."

"He's standing in an alley with a trumpet."

"That's cool!"

"He doesn't know how to play a trumpet."

"That just makes it cooler."

"It's the exact opposite."

"You're too cynical," she said.

"If I walked into a bar with a trumpet and somebody asked me, 'Do you play?' And I was like, 'Nope. I just like walking around with a trumpet,' the entire bar would be justified in getting off their stools and collectively beating me into a bloody pulp."

She turned the record over, holding it delicately by the sides, and then placing the needle onto the vinyl like she was pulling a sliver out of a child's finger.

"Well, I thought you were cool," she said, almost absentmindedly.

"You're saying that to make me feel good."

"Well, what did I know? I listened to this." She pointed to the Bon Jovi record. "Billy Joel seemed more mature. Kids our age weren't supposed to like guys who wore ties. You were the only guy I knew who was into him. And that was intimidating."

"Stop it. Why am I just hearing this now?"

She smiled, but I don't think she was really listening. Her head was swaying in little figure eights as she mouthed the words like she was reciting the Lord's Prayer.

I still couldn't wrap my head around what she'd just told me. It was the exact opposite of everything I'd been bracing myself for. I was prepared to have her tell me that I ruined any romantic future we might've had because of that thing I grew on my face that I thought looked like a Hüsker Dü album cover. Or that pretending to like Bon Jovi so that I could touch a girl's boobies is exactly as creepy as it sounds. But this was not on the agenda. This was like opening up an old high school yearbook and realizing that you actually did look like Ferris Bueller.

We kept talking, and playing records. Sometimes we talked about the records, and sometimes the records were just background noise.

While we listened to the Police's *Ghost in the Machine*, we talked about what her room looked like in the other house, a few miles from here.

"It had rainbow wallpaper," she said. "Which perhaps, in retrospect, should have been a clue."

"Weren't there unicorn posters?" I asked.

"Oh yeah, a whole lot of unicorn posters," she said. "And Duran Duran posters. It was like a sea of magical horse horns and John Taylor haircuts. Oh, and also posters of gymnasts from the 1984 Olympics. I was living the life."

During side one of U2's *The Joshua Tree*, we talked about my car, the one I drove during high school, which I'd inherited from my grandmother. A Plymouth Valiant from the midseventies that Heather had dubbed the Shit-Mobile. During the entirety of "With or Without You," we debated whether it was maroonish or a dehydrated poop color.

For side two of *The Joshua Tree*, we talked about my hair, which was apparently something that concerned me as a teenager. "You used to get so upset about it," she told me. "You didn't know how to get it cut, and you said if you let it grow it would stick out all over. It was a thing. You kept it short on purpose so that wouldn't happen."

We skipped around the Monkees' *Greatest Hits*, bypassing songs like "She" and "Listen to the Band," and playing "Pleasant Valley Sunday" three times in a row. During those repeated plays of "Pleasant Valley Sunday," she told me about the time she and our mutual friend Christine inadvertently discovered Christine's mom's vibrator.

I didn't hear a single note of Genesis's *Invisible Touch*, I was so engrossed in Heather's explanation of her first marriage, to a guy who loved Phil Collins so much that "he used to say that Phil Collins was the only man he could picture himself fucking." He also argued that they should name their first child Collins, as a tribute to the little bald British man who invented the word *sussudio*.

"We had a deal," she told me. "I'd pick the girl's name and he'd pick the boy's name."

"You were actually going to let him do it?" I asked.

"He was really passionate about it. What could I say?"

"Your daughter has no idea how lucky she is to have not been born with a penis."

"Oh, she knows."

While trying to play the "Hungry Like the Wolf" forty-five—which was so badly warped, it was like dropping the needle onto an undercooked pancake—she told me about her first date with a woman, which just so happened to be at a Duran Duran concert. And that her taste in women was "more Pierce Brosnan 007 than Sean Connery 007. Not really masculine but not super feminine either. A little dykey, but with softer features."

"Pierce Brosnan is dykey?"

"Well, of the James Bonds, he's the dykey-est."

During Prince's *Sign o' the Times*, we talked about our respective wives, and how amazing they were, and how much we loved them, and how they were likely the only two women in the world trusting enough to let their respective spouses spend an evening drinking wine and listening to records with a former lover.

"Amanda said, 'What are you doing today?' And I was like, 'Eric's coming over.' And she's like, 'Oh yeah, you're going to relive your high school days, right? Should I worry about you guys making out on the couch?'"

I shrugged and slowly pulled a record from out of the stack. "Well, that is kinda why I brought *Barbarella*."

Heather laughed so hard, I swear I saw a little wine come out of her nose.

"Wait, we're not making out to *Barbarella*?" I asked. "Well, why the hell did I drive out here?"

"Absolutely," she said, pouring us both another glass. "I put my date underwear on and everything."

"You've still got date underwear?"

There was no sexual tension. But there was intimacy, in a way I hadn't experienced with an old friend in longer than I could remember. I'd been Facebook friends with Heather for years. I "liked" her pictures, read all her updates, thought I knew her. But I knew nothing about her. She was a stranger to me. It took three hours, two bottles of wine, and a bunch of records coming apart at the seams to find her again.

Were the records really necessary? Couldn't we have just met at some local bar and had the same experience? Maybe, I don't know. Maybe just talking would've been enough. But the records felt like an indispensable part of what happened.

There's an old tavern near our apartment that Kelly and I used to visit almost every week. It became a fixture for us. It's where we went for birthdays. It's where we brought friends when they visited. It's where we've commiserated over scary news, and celebrated when that scary news became awesome news. It's where we came during winter storms when we just had to get out of the house, and where we came during spring when we just had to get out of the house. Charlie had his favorite table, and his favorite waitresses who all knew his name. When you went upstairs—and we always went upstairs, because that's what Charlie demanded—you had to be careful at the top step, because it was weirdly shaped, and a little higher than the other steps. When the host seated most people, they warned them about the step. But we'd been there enough that they stopped warning us. And even Charlie started saying, "Look out for the step!" And the waitstaff would all laugh.

One day, the tavern burned down. We heard conflicting stories about what happened—it was either a grease fire or a rogue cigarette, or some combination of the two—but the building just . . . disappeared. I didn't know how to explain to Charlie. It was like having to explain death to him, but more difficult, because I had to explain how walls and buildings are important, and why it's okay to miss them when they're gone.

The owner promised that he'd rebuild, but that seemed pointless. The thing that was lost, it was lost forever. You couldn't rebuild what burned down. How could you do that? It wouldn't be exactly the same. It'd be something different, something that looked vaguely similar but unconvincing to anyone who actually knew better. There wouldn't be the same badly constructed step that only regulars know not to trip over.

The step was important. The step is what made it feel like our own. Without the step, it might as well have been an Olive Garden.

That's a hard truth you learn pretty quickly with adulthood. The things that make experiences unique disappear. Because it's not the broad strokes that matter. It's the top step that's just an inch too high, that catches your foot if you're not paying attention.

It's the scratches on a Billy Joel record.

Heather put on *Cold Spring Harbor*. Because she wanted to hear "She's Got a Way," which is apparently a song I should have paid more attention to. (The song, not the mustache that Joel sported on the album cover. Somehow, this rock 'stache had snuck under her radar.)

She told me about the summer after we broke up. I was up in Michigan, at my family's cottage. And she was back in the suburbs of Chicago. I'd sent a mix tape to Christine—our mutual friend, with the mom who didn't hide her vibrators all that well—which I'd asked her to share with Heather. I'd included a special song, just for her.

It was "Total Eclipse of the Heart." Because I was a dick. A dick with a broken heart, but a dick nonetheless.

"I just burst into tears," she told me. "I was like, 'Oh my god, I'm so terrible. I'm such an awful person.'"

I made up for it, thank god. I sent anther mix tape before the end of the summer, this time with "She's Got a Way," along with a letter of explanation.

"You said something like, 'This was the song I meant to send when I sent you that other song.' Which sounded to me like, 'I was really pissed off at you then, so I sent you that mean song, but this song is what I really meant.'"

"I'm pretty sure that's what I meant," I said.

"Well, it was too little too late," she said. "To be honest, it might have tipped me over the edge if you had sent me 'She's Got a Way' the first time."

And then, without even thinking about it, she leaned toward the record player and nudged the needle, like she was pushing it past a scratch. I know exactly why she did this. Because my copy of *Cold Spring Harbor*, the one I played for her back when we were teenagers, had a scratch in "She's Got a Way," right around the point where Joel sings about the "million dreams of love" surrounding her. I hadn't remembered that scratch until I saw Heather instinctively reach out, like she'd done a thousand times before, a million years ago, to save the song from getting stuck in an endless loop.

But this wasn't my record. It was just something that I'd picked up at a record store in Chicago. It didn't have that specific scratch she remembered. But she nudged the needle anyway, like she was scratching at the empty space left by an amputated leg.

She didn't even notice what she was doing. But I did.

And that was it. That was all I needed. It's what I came looking for, even if I wasn't exactly sure why.

The bar had burned down. The old stone walls were gone. I was a different person, and so was she. Nothing was the same anymore.

But there was still that little misshapen step, the little flaw you had to know to look for. Somehow, miraculously, that survived. Even if it wasn't technically there, it was still there.

I wasn't drunk—which was kind of insane, given the volume of wine we'd consumed. But it was also almost 10:00 p.m., which meant I'd been sitting at her kitchen table, listening to records, for over six hours. I made up some excuse about having to get up early, and she helped me carry my records and the record player to the car.

"Give me that for a second," she said, pulling the *Slippery When Wet* record out of the stack. She found a pen and scribbled something on the front sleeve.

She'd crossed out the old phone number and written a new one.

"Let's get together again," she said. "Maybe bring the wives."

"I'd love to meet her."

"And the kids. Your Charlie is adorable."

Driving home, I let Billy Joel's "Angry Young Man" blare through the car speakers. I'd forgotten how badass the droning C note opening in "Angry Young Man" really is. The lyrics don't get much more complex than "I'm young and angry," which is the least original observation made in pop music since "I'm young and horny." But goddamn, those pounding thumbs sound great.

At every stoplight, I was air-pianoing to "Angry Young Man" with the same manic and unironic glee I did as a teenager. And for the first time in a long, long while, I was okay with that.

Eight

It shouldn't have worked. There was no reasonable explanation for it. I could see the boot print with my own eyes—thick chunks of dried mud that had coagulated over time. The record should be useless—unplayable junk. The fact that it'd survived this long, stored for future generations to puzzle over, was a laughable lack of good judgment. You didn't need to understand the science of how the grooves on a vinyl record create sound—which has something to do with electrical energy converted into vibrations—to realize that, nope, this record was fucked.

But there it was, spinning on the turntable, the stylus drifting effortlessly across its warped surface, and somehow, miraculously, creating a more crisp, vibrant, testicle-rattling sound than I'd ever heard coming from a Rolling Stones record.

Robert was on his feet, assuming that rock-front-man pose that always seemed to come so naturally to him—his groin the magnetic center of his body—and the lyrics burst from him like a painful wailing.

"Waaaaaaar, children," he sang, a bit more late-seventies Elvis than a young Mick Jagger. "It's just a shot away! It's just a shot away!"

Robert was a little puffier than he'd been in his twenties, when he and I had first become fast friends. His belly was a little more pronounced, his hair a little grayer. But you could say the same about me. I hadn't aged any more gracefully.

Let he who is without paunch cast the first stone.

The music was coming from my Crosley three-speed portable turntable. And the sound, oh, it was spectacularly shitty. But it filled the room just enough to cast the shadows we needed to see again.

Robert and I were in the basement of a fraternity that hadn't been our home since we were barely of legal drinking age. It was familiar in all the predictable ways—I recognized the checkerboard floors, the battered staircase, the empty bottles of Milwaukee's Best lining the halls like bread crumb trails. But it also felt cold and distant, like visiting the wake of a dead friend. At least until we turned on the music.

Then I started to recognize where I was, and why it had once meant something to me.

A few months earlier, I'd called Robert, who I hadn't talked to since at least the late nineties. I knew he was in Chicago, but we ran in different circles now—I had a kid, and my friends were all parents who only socialized with other adults for "playdates," where we hid in kitchens and drank too much wine and occasionally shouted, "It's his toy and you need to share."

Robert was a relic from another era. The last time our friendship wasn't mired in the past tense, we were both young and single and embarrassingly broke. In my memory, he'll always be the guy from college, the sinewy dude from Wyoming who wore leather jackets graffitied with spray paint. The guy who had once karate-chopped a car's headlight because the owner had poured beer into my ashtray at a local pub, and Robert took it as a personal offense. The guy who loved Elvis and Tom Jones and Engelbert Humperdinck, not because he was being ironic or trying to prove how clever or unique or un-mainstream he was, but because he honestly loved Elvis and Tom Jones and Engelbert Humperdinck.

I asked if he wanted to join me for a day trip to Beloit College, our alma mater—a tiny liberal arts school in southern Wisconsin that likes to bill itself as the "Yale of the West." I wanted to visit some of our old college haunts, listen to music the way we used to listen to it, and . . . well, that was pretty much it.

Robert said yes immediately. He even offered to drive. I'm not sure why he agreed so easily, and so enthusiastically. Nothing about this was convenient, and all I was offering was a chance to wander aimlessly around a campus that wasn't our home anymore, where we knew no one. But that didn't seem to faze him.

The frat guys gathered around us were twenty, maybe nineteen. There was Alex, in the oversize sweatshirt with the Greek letters on the front. And Ulysses, dressed in a tie and button-down like he was a college student in the 1950s. They were smiling and nodding along to the music, but they did it in the way an eight-year-old nods along to "American Pie" when their parents insist on turning it up too loud when it comes on the radio during a road trip. They don't really care, but that song seems to be the consensus for the moment, so what the hell, let's do this!

"This is kind of blowing my mind," Alex said, with a smile I wasn't sure if I could trust.

"It's insane, right?" I said, turning to him. "This shouldn't be happening. It's defying all the laws of physics and common sense. Best-case scenario, it should sound like a power drill dropped in oatmeal."

"This is your record?" he asked.

"Well, no," I admitted. "I stole it."

"Seriously? That's so cool. Like how long ago?"

"About twenty minutes."

Alex seemed shaken by this news.

"Twenty minutes from right now?"

"Yep," I said. "You know the radio station on campus?"

"Yeah," he said tentatively.

"Totally stole it. I'm not sure if they noticed yet, but that's why we're here. Just laying low. In case they're looking for us."

Alex laughed nervously. Just as "Love in Vain" was really turning into something gritty and soulful. Why was Alex getting so caught up in the stealing part of the story, and totally missing the really remarkable part, the fact that a vinyl record—a really battered and bruised copy of the Rolling Stones' *Let It Bleed*, caked with mud from another century—was not just playable, but appeared to have somehow improved with age?

There was a story behind it. A story I hadn't bothered to mention to Franny and Maureen, the friendly twentysomething station managers who'd been so accommodating when I contacted them several weeks ago and told them I was an alum, writing a story about college radio or something. I don't remember exactly what I told them. What matters is, they said yes! They invited me to tour the station, to see the old soundboard where I'd worked briefly as a DJ during my college years, and even check out the shelves of vinyl records that were inexplicably still kept in the back.

I knew what I'd find on those shelves. The only question was, how could I get it out? Without, you know . . . stealing.

When we happened upon the footprint-scarred *Let It Bleed*, I told them about my decades-old feud with the station manager, which resulted in him grinding his muddy boots into the radio station's own copy of *Let It Bleed* with extreme prejudice. But I avoided getting into too many details about how it was probably mostly my fault.

During my junior year, I was invited to host my own radio show, despite my insistence that it should be entirely devoted to the Rolling Stones. And not the familiar stuff. All the deep cuts and outtakes and bootlegs and non-hits. The manager told me no. Their listeners (my peers) weren't interested in obscure Stones, he said. I could host a classic-rock show, with occasional songs by the Stones, but also other artists old enough to be called "classic." I defied him. I hosted the show I wanted. I played too many songs from *Brussels Affair*. I played *Jamming with Edward!* in its entirety. What were they going to do, dock my pay?

The manager sent me a message. He knew my affinity for *Let It Bleed*. So he made the record disappear. I found it in the Dumpster behind Pearsons Hall—thanks to a tip from a sympathetic colleague. I saved it, plucked it from its disgusting grave, smelling like rat piss and Tater Tots from the cafeteria, and shoved it back into the shelves. The manager—I wish I could remember his name—accepted my challenge. He took the smelly *Let It Bleed* out to the parking lot behind the station and, with a few witnesses, repeatedly stomped on the raw vinyl with his Doc Martens, thrashing it like a bouncer teaching a lesson to a belligerent drunk.

He returned it to the station, left it where he knew I'd find it, and scrawled "NEVER AGAIN" across the cardboard sleeve in red ink.

The message was received. I officially retired my *Rolling Stones Radio Hour*. I decided then and there that maybe I didn't have the constitution for radio work. I was too stubborn. I would focus on my side career as an amateur mixologist, creating mix tapes for women I wanted to sleep with. I considered giving *Let It Bleed* a proper burial, but that felt like admitting defeat. So I just put it back with the other Stones records, and left the dirty work of dumping the body to somebody in authority.

Twenty-five years later, it was still there.

Franny and Maureen—tall and thin and pale as bedsheets—

were as amazed as I was. Especially when they put it on the station's turntable and gave it a test drive. The turntable was sleek and metallic, so modern that the tonearm looked like a robot arm, the stylus its angry fist, ready to smash a record into accepting progress. The filthy, bedraggled *Let It Bleed* looked so out of place on top of it, like a train hobo who'd wandered into a spaceship.

But the unlikely union created something amazing. The record played! And not just begrudgingly. It came alive in ways it never did when I was younger. The vinyl's youthful sneer was gone, but all that time in neglected darkness had brought out something feral in *Let It Bleed*. It was frightening in ways it never had been when I was nineteen.

As I stood there and watched *Let It Bleed* make impossibly beautiful sounds, I made the conscious decision: I had to have it. I needed to liberate it from this graveyard, and bring it home with me, where it belonged.

I plucked the record from the turntable and said something vague about putting it back where I found it. I disappeared into the other room, through a maze of shelves filled with records that hadn't been played, much less touched, in ages. As I flipped through the stacks—pretending to look for its alphabetical nesting spot—I could almost hear the vinyl squeal with glee. They were like old dogs at a pound, watching a child walk past their cage. "Pick me! Pick me! Pick me!"

I listened to Robert talking to Franny and Maureen, asking them about their future plans and musical tastes, and waited for my moment to strike. I could hear my heart pounding in my chest, on the cusp of a full-on panic attack. Logically, I knew this was a victimless crime. I was stealing an old piece of forgotten technology—with a street value of maybe twenty-five cents, and that's being generous. But still, this felt wrong. I've never stolen anything in my life. Sure, the occasional MP3 online. But nothing tangible. Nothing that required stuffing something into my shirt and trying to seem inconspicuous. As a teenager, I once almost stole a porn magazine from a mall bookstore. But at the last minute, I chickened out.

I held on to the muddy *Let It Bleed* sleeve, and watched my fingers visibly tremble. And then, with a burst of adrenaline, I took it. I stuffed it . . . I don't even remember where. I walked back toward Franny and Maureen, talking way too fast, my eyes a bit too wide, tugging at Robert's sleeve. "Thanks so much, this was great, gotta go!"

I didn't tell Robert what I'd done until we were several blocks away. And by then, I was giggling. I'd gotten away with it! The perfect crime!

We went to the first place we thought we'd be safe: the fraternity house that hadn't been our home since 1991.

"We need to lay low for a little bit," I explained to the confused-looking fraternity members. "Just until the heat dies down."

They smiled and shrugged. Like the women at the radio station smiled and shrugged. I couldn't tell what those smiles and shrugs meant. Was it condescending? Were they being like "I wonder how much longer I need to listen to Grampa rattle on about this shit I don't care about before I can slip away and get back on Instagram"?

We'd almost reached the end of *Let It Bleed*'s side one, and it hadn't hit a single skip or muddy roadblock. That was a miracle. Not like the Virgin Mary on a grilled cheese sandwich, but a real miracle. One that gives you faith in a higher power, and that higher power's enthusiasm for Keith Richards guitar licks.

"Anybody want to hear some Boswell Sisters?" Robert suddenly announced.

The three frat guys laughed, but Robert wasn't trying to be funny. He honestly wanted to put on a Boswell Sisters record from the thirties and see if we could turn this party into a keen wingding.

This wasn't something he'd stolen from the station. These were records he'd brought with him. I'd heard more Boswell Sisters in the last few hours than I had in my entire life.

Robert had volunteered to drive us from Chicago up to Beloit in his Dodge pickup—a beast of a truck that he liked to aim toward medians—and his tape deck was exclusively devoted to Boswell Sisters compilations. Which was strange enough for the first hour of the trip, but got even weirder when Robert insisted on making a quick stop at a mall off the highway to pick up a pellet rifle and a thousand rounds of ammunition.

"You need this now?" I asked him.

He smiled impishly, and slipped another Boswell Sisters tape into the car deck. We listened to "Heebie Jeebies" at a volume better served for heavy metal, and Robert jerked his head along to the beat, pushing down on the accelerator far beyond the posted speed limit. I tried to enjoy the music and pretend there wasn't a loaded rifle sitting on the seat between us.

"The thing about the Boswell Sisters is, they're kinda dirty," Robert said to the frat guys, who didn't seem entirely sure if this was a joke. "I mean, listen to this . . ." He paused as we all pondered the scratchy harmonizing coming from the record player. Robert laughed, hearing something we apparently didn't. "You see what I mean? 'If you see me necking with somebody new / I'm in training for you!' That is insane, right? It's really dirty for their time."

This unsolicited music lesson, which he soldiered on with despite the glaring lack of interest from everybody around him, is exactly why I first became enamored with Robert. He made people uncomfortable, but for all the right reasons. Because he was *just so excited* about this thing you couldn't care less about.

I met Robert on my first day at college—we made each other laugh with our impressions of Buddy Holly doing a bubbly cover of Prince's "Darling Nikki"—and together we ended up joining a fraternity, TKE, mostly because their cafeteria was clearly superior to the dorm options. He was the one constant during my four years of college, despite the fact that our musical tastes were on opposite ends of the spectrum—he was to Engelbert Humperdinck what I was to Paul Westerberg—but we were just entertained enough by the other's animated enthusiasms to sit through music we might normally ignore.

Being down in that basement again, listening to records like we used to, getting way too excited about songs we were convinced mattered only to us—it was exhilarating. But not just because of the rush of memories. It was the audience. We weren't two old geezers having a private moment, reminiscing about the past. We were reenacting the past for a younger crowd who had to take our word for it.

We didn't come here to relive our past, because you can't do that. I'm not stupid enough to think I get a do-over. But I do like telling stories about myself. "You know that Bob Marley song, 'No Woman, No Cry'?" I asked them. "What do you think that's about?"

Ulysses was the first to answer. "Not wanting your woman to cry?"

"No!" I countered. "That's the thing! It's the opposite. It's more literal than you think. You're adding too many extra words. It's not, 'No, woman, you shouldn't be crying.' It's saying exactly what it seems to be saying."

I got closer to Ulysses. "It's about cause and effect," I half whispered into his ear. "One thing leads to another. No woman . . . no cry. You don't have a woman, ipso facto, you won't be crying. You see what I'm saying?"

"I think so," he said.

Robert and I weren't stoned, but we were trying to show these guys, as accurately as possible, what it looked and sounded like to be stoned in a Midwestern frat basement in 1989. And that was somehow better. We didn't need the actual drugs. We didn't need the younger bodies. Because we got to romanticize it. We got to play the part of us as we wanted to remember it. It was our personal Easter pageant.

It didn't last long. A good passion play requires an audience that sits in hushed silence and lets you finish the goddamn story. But this one didn't. They had their own stories, their own memories of college and music, most of which involved iPods or smartphones.

We watched the two of them stare down at their screens, scrolling through their massive MP3 libraries, looking for the perfect song to soundtrack this moment. But that's the problem when you've got instant access to forty thousand songs. You can't possibly pick just one without wondering if a better one is a few strokes away. So you keep scrolling and scrolling and scrolling, and then the moment's over and whatever, might as well see what's happening on Twitter.

The perfect song for the moment is whatever happens to be playing.

We talked for at least an hour. They told us about their majors. And how the TKE kitchen doesn't have a cook anymore, so it's really just a place to keep a fridge. We told them about mix tapes, and how you won't win back somebody with a tape full of the Cure and Cocteau Twins songs. We talked about women, and whether college sex is as crazy for them as it was in the late eighties, when we just had regular gonorrhea and not "super" gonorrhea.

They told us their sex stories, and we told them ours, except ours came with epilogues, where a few of the women we had crazy college sex with went on to become Facebook friends who "like" our baby photos, or get breast cancer and then die in front of you on social media.

"That's the thing nobody tells you about growing older," Robert says. "Nobody tells you that the girl you titty-fucked in the bar restroom when you were twenty is going to get breast cancer in twenty years, and you're going to go to her funeral with very complicated emotions."

This information seemed to bum them out.

Eventually they went away—they had classes to go to, exams to study for, Instagram accounts to update—and it was just Robert and me, alone in the basement. We wandered upstairs and sat out on the back porch—which wasn't really a porch, just a glorified step with enough room for folding chairs and an ashtray. We plugged the Crosley into the electric socket just inside the back door, like we'd done with countless boom boxes back in our youth, and Robert pulled out another record: Elvis Presley's *That's the Way It Is*.

"Nice," I said.

He went directly to the song we both needed to hear.

The first time I can remember listening to "I've Lost You"—side two, track two—I was nineteen and rip-roaring high.

Until that moment, I was not an Elvis fan. I knew his songs—I could probably hum a half dozen melodies from memory—but I had absolutely no interest in them. It wasn't until I was in a college dorm room, listening to "I've Lost You" on a record player that was made of cheaper plastic than a Happy Meal toy, as this ode to a crumbling marriage was narrated, and occasionally performed, by a wildly enthusiastic and equally stoned friend, that I realized an Elvis song—a fucking Elvis song—could make the hairs on my forearms stand on end.

"It's so clearly about Priscilla," Robert told me, shouting over the drums and trumpets, his eyes practically glowing in the dark, smoke-filled room. "His marriage is falling apart, and he doesn't want to admit it, and he's fighting to keep her, and the baby's crying in the next room, and . . ."

The song surges, and Robert leaps out of his chair, assuming an Elvis-esque posture.

Oh, I've lost you, yes, I've lost you
I can't reach you anymore

I'd laugh and nod my head along to his epic pantomiming. Because at nineteen, I could appreciate the kitsch of a marriage falling apart melodramatically. I felt enough heartbreak to feel that sting of romantic disconnect. But the way Elvis was singing about it—with campy emotional devastation—it wasn't something that had anything to do with me. Even though it kinda did. I heard the song at the perfect moment, while grappling with the second major heartbreak of my young life. I knew what he was talking about, even as I wanted to laugh at his theatrical mawkishness.

It was my first experience with how emotional resonance can be even more powerful with ironic detachment.

That was in 1988. Almost twenty-five years later, I was hearing "I've Lost You" again, with the same guy from Wyoming who introduced me to it, just a short walk away from the dorm room where our weed-addled brains first decided that no song understood our pain—and was more worthy of being mocked for understanding our pain—quite like Elvis singing about his shitty marriage in 1970.

We sang like you might sing along to a Black Sabbath song. With pumping fists and thrusting groins. More appropriate for a song about Satan or recreational sex than a sad tale of a marriage on its last legs.

I sang it with a little more force than I did when I was nineteen. Because I understood the song a little more now. It made sense to me in ways it couldn't possibly when I'd just had my heart broken a measly two times. When you know what it feels like to feel friends slip away; or have careers not work out quite the way you intended; or parents who drop dead on you out of the blue, leaving you confused and angry and scared; or a partner you've committed yourself to for the long haul start to grow distant—not in big, knuckle-clenching, impossible-to-miss ways like it does in the movies, but in inches, just enough to make you wonder if you're crazy.

That's when you realize how bellowing, "I've lost you, yes, I've lost you, I can't reach you anymore" at the top of your lungs can be so cathartic and satisfying.

The song ended and Robert and I continued to talk. But our conversation drifted from bittersweet nostalgia into the murky details of our lives since we'd fallen out of touch. We told each other things that were awkward and embarrassing, things we regretted, things we were proud of, and more often than not, things we wished we could forget. AA meetings and mistresses and bad decisions and career missteps.

"It was like a music thing," Robert told me, about the affair that nearly toppled his marriage. "It felt like this was my last love experience. Not real love, but the bullshit kind of obsessive love. I'd come home after seeing her, and listen to 'Nights Are Forever Without You.' You know that song?"

"Yeah," I said. "England Dan or something?"

"England Dan and John Ford Coley. It was probably their biggest hit." Robert burst into the familiar melody, belting out the chorus: "'I didn't know it would be so strong, waiting and wondering about yooooooou!'"

A few students walked past us, looking worriedly in our direction. We smiled and waved, and they moved on.

"I used to come home and crank that song and start rolling on the floor," Robert told me. "I was like a teenage boy or something."

I didn't ask him why he cheated on his wife. Or why she took him back. The only explanation he gave me was that song. And that was enough. I understand what he meant. And that was really all I needed.

We played our records while basking in the late winter sun, and watched people twenty-five years younger than us sit on the grass and do nothing. They did nothing spectacularly. Joyfully. I missed doing nothing like that. Where nothing felt like something. Now, doing nothing seems laughably irresponsible.

I looked at them and felt jealous. Not for their youth, but for how much they seemed to enjoy doing nothing. They stretched and purred, like cats having their belly scratched, and ignored the books on their blankets, and yawned triumphantly.

I tried to think of the last time I let myself get away with doing nothing. I thought back on the year—the last several years—and all the endless busywork that dominated every day, the constant fear that I wasn't trying hard enough to be the best employee, the best husband, the best father.

I'd so forgotten what it felt like to do nothing that I didn't even realize I was right in the midst of doing it. Or not doing it. Doing nothing.

Robert dug through the records and pulled out a Cure album, *Disintegration*. I smiled in agreement and waited for those familiar chords.

"You know what's weird?" I asked Robert.

"What?"

"I can still remember my college mailbox locker combination."

"The one from the mailroom downstairs?"

"Yep."

"That's pretty impressive," he said.

"Not really. It's also my debit card pin. It's my e-mail password. All of them. Every secret code I've had since my freshman year of college, I've used those four numbers.

"I feel like it might be a problem," I said.

"It's a problem if you're concerned about being hacked."

"It feels like a metaphor for my inability to let go of the past. I cling to those four numbers like I cling to everything else, like if I just hold on hard enough and don't let anything slip away ever, I'll be okay."

"Are you worried about being a hoarder?" he asked.

"A selective hoarder. One who has emotional attachments to old mailbox combinations and very specific vinyl records."

"I think you're being melodramatic. You're fine."

"I'm a forty-five-year-old man listening to a Cure record on a college campus I graduated from twenty-four years ago."

"Yeah? So?"

"On a Wednesday afternoon! It's not even like it's a weekend."

"Why is that a big deal?"

"I have a family! A child who's probably wondering where the fuck I am. What am I doing here?"

Robert considered this, nodding thoughtfully like he knew the answer but he had to find the right words to make me understand.

"You know what would help?"

He paused, letting the Cure finish their thought before continuing.

"If we played some Boswell Sisters really, really loud."

And so that's what we did.

A few weeks later, I was in the office of my apartment in Chicago, Charlie napping in the next room, having what I thought was a productive conversation with Kelly, my wife. At least it seemed productive until she threw the *Cocksucker Blues* VHS tape at me.

Even as the tape was hurtling toward me, I could tell by the expression on her face that it was an accident. The way she gasped, and put her hand over her mouth, like she couldn't actually believe what was happening.

I ducked, and the tape hit the wall behind me, and it exploded in a most spectacular manner.

A most spectacular manner—that's how my friend had described the way his wife's adult diaper had exploded when he'd thrown it against the wall. She was dying from cancer, and one night, the frustration and anger about everything that was happening to him and the woman he loved got the better of him, and he threw the diaper against the wall. And it exploded. Like a water balloon. In a most spectacular manner, he told me later.

Kelly and I both looked at the shards and tried to think of what to say.

"I'm sorry," she said. "I didn't mean . . . That was . . ."

"I know," I said.

"I'm just a little upset."

"I know," I agreed. "I can see that."

"I'm trying to be supportive of this thing. This . . . record-collecting thing, or whatever it is you're doing. But it's starting to get irresponsible."

"Because of *Cocksucker Blues*?"

I watched her face scrunch up, like she was wincing from a migraine. "No. No, it's not the— I mean, yes, I don't get the tape. I thought this was just about old records."

"It is," I said. "Nothing has changed."

"I'm trying to understand," she said. "You're not going to start bringing home VHS box sets of *Bosom Buddies* or something, are you?"

"Absolutely not," I said. I reached for her hand and squeezed it gently like I'm pretty sure guys do when they've been caught cheating.

She pulled her hand away. "This has just not been a good time for this."

I knew what she meant. Money was tight. Money's always tight when you're a freelance journalist, but it was especially so in recent months. We had an IRS bill that somehow managed to get larger every month. Our health insurance—which I'd gotten because of my column for MTV Hive, a website whose continued existence surprised even its full-time staff—would sometimes sporadically disappear without notice, usually just before a pediatrician visit for Charlie. Some weeks, we could afford to grocery shop at Whole Foods. On other weeks, we were at the grocery store with a "cheap meat" special on Tuesdays. We had no savings, no nest egg, and owned literally nothing. The bank even had the title to our car.

I had just spent a weekend in Nashville. Not for pleasure, for work. I flew down to interview Dolly Parton for a German magazine, *Süddeutsche Zeitung Magazin*. The whole experience was epically awesome and weird. It's weird enough meeting Dolly Parton, but especially so when you go into it knowing that the conversation will eventually be translated into German. It makes you self-conscious about the way you speak. Which is something you're doing anyway, being in the same room with Dolly Parton. But the German thing adds another layer to it.

The trip was completely paid for by the Germans, of course. The plane, the hotel, the rental car, all of it was covered. And eventually, somewhere down the line, I'd actually be paid for the interview— maybe when it got published, maybe before, maybe long afterward, it was anyone's guess. But all in all, it was good news. In our financially unstable world, it was a win.

Or it would have been, if I hadn't visited those three record stores in Nashville, and made those completely unnecessary purchases.

It had been a bad decision from the beginning. Logically, I knew there was no way that any of my records were in these stores. But sitting alone in a hotel room, in a city where music is literally everywhere—they pipe in country tunes at the crosswalks—my brain started to play tricks on me. Two decades is a long time, and it wasn't outside the realm of possibility that something from my old collection made the cross-country trip. Maybe not in one shot, but state by state, over the course of a dozen or so years. It could have made the five-hundred-mile journey in the back of a U-Haul truck, or many U-Haul trucks, as it got passed along and resold and donated, several times over, until it found its way to Nashville.

In my head, it made sense.

I spent almost an entire morning at a store called Grimey's, where both the customers and the employees looked like Bon Iver, and all the college girls wore black jeans and tiny black shirts that exposed their shiny navel rings. The Rolling Stones section had only a copy of Mick Jagger's *Primitive Cool*, but a pristine-looking *Exile on Main St.* hung on the wall, out of reach for anybody without a ladder, next to a price tag that read ONLY $169.99.

I'd bought a few things that I shouldn't have. Like a Temple of the Dog record. It wasn't mine, and I knew as much. But I couldn't imagine a scenario in which I'd ever hear "Hunger Strike" again, and I really wanted to.

I also picked up a copy of Cheap Trick's *At Budokan*. It absolutely wasn't mine. This was made abundantly clear by the graffiti written on the back, which read: "This is Richard's. Steal it and I will poison you." But I know a few Richards, and I'm pretty sure they're all Cheap Trick fans. So on the off chance that I could reunite one of them with his record, it seemed like a good risk for five dollars.

The biggest purchase was the VHS copy of *Cocksucker Blues*, the 1972 documentary about the Rolling Stones. I just stared at it for what must have been thirty minutes. I couldn't believe what I was seeing. My logical brain was saying, "Stop, you don't need that. Certainly not for fifty dollars." Also, I can't remember the last time I owned a VCR. It's been ages. But despite all the evidence against it, every cell in my body was propelling me forward, forcing my hand to yank away that VHS tape before somebody else saw it and bought it first. If I didn't get it now, I'd never get another chance!

The first time I saw *Cocksucker Blues*, it felt like a miracle. The series of events that needed to happen for me to witness even one frame of it was nothing short of alchemy. A friend of a friend knew a guy who lived with a guy who owned a third-generation copy he'd borrowed from some Russian mafioso. I watched every tedious, un-edited, horribly produced, unbearably grainy second in grateful hushed silence. I watched it with the same reverence I had when I witnessed the birth of my son. "This is something that will never happen again. Don't you fucking dare even blink."

But as much as my old brain was shouting at me to "GET IT GET IT GET IT NOW NOW QUICK," my new brain, the one with Wiki-cynicism, who'd seen too much on Google to ever go back, knew that there was nothing special about *Cocksucker Blues*. I could go home right now and watch it on YouTube. I didn't need to pay for it. I cer-tainly didn't need the movie in a box as big as a hardcover novel.

It wasn't precious anymore. It wasn't something you took the subway to the bad part of town to watch in a guy's garden apartment that smelled like rotting broccoli but you didn't care, because this moment wasn't going to happen again, and you could tell all your friends about it tomorrow and they'd be like "Holy shit, dude. What was it like?" And you'd talk about the sad and bored debauchery like it was life-affirming poetry. You talked about it like you talked about that time you saw *Faces of Death* and nearly vomited and then had nightmares for months, but it was worth it because you were part of an exclusive club that saw the thing that existed only in shadowy dangerous underworlds. It was a scar on your skin that was unique, and left a mark that was different from other people's scars.

That's not what *Cocksucker Blues* was anymore. It was just an-other thing you can watch on the Internet until you got bored after two minutes and went looking for something else.

But I bought it anyway.

All told, I didn't spend a lot of money. Maybe seventy dollars for everything, the records and the VHS tape. But the house of cards that was our current financial situation meant that the unannounced disappearance of seventy dollars from our checking account was a recipe for disaster. While I was gone, Kelly had written a check for Charlie's day care, assuming there was exactly enough money to cover it until my next sporadic paycheck arrived, but now we were twenty dollars short, and so the check bounced, and she had to come up with an elaborate web of lies for the day care administrator.

"It was humiliating," she said.

"I know," I said.

"No, you really don't. I am an adult woman. I do not appreciate being in a situation where I'm having to apologize for being broke because my husband emptied our bank account to buy records."

"I totally get it," I assured her.

"We are goddamn adults now. We need to start acting like goddamn adults."

"It was a one-time thing," I said, "and I promise it will never happen again."

Her eyes were starting to glass over. "You can't promise that. You just can't. And that's fine, I understand, it's just . . ." She ran a finger across her eyes. "I'm just so tired."

I knew what she meant. I was tired too.

Back in our twenties, an unpredictable money situation was just something we dealt with, rather than something we worried about constantly, or felt the weight of it crushing down on us. A few months after we started dating, I moved into her studio apartment— not officially, but it's where I slept every night for the first year we were together—and it was maybe five hundred square feet at most. But it never felt small. It was the perfect size, just as much as we needed. We'd lie in her bed all weekend, listening to music and having sex and laughing at jokes that were funny only to us, and it never felt like a jail cell.

Today, with a family and adult responsibilities, a dining room that's five hundred square feet feels oppressively small.

Kelly was right. We were goddamn adults now. And being a goddamn adult is no goddamn fun.

"I'll take the job," I said.

"That's not what I'm saying," Kelly stopped me.

"No, no, it's the right decision. It's the adult decision. I should do it. This freelancing thing is killing us."

I'd been offered a job at *Men's Health*. As their deputy online editor. It would require moving to eastern Pennsylvania, where their offices were located. And commuting to an office every day, five days a week, and keeping regular hours. And wearing pants. (Not something I was required to do as a freelancer.) Also, the magazine was *Men's Health*, which meant I would likely be required to edit and write stories about fitness and nutrition and healthy lifestyles and glamour muscles and other things I had absolutely no knowledge of or interest in.

But, the salary was sizable, with more zeros than I was accustomed to. Money would just magically appear in our bank account every few weeks, in a predictable pattern, so that we could ostensibly plan a budget and have some financial stability and maybe even start a savings account.

This is what goddamn adults do.

"I don't want you to do it if you don't want to do it," she said.

"I want to do it."

"I don't believe you."

"We can't live in this house anymore," I insisted. "We're suffocating in here."

"This isn't about the house. It's about leaving Chicago and moving to Pennsylvania and you wearing a tie every day. Are you sure this isn't what the records are about?"

I tried to look distracted, suddenly deciding that I had to start unpacking my bag from Nashville. "I wish you wouldn't keep bringing that up. One thing has nothing to do with another."

"I think it does."

"I've got something for you," I said, digging deeper into my suitcase.

"I think you're freaked out about saying yes to this job, so that's why you're doing this record thing. You're clinging to the past because you're terrified of the future."

I found it. Right at the bottom of my bag, under the clothes and the Dopp kit. I'd been hiding it, waiting for the right time to show her.

"This is for you," I said, handing it to her.

She paused, staring disbelievingly at it. And then, just as I hoped, she burst into laughter.

"Seriously?" she asked. "Journey?"

Not just any Journey record. Journey's *Escape*. Or *E5C4P3*, if you want to get technical about it. The one with "Don't Stop Believin'" on it. The song that we'd played at our wedding in 1999, as the recessional.

It was a private joke, one that everybody at our wedding laughed about, but nobody but the two of us really understood.

Years before, when Kelly and I were barely dating, I invited her to join me for a party hosted by my then literary agent, at her summer home in Lake Geneva, Wisconsin. It was a preposterous thing to ask somebody you've known literally a week. "Hey, do you want to drive two hours up to Wisconsin to eat cheese and drink rosé with a seventy-year-old agent and a bunch of trade paperback writers?" But she said yes, and we borrowed a mutual friend's car, and made a weekend of it.

After the party, which was Gatsby-level ridiculous, we ended up driving around Lake Geneva, looking for a bar open past midnight. We found nothing, so we bought some beer from a gas station and drank in the car outside our hotel. We listened to the radio, and when the local DJ invited callers to make a request, Kelly—lightheaded from too much beer—came up with a scheme.

She called the station, and using her best redneck voice, requested "Don't Stop Believin'" for her fiancé, who was serving overseas in the army or navy, she forgot which.

"'Don't Stop Believin',' is our song, and we were listening to it when we made love the last time, so could you play it so he knows I'm thinkin' of him and he's gonna be a daddy and I miss him so goddamn much?"

When the song came on, we cheered and laughed and sang along, throwing open the car doors and dancing around the empty parking lot, screaming "Hold on to the feeeeeeling" to the night sky.

That night seemed like a lifetime ago. Many lifetimes. And here we were, several decades later, in an apartment we could barely afford, our four-year-old napping in the next room, feeling giddy about that same song.

"Where did you find this?" Kelly asked, pulling the black disk out of its sleeve.

"In Nashville," I said. "Look at the sticker."

There was a small orange circle on the front that just read FIRST COAST DJ.

Her eyes went wide.

"Was that our wedding DJ?" she asked.

"I'm pretty sure it was," I said.

I was basing this on absolutely no evidence, other than that we had a DJ at our wedding, and we provided him with a Journey record to play during the ceremony—this was back in the neolithic days when DJs still used vinyl—and we never saw that record again. We just assumed the DJ had stolen it, but we didn't care. We had long since moved on to CDs.

I tried searching my old e-mails, to see if I had anything from a

"First Coast DJ" around the time of our wedding. But I used AOL back then, and that account was long gone. Even my Yahoo e-mail, which I rarely checked anymore, had nothing. There's a First Coast DJ doing weddings in Florida, nearish where Kelly and I got hitched, but when I contacted him, he sent back a terse e-mail, writing only "I think you have me mistaken with someone else."

I told none of this to my wife.

"I can't believe you found it," Kelly said, admiring the faded album sleeve like it was an old high school yearbook.

"You want to hear it?" I asked.

Kelly laughed, and she blushed, like I'd just suggested we have sex on the kitchen floor.

"I don't think I've listened to this song since our wedding," she said.

Of course that wasn't true. We'd heard "Don't Stop Believin'" at least a thousand times since then. It gets played incessantly. We'd heard it on satellite radio, in TV commercials, in movies and reality shows and TV shows about teenagers who weren't even alive when we sat in that borrowed car in Wisconsin. But I knew what she meant.

She didn't mean the song in general. She meant *this* song. This specific piece of plastic, which we both agreed to believe, at least for today, was the same object used during a formal ceremony many, many years ago—which, if we're being honest, was mostly for our mothers—to play a song that symbolized something true about our relationship, that wasn't about "for better or worse," or fathers giving away brides, or drunken toasts about "true love" and "she gets you" and all the other well-intentioned wishes that meant nothing, really. This was a song that would only feel significant if you were in that car with us in Lake Geneva at 2:00 a.m., laughing ourselves dizzy as the radio blared "Don't Stop Believin'." That was where it happened, when we became a *we*, and I knew I'd be with her for the long haul.

I remember feeling weightless, and thinking, "We could go anywhere right now. We could just drive and drive and see where it takes us."

Charlie was still napping, so we put the record on the Crosley. We laughed at the guitar arpeggio—so epic and self-important—and clapped along with Steve Perry, right between "don't stop" and "believing." We didn't talk about the wedding, or that night in Lake Geneva, because we didn't need to. The song was enough.

At some point, we started dancing. Not in the awkwardly self-conscious way you do at weddings. We just fell into each other's arms. I can't remember the last time I danced with my wife. Most days, we're focused on the tiny human being we created, and how to keep him from breaking things and/or himself. When we're alone, it's all about logistics, and then TV. But this, for once, was just about us. I'd forgotten how much of us we'd let slip away.

We could've stayed like that forever, swaying along to those familiar notes, laughing at twenty-year-old jokes. But then we belted out the "some were born to SING the blues" part and woke Charlie up from his nap. We always belt out that part, as loud as humanly possible. Because that's the only way your baby daddy will hear it.

Nine

I was back at the Record Swap in Champaign. It was just six months ago that I'd first walked through these doors, but it felt like a lifetime. The last time I was here, the weather was still warm, and Bob treated me like an insane person. But something had changed. Winter had come, for one thing. I'd driven through a blizzard to get here. And something had definitely shifted for Bob. He greeted me like an old friend. Somebody to be trusted.

"Let's see what we've got here," he said, as he peeled off the plastic tarp, like a homicide detective showing a dead body to relatives. The tarp crackled angrily, spitting dust into the air.

Underneath were boxes. Dozens of boxes. Shapeless, squishy, sad-looking boxes.

I'd been looking for my old records for, god, I don't even remember how long it'd been. Almost a year? I'd started in earnest last spring, and we were already deep into February. Since then, I'd looked through at least a thousand boxes, bins, racks, and milk crates. That's a ballpark figure, but I think it's pretty accurate. I'd been to a lot of places. I'd been to every record store in Chicago still in operation at least four times. And I'd expanded the search outside Illinois, into eight states in every direction.

I'd traveled out to Pennsylvania, into New Jersey, and eventually upstate New York, visiting stores that all looked the same—the same fading Pink Floyd and Kurt Cobain posters on the same cement walls, the same plastic dividers with band names drawn in Sharpie, the same skinny guys with scraggly beards buying and selling the same records from and to one another.

And I flipped and I flipped and I flipped.

I'd been out west. Well, Saint Louis. That's west, right? I'd been to a store in East Saint Louis—no bigger than some of my first post-college apartments—and eavesdropped as a guy with an armful of Boz Scaggs albums loudly explained how to solve the Israeli–Palestinian conflict. And then he got into an equally intense argument with another middle-aged guy with a white beard about whether Jethro Tull was better pre- or post-*Aqualung*.

"I believe two things," the Boz Scaggs–loving guy announced. "The Jews should have their own homeland, and 'Lido Shuffle' is the greatest song of the seventies."

And I flipped and I flipped and I flipped.

I'd been to a lot of record stores. And here's something you learn when you go to enough of them. Record stores—at least the good ones—are always in bad neighborhoods. You're always worried about whether it was a good idea to park your car nearby. It's always on the same street as a thrift store or a McDonald's where kids are doing whippets in the parking lot, or there's a middle-aged guy sitting at a bus stop who clearly has nowhere else to go. You're always within a short walk of a discount tobacco store or a place that buys gold.

And I flipped and I flipped and I flipped.

I flipped through so many records, I had calluses on my thumbs and index fingers. I got such a big blister on one of my thumbs that I actually went to a dermatologist.

It was my record-store stigmata.

There were times when I felt despondent. Not that I had any reason to be. I'd been absurdly lucky. I'd already tracked more of my original records than I could have reasonably hoped to find. But it does something to you, all of that flipping. The victories don't come very often. And when they do, they're quickly forgotten. I was always looking ahead, wondering what buried treasure was hidden in the next box.

I flipped, and flipped, and flipped, and flipped, and flipped. And almost always came up empty-handed. It can break your spirit after a while, all that flipping. You want more wins. You want something more to show for your effort than a few mud-splattered records and a callused lobster claw grip.

Crate digging is like driving through Nevada. Every once in a while, you stumble upon something miraculous. An impossible city of lights in the middle of nowhere. But then you're back on the highway, and it's just desert again. It's mile after mile after mile of nothing. You keep looking to the horizon, waiting for those lights to appear again. But they come too infrequently.

Just when I was beginning to have my doubts, when the constant flipping was starting to feel meaningless and stupid, a sure sign that I was wasting my life, I got the call from Bob.

Less than six hours later, I was in the back room of the Record Swap.

"You can look through everything, if you want," Bob offered, watching me look at the boxes. "I don't want to interrupt you."

He glanced toward the front of the store. There was nobody there. Not a soul. And not much hope that any customers would be arriving anytime soon. Outside, it was a blustery white. An angry wind pounded snow against the glass.

Bob looked back at me and waited. He had nowhere else to go, and he seemed as curious about what was hidden in those boxes as I was.

I crouched on the floor. My calves were already quivering, threatening to collapse. It was cold; the room wasn't heated, other than a tiny space heater, which wasn't currently turned on. Other than the records—which hadn't seen sunlight in at least a decade—there wasn't much back here. Just gray walls that were probably cold to the touch in July, and lights that seemed designed for a coal mine.

I opened the first box, releasing a dust cloud of disintegrating cardboard. Inside were dozens of classical records, some Perry Como, and fourteen copies of Phil Collins's *Hello, I Must Be Going!*

A gentle thud moved across the ceiling, sending a trickle of dust down toward us. I looked up nervously, but Bob didn't flinch. "There's an apartment upstairs," he said. "I don't ever see them, wouldn't even know they're there other than the footsteps." We listened as the thud kept moving, until it settled on a spot. "Sometimes I pretend it's a ghost," Bob said, with a half smile.

The wind pounded more snow against the window out front, perfectly timed to make Bob's ghost wish extra creepy. I was acutely aware of how alone we were, and how nothing about this made me comfortable.

Four boxes down. Only about a hundred or so left to go.

I'd spent almost a year trying to make this happen. It was a gentle operation. I had to take my time, not come on too strong. If I'd asked for what I actually wanted—"I WANT TO COME TO YOUR BASE-MENT AND LOOK THROUGH YOUR THINGS"—that would have scared him away. I had to be seductive about it. Send e-mails just to say hello. Make conversation. Show him I was a friend. And harmless. Demonstrate that I shared his love of records, but not in an aggressive or demanding way. I couldn't let him see the desperation in my head, the way my body vibrated when I thought about what records he might be sitting on, in some moldy basement, just waiting for me to come and liberate them.

I came up with plots. I asked if maybe I could spend a weekend working at the store, so I could write about what really happens behind the scenes at a record store in the new millennium. After we became colleagues, it wouldn't be weird if we went out for a beer after work. And then, hey, let's get a nightcap at your house! I'll pay for the six-pack! And once we were in his living room, hey, didn't you mention that you had a bunch of records downstairs? Mind if I take a look?

I didn't mention all of that, obviously. Just the part about being a free-of-charge employee. But he never responded.

Months passed, and I decided to be bold. I sent him an e-mail, told him I was coming back to Champaign and would be visiting the store. I laid it on thick, telling him my magazine story about the record industry was taking a new turn. It would now feature him, "a survivor who stuck through the lean years and saw how the industry changed and evolved, going from the near-extinction of the late 1990s to the recent resurgence." Who knows, I might even write that story one day.

I heard back from him within twenty-four hours. "I've been working hard on organizing the basement (or at least my LPs) and it is just about presentable so you are welcome to take a look," he wrote.

I wrote back: "I can be there tomorrow."

My trip up there was treacherous. For several reasons. One, it was Valentine's Day. Which is really a terrible time to leave your wife to take a road trip to southern Illinois to hang out in the basement of a guy who owns a record store. Even if she says she understands, and of course you need to do this, and it's such a commercial holiday that neither of you believe in anyway, you still look like an asshole.

Second, there was that winter storm. A major one. The kind that any reasonable person wouldn't consider driving two hours through unless it was an actual emergency. The snow was like something from a stop-motion animation special where Santa Claus has to cancel Christmas.

And now here I was, in the back room of a cold record store, looking through boxes of records, while the owner watched me and talked on and on about god only knows. I nodded like I was listening and kept flipping, hoping that this was just the beginning, and eventually he'd let me come back to his home and look through the real stuff in his basement, which would likely take most of the night.

And for what? Why was I doing this? I was starting to feel foolish. Who the fuck wastes an entire year of their life chasing down old records, especially records that are easily replaceable? I could buy them all on Amazon in about fifteen minutes. This was crazy!

"Your thing is not that crazy," Bob said.

Excuse me?

"I've talked to some people about it," Bob continued. "I talked to a guy last weekend. I told him about what you're trying to do, and how I thought it was kinda nuts. And he was like, 'No, he's completely right. Every record that you own is a unique thing. It has a pop here and a click here, and this and that. You can't just replace it with something else. Because it won't be exactly the same.' I thought about it, and I realized he's right, it totally makes sense."

I looked up at him, waiting for the punch line. But it didn't come.

"I've been digging up some records I had when I was a teenager. Some of them have been with me for most of my life. And I never thought there was anything important about them. I mean, I loved them, but I loved the music. I didn't love the actual record. That was just the container. What's the difference between a new copy of *Born to Run* and your old scratched copy? But now I understand."

He reached out and put a hand on my shoulder. "You've opened my mind to that."

Bob helped me pull down boxes and line them up on the floor. Most were unmarked, but some were labeled with genres, like "alt-rock," "CDs," and one that just read "MINE." An especially water-damaged box was marked "scratched smelly records," which seemed like a promising sign. But when I tried to open it, Bob waved me away. "These are not yours," he said. "I remember buying these myself. They still smell. They're bad, man. Really, really bad."

"So why'd you buy them?" I asked.

"Well . . . they're cool albums."

I kept digging. He saw me lingering over one album a little too long. "Is that yours?" he asked.

"It might be," I said.

"Well take it," he said. "Take it home and listen to it. That's the only way you'll know."

I was pretty sure it wasn't mine. Positive even. But that's not why I stopped when I saw it.

It was Neutral Milk Hotel's *In the Aeroplane over the Sea*. Which was an odd record to see in these boxes, buried under the mountains of abandoned, unloved vinyl. It was nestled between a Night Ranger album and Tammy Faye's *We're Blest* (with a sticker price listed at twenty-five cents). It so clearly didn't belong here. It was like some Brooklyn hipster kid who wandered into a church basement and decided he preferred it here, snacking on cold coffee and kuchen with seniors.

I knew the record wasn't mine. But seeing it again, being reminded of that amazing cover—the woman with a cucumber-slice head doing a *sieg heil* salute, or whatever the hell is happening—it reminded me of my uneasy early courtship with the album. It was 1998 or thereabouts, and I'd heard nothing but good things from friends. But my first impressions of Jeff Mangum's magnum opus weren't promising.

"This dude is really into Jesus," I remember thinking. "Whoa, whoa, did he just say 'Semen stains the mountain tops'? Ho boy."

Despite my initial misgivings, I listened to it again. I listened to it at every opportunity. Because that's what you do when you're in your twenties. You give new music a fighting chance. Because you know something might not click until the fourth or fifteenth or even fifty-second listen. That's how long it takes sometimes. You have to let music live with you for a while. You have to listen to it when you're not really listening to it. It has to sneak up on you when you're doing something else, or it finally starts to trust you. Because music is alive, and it's as wary of you as you are of it.

These days, I'm old and lazy, and when I listen to new music, I want to be swept off my feet right away rather than doing any hard work. Even before I started looking for my old records, I noticed that I'd lost some of the patience you need to forge an emotional connection with a slightly different combination of rhythm, melody, and harmony. Not even with artists I was hearing for the first time. I'm talking about bands and musicians who I already had chemistry with.

I feel about *OK Computer* like some people feel about family members. But when Radiohead put out *In Rainbows*, I thought it was just "meh," and the band hasn't meant as much to me since. There was a seismic shift in our relationship.

I had something special with Ryan Adams's *Heartbreaker*, but *Gold* felt forced, like date night in a loveless marriage. Has Adams made more albums since? Probably, I don't know.

And that's just two of countless artists—Clap Your Hands Say

Yeah, the Strokes, the Gaslight Anthem, the National—who had my unconditional love until they made a semi-okay album that left me empty, and I haven't returned their phone calls since.

I used to actively seek out new music. I used to read *Pitchfork* religiously, and make a commitment to a new album based on the cover art alone, and spend money I couldn't afford to lose on music I'd never actually heard just because a woman with a bleach-blond fohawk and a *Death to the Pixies* half shirt told me that it was her new religion. But now, I'm in record stores looking for names I recognize, cruising eBay for albums that might be battered and bruised enough to be former friends, and sitting in cold storage rooms in the middle of blizzards, looking through boxes of records that are warped not just from years of being stored in moldy boxes, but from a total lack of human touch, like newborns in a Romanian nursery.

Seeing that copy of *In the Aeroplane over the Sea* isn't a reminder of what I'm searching for. It's a reminder of what I'm turning into. If I find one of my lost records in these boxes, so what? How is it not the burning sled at the end of *Citizen Kane*? Isn't it just more evidence that I've stopped evolving, that I'm stuck in some past idea of self that I can't break out of?

After Kelly and I got married, we'd joke about how the only thing we'd miss about being single was the excitement of a first kiss. The not knowing, the butterflies in your stomach, the flush of excitement when you lean in and you feel your lips on a stranger's lips for the first time, and it's all so new and perfect and terrifying and awesome. After two decades of marriage, you're not even romanticizing the first kiss anymore. It's so far in your rearview mirror.

That's what it feels like is happening with my relationship with music. And I don't know if I'm okay with giving up the first kiss.

I kept flipping, because it was all I could do.

Until I'd gone through everything.

There's a panic that sets in when I'm on the last box. It was a feeling I felt as a teenager, after I'd spent an entire Saturday flipping through endless crates of vinyl at the old Record Swap in Homewood, walking down row after beautiful-smelling row, drunk on possibilities, until I realized I was on the last crate, and there was nothing else to look at—except maybe the VHS section—and I was gripped with the existential panic of a record-store browser, the opposite of buyer's remorse—the non-buyer's remorse, when you wonder what you missed from flipping too fast and looking so far ahead that you weren't paying attention to what was right under your nose.

I felt it now, as Bob carried over the last few boxes, and my flipping finger had slowed from a manic "I don't know how much time we have" desperation to a lumbering "what if I walk out of here with nothing?" crawl. The terror that I couldn't possibly search through all these records had turned into a terror that I had searched through them too quickly.

"You want to go back to the house?" Bob asked.

I was flipping slowly, meticulously, through the last dozen or so records in the last box when he said this, and it sent a chill down my spine. I didn't want to seem too eager, but also didn't want to seem in any way hesitant. So I blurted out "Sure, yeah."

"That's where all the good stuff is," he said. "That's probably where your records are. We'll look through them, maybe smoke a little ganja . . ."

"I don't see any reason why we shouldn't," I said, shoving the last box away.

This was my moment. And I knew it was my moment. I hadn't felt something like this since the last time I was single, and I was out on a date with somebody, and I knew she wanted me to kiss her, and there was that electricity when you knew you were going to kiss but it was just a matter of how long it'd take for your lips to finally fall into each other. And that was the good part: the waiting, the anticipation, the knowing that something amazing was going to happen, as long as you didn't do anything stupid.

"So," Bob said, breaking the silence. "You think you could give me a ride?"

We were somewhere around the middle of side two of *Rubber Soul* when the drugs began to take hold.

At first, I didn't think anything of it. I just assumed I was getting lightheaded from too little food. I hadn't eaten since breakfast, and the last time I checked my watch, it was 2:00 a.m. The only thing I'd had in my system all day were the fumes of disintegrating cardboard sleeves. But then it occurred to me, maybe this weird feeling washing over my body, making me feel like I was soaking in a warm bath, had something to do with the five joints I'd just ingested.

When Bob offered me some "ganja"—he said it just like that, "ganja," which sounded like an undercover cop trying to buy drugs— I was hesitant. I like the idea of marijuana. God knows I'd spent the better part of my youth consuming it. But it wasn't a part of my usual routine anymore. I was out of practice. I wasn't even sure I remembered how to hold a joint, much less hold in the smoke correctly.

It wasn't a conscious decision to stop using it. It happened gradually. You go a few days without smoking, then a few months, and then blammo, you don't even have an emergency nickel bag hidden in your underwear drawer anymore. When you're in your forties and it's been over a decade since you've smoked weed, you can't just wake up one day and decide you want a joint. If you've been off wine for a decade and feel like a glass of cabernet, you just drive down to the wine store and pick up a bottle. But pot? This forty-five-year-old guy would have better luck finding enriched uranium than skunk weed.

I hemmed and hawed when Bob started rolling, because I was nervous.

He finished the blunt and handed it to me. I looked at it, considering my options. I was in a basement in a small house in southern Illinois, in a room with an oppressively low ceiling, exposed pipes perfectly situated for head bonks, and only one exit that I was aware of, a rickety flight of stairs—with plenty of loose boards, making escape difficult at best—leading up to the first floor. It was snowing outside, and I was pretty sure my car was stuck in his driveway, submerged in a snowdrift. I wasn't going anywhere for a while.

I texted Kelly the address, told her what was happening, and asked her to stay by the phone, in case I needed her to call 911. She called me immediately, and I asked Bob if I could use his bathroom.

"I don't like anything about this," she scolded me.

"I'll be fine," I whispered, picking at the peeling wallpaper. "But we need a code."

"A code for what?"

"If I'm in trouble. I can't call you and say, 'He's handcuffed me to a radiator.' It's got to be subtle."

How quickly the tables had turned. It wasn't that long ago that I couldn't believe he was being so trusting of me. And now here I was, worried that he was plotting something sinister.

"This is making me very uncomfortable," she said.

"How about this. I'll tell you, 'I wasn't able to find that Bananarama song you wanted.' That good?"

"Bananarama?"

"What's wrong with that?"

"I don't like Bananarama."

"What does that matter? He doesn't know you."

"Can you make it something other than Bananarama? They had one good song."

"Bananarama is easy. I've seen a half dozen Bananarama records today. They're in my head already."

"But it makes me look like an idiot. Can you make it Arcade Fire?"

"These are records from a store that closed in the late nineties," I said, my voice rising a few octaves. "They're not going to have anything by Arcade Fire."

"How would I know that?" she asked. "Maybe I think it's a new record store. Someplace with music for people not living in the past."

"We're doing Bananarama," I whisper-barked at her. "It's less suspicious."

After I hung up, I took the joint. If I was going to die here, in the creepy basement out of a horror movie, in an epic snowstorm that was like an icy prison, with a wife unwilling to pretend-like Bananarama to maybe save her husband's life, I should at least go out with a smile on my face.

I smoked it tentatively, inhaling the smoke through pursed lips. I wasn't breathing much of anything in, but I bulged out my cheeks like a stoner Dizzy Gillespie.

I waited. Nothing.

Bob rolled another joint. I tried this one in earnest, letting some of the actual weed enter my lungs. It tasted awful. Like the exhaust from a city bus on a humid summer afternoon. I tried to hold it, but I ended up coughing most of it out.

I waited. Still nothing.

As if he'd been expecting this, Bob rolled a third joint while I was still hacking into my fist. And then a fourth. We passed them back and forth, wincing through bloodshot eyes.

"This stuff doesn't really work too well for me anymore," he said.

"It's a little harsh," I admitted, my voice reduced to a gasping croak.

"You have to smoke a fair amount of it," he said.

"Like how much?" I asked.

He didn't answer, just went back to rolling joints.

I went back to the boxes. I wasn't sure how many I'd been through, or how many there were left. Bob hadn't given me an exact number. I knew there were a lot. I'd been down in his basement at least four hours, flipping constantly, and there was no indication that we were nearing the end, or even the middle.

I sat on his couch—which had the texture, color, and consistency of a giant turd—and leaned over the boxes that Bob would carry out, one after another, from some back room, or from a pile in the corner, or wherever he happened to shove them when his brother dropped them off. He brought out boxes faster than I could get through them.

There were two pillars, surrounding me like pieces in a game of Jenga. Satisfied that I had enough to work with, Bob ducked under the industrial work lamps—the only source of lighting down here, which hung from the ceiling from extension cords—to look at his own record collection. And, of course, to tell me about it. Because that's why any human male collects music in any format—whether it's vinyl records, CDs, or even meticulously curated MP3s on his iPod. He does it in the hope that somebody will come to his house and want to know the philosophy behind his cataloging system.

Show me a man who doesn't want to explain to you—in a monologue not dissimilar to a TED Talk—why he decided to organize his records by genre rather than alphabetically, and I'll show you a man with no soul.

"This is various artists," he says, his voice echoing from a maze of shelves. "This is rock. That's Christmas. This is country. This over here is my reggae. This is my reggae twelve-inches. I like to keep those separate."

"Obviously," I said.

"This is Zimbabwe albums," he said, moving on. "This is African albums. This is other international stuff. This is Arabic stuff. This is folk/rock/blues/jazz."

"All together?" I asked, looking up from my box.

"Yeah. It makes more sense that way."

It maybe didn't make a lot of sense to devote entire sections in his music library to Africa and a country within Africa, and yet lump together Pete Seeger, Marilyn Manson, and John Coltrane into some sort of musical goulash. But something about it was calming to me.

"I have this theory that if your records are not in order, then your life cannot be in order," he said, so quiet that I wondered if he was talking to me.

"I really think that's true," I said.

"If you're going through a real hard time, you rearrange your records," he said, pulling out a record to examine it, touching it gently. "That helps. It makes things make sense again."

We had that moment, that quiet moment when you realize somebody gets you, and you feel a little less alone in the universe, and you don't want to say anything else, because saying anything else would just muddy it, and it's enough to just be quiet in the same room with somebody who thinks like you.

We did this for a minute, and then Bob said, "You want some more ganja?"

"Fuck yes," I said.

He rolled another joint, and we smoked it, and then he put on more music. I had no idea what it was. Possibly something from Zimbabwe.

I kept flipping. There were amazing records in these boxes. And also, some really awful ones. Records that deserved to be abandoned and forgotten. And yet here they were, sharing space, like Albert Einstein living in the same retirement community as a guy who used to work at Costco.

I wondered how these records ended up in the same box. How had *Christmas with Nat & Dean* come to live alongside David Lee Roth's *Crazy from the Heat*? Or *Jane Fonda's Workout Record* managed to share an eternal resting place with *De La Soul Is Dead*? What were the circumstances in which anything by Dan Fogelberg would become box besties with the Jesus and Mary Chain?

Does something like that just happen on its own, by accident? Or had these particular albums been placed together on purpose? The way Bob described it, they'd just been dumped into boxes without any attempt at order or clarity. So maybe this was how they had arrived at Record Swap—cardboard snapshots of the previous owners' lives at a very specific time. It was like looking at deep-sea photos of the sunken *Titanic*, and being transfixed by a rusty old stopwatch, still sitting at the bottom of the sea, right where it'd been left by its owner before he went and drowned. You see something like that, and you feel like you know somebody that you never actually knew.

Bob reappeared from behind his shelves, carrying another box over to me. I didn't know where he kept finding them, or where he brought boxes when I'd rejected them. There seemed to be more boxes down here than actual square footage.

"She only listens to boy bands," he said, as he dropped the box at my feet. "It's all got to be Top 40 radio hits. That's the only thing she's interested in."

My mind had wandered, but Bob had kept talking. "Your . . . daughter?" I asked, making a lucky guess.

He nodded, solemnly. "She's in high school now," he said.

"It's a stubborn age," I said, as if I had any idea.

"I bought her a turntable and she broke it right away. She doesn't want anything to do with it. She doesn't even understand why you would want a record."

"It's not just her," I said. "It's all of them."

"You know what's going to happen?" Bob said, pinching what was left of the joint and relighting it. "Eventually we'll all just have a chip in our head. We'll download a book, or a song. It'll be uploaded while you sleep so it'll go directly into your head. You won't even have to listen to it! You'll just remember it. You'll know the song without ever having to actually have the experience of listening to it."

I paused on a battered copy of Prince's *Around the World in a Day*. A record that always makes me think of my dad.

It was 1985, maybe 1986. I was supposed to be going to prom with Heather, but she'd recently broken up with me for another guy. Rather than ask somebody else, I opted just to skip prom entirely, and spend the evening instead alone in my bedroom, with the lights out, quietly flagellating myself for being unlovable, feeding buckets of chum to my self-made beast of self-pity.

But my dad, recognizing the signs of teenage ennui, wouldn't let me do it. He dragged me out of my room, took me on a "guys' night out," which included eating fast-food burgers in a parking lot and then going to the Record Bar in Lincoln Mall to buy records. We shared no musical interests, so the idea of browsing a record store with him seemed awful. I just assumed it'd be like smoking a joint with a parent (which, for the record, I've never, ever done); something I normally enjoy rendered totally unfun, self-conscious, and awkward.

But he proved to be the perfect vinyl wingman. He stuck to his sections—country and western, mostly—and I stuck to mine. He didn't pretend to be anything he wasn't, and he didn't ask questions I didn't want to answer. When I settled on *Around the World in a*

Day, he just nodded and said, "Looks cool." He didn't make me explain that I didn't really like Prince all that much, except for that "Let's Go Crazy" song, but liking Prince seemed cool, or at least cool among the handsome, athletic, self-confident guys at school who had girlfriends, and I wanted to be like the handsome, athletic, self-confident guys at school who had girlfriends. Prince was a little freaky to me. He seemed like an oversexed midget who needed to take a chill pill and relax with the thrusting. But when you're spending prom night in a mall with your dad, it's hard to be judgmental of the pop singer who seems to be getting laid constantly.

My dad bought it for me, and we drove home saying nothing, which is exactly what I needed at that moment. I couldn't tell you a single song from that record. I think one of them was about a beret. But I remember riding shotgun in my dad's car on a weirdly hot night in April, through the shitty Chicago suburbs that I hated and couldn't wait to leave, not listening to the radio and not even saying much of anything to my dad, just holding on to that Prince record, feeling a little more comfortable in my skin because I was cool enough to buy it, and maybe I wasn't getting cool enough to get laid in the back of a limo after prom, but goddammit, I was getting closer.

"Is that yours?" Bob asked.

I pulled out the disk and tried to study the markings.

"I don't know," I said. I really didn't. I remembered scratches—many, many scratches—but were any of these mine? How could I possibly know?

"Did it have the perforated flap?" he asked.

The flap! The unnecessary cardboard flap that served no purpose other than making the gatefold feel like a big, awkward manila folder. I remembered the flap! And I remembered not tearing it, not out of respect for maintaining a mint condition for future collectability, but just because I didn't understand why it was there and what tearing it off would mean. Removing it seemed as dangerous as cutting off the DO NOT REMOVE tag on a mattress; an act with likely no consequence, but better to be safe than sorry.

"I definitely had the flap," I told him.

"You're sure?" he said. "I've seen a lot of these records without the flap."

"No, I know the flap was there. I wouldn't get rid of the flap."

"You need to listen to it," Bob offered.

"Right now?"

"No, just take it. Take it."

"I couldn't."

"Take it home," he insisted. "You won't know until you play it at home, be alone with it for a while."

"This is nuts," I said.

"It's not nuts," Bob said, firmly. "You have to believe in it. You have to believe."

I don't know why it mattered so much to him. It was like once he changed his mind about me, once he decided that I was doing something worthwhile, that I was righting an injustice, repairing some wound that wouldn't scab over on its own, it became personal for him.

I was the sick dog he'd found shivering under an overpass during a storm. When he brought me home, wrapped me in a blanket, and put me in his car, he'd made a commitment to nurse me back to health. If I didn't walk out of here, with all my records, it would haunt him.

Or maybe I was projecting. I was pretty stoned.

A half dozen joints had done the job!

Bob did a lot of talking as I flipped through records. We were long past the stage of polite banter and "can you believe this snow?" superficialities. When you're stuck in the same room with a guy for enough hours, listening to records and smoking weak dope, it acts as a social laxative. You forget that you're essentially strangers, and you start sharing things you probably shouldn't be sharing.

He told me, for instance, about his brief career as a concert promoter during the nineties—while he was still running the Record Swap—for Zimbabwe singer Thomas Mapfumo, who was apparently very popular with prostitutes and criminals back in his own country.

"I remember once, at one of the gigs in California, he was trying to impress these girls," Bob said. "He told them, 'I paid five hundred dollars for these Italian shoes.' I pointed out that he should probably invest in a better sound system. He put a death threat out on me."

He told me about the home he owned in Zimbabwe, which he'd been trying to sell to pay for his daughter's upcoming college tuition. But he had no takers, since the place was in a dangerous part of Zimbabwe and, by Bob's own admission, "The police don't come out there."

He told me about his marriage to a woman named Patience, a backup singer in Mapfumo's band, the Blacks Unlimited. He told me about visiting her family in Zimbabwe, and how her dead grandmother possessed her one night while they were sleeping in the guest room, which really freaked Bob out, but then the grandfather had a talk with Patience and he realized why his wife had possessed her.

"He went out to his front yard and he started digging," Bob said. "He dug and he dug and he dug. And he found this little packet of herbs that somebody had put in his yard. It was a curse, and the grandmother had used Patience as a conduit from beyond the grave to warn him about it. At least that's what he said."

These were hard stories to compete with. But I tried. I told him about my own marriage—how I met Kelly in Chicago, and invited her to a Soul Coughing show in 1996. That was our first date. Every time I hear "Uh, Zoom Zip," I still get the goose-bumpy thrill of wondering if I'll get to see my wife's boobs that night. I made her a mix tape before the show, to impress her with my knowledge of Brooklyn hipster musicology. It did the job—obviously, because she married me—and I never made another mix tape again. Partly because it's never a good idea to make a mix tape for somebody you're not fucking or trying to fuck, because a mix tape is nature's way of saying "I totally want to fuck you. Please allow these songs to explain why."

Also, there is no such thing as mix tapes anymore. If you say to somebody "I would like to make a mix tape for you," their first reaction—if they're older than thirty—will likely be: "You're married. Stop trying to fuck me." And if they're under thirty, they'll look you right in the eyes and ask, "What is a mix tape?" And then you can either explain what a cassette tape is or slink toward the nearest exit, the latter of which is probably a better idea, because she's right, you're way too married to be flirting with her that hard, and she's far too young to give a shit about "Super Bon Bon."

John Coltrane's *A Love Supreme* was blaring from Bob's turntable. And I'd never liked the album more. Growing up, I'd pretended to like this record on numerous occasions. Like how I pretended to appreciate *Bitches Brew* or *Kid A* or anything by Captain Beefheart. But in this basement, as a soundtrack to this conversation, Coltrane's screeching saxophone added just the right amount of gravitas. It made the whole room dissolve into gritty black and white.

"Are you EJS?" I heard Bob ask.

He pointed toward Guns N' Roses' *Appetite for Destruction*, the album I was holding without even realizing it. And sure enough, right there at the top, were three letters that looked like initials. Which just so happened to be my initials.

"Holy shit," I managed to say.

"That's yours, right? It has to be yours." Bob's voice had risen a few octaves.

"It might be mine."

"Of course it's yours! Why would it not be yours?"

I traced a finger along the Sharpie trail. "It doesn't feel familiar," I said.

"What does that even mean?" Bob exclaimed.

"Maybe it's somebody else's. I'm not the only one with those initials. If I'd just written my whole name, this wouldn't—"

Bob disappeared behind the shelves and reappeared with a notebook and pencil. "Write your initials and we'll compare them," he said.

I did as he asked.

"You're not trying," Bob insisted.

But that wasn't true. If anything, I was trying too hard. I was trying to focus on what was unique about my handwriting. And that's like trying to think about riding a bicycle while you're riding a bicycle.

My initials back then—if it was indeed my actual initials—were more carefree, with softer corners and bigger, cartoonish loops. Today, my initials are kind of severe, with sharp, unbending lines. Or maybe I just don't know how to write my own signature anymore. Why would I? You can do all that stuff with computers now. I haven't signed a document with my own name since I was young-enough looking to get carded at bars. I knew as much about signing my own name as I knew about how to find a checkbook in my home office.

"Maybe my handwriting has changed," I said. "Like how your fingerprints change."

"Your fingerprints don't change," Bob said. "Unless you get your fingertips cut off in a shop accident."

"I thought the epidermis could peel off."

"The epidermis can, sure. But not the dermis. That needs to be scarred before your fingerprint changes."

"Didn't John Dillinger have his fingerprints removed?"

"Yeah, I think I read that."

I eventually conceded to take the *Appetite for Destruction*, just to keep things moving. And as the search continued, any time I hesitated, he insisted that it might be mine, and I set it aside to take home with me. I had a stack of records by Big Star, R.E.M., Curtis Mayfield, Paul Simon, Talking Heads, Jane's Addiction, Buzzcocks, and Echo and the Bunnymen—all with small and almost undetectable blemishes, rips, stains, frayed edges, and zigzagging scratches that were like mini–Rorschach tests. He didn't care how much I protested, or how much I said they weren't mine. When I tried to shove them back into the box, he'd just pull them out again.

"It'll be interesting, when you get them home and play them, if you remember the pops," he said. "Look for the pops. Look for the pops."

"What if I don't recognize the pops?" I asked. "How do I know they're my pops?"

"You'll know," he said. "Just make sure you're using the right record player."

"Like a really good one, with a lot of wow and flutter?"

"What? No. No, no. Here's what they don't tell you. The cheapie record players—the little plastic ones?—will actually play scratched-up, damaged records better. They won't give you the same fidelity. But if you have a super-good needle and a super-good audio system, it's going to pick up every imperfection in the vinyl. If you have a crappy setup, it's not going to pick that stuff up. It just slides right over it."

I thought of my old puke-green plastic record player, the one from Fisher-Price or Tele-tone or whatever. I don't remember music ever sounding as sweet as when it came from those tiny, shitty speakers. I thought it was just nostalgia. But maybe I had it all wrong. Maybe this was how the songs that mattered to me were supposed to be heard.

"I used to have two turntables hooked up to my receiver," Bob said. "One of 'em was a nice one and the other one was not as nice. And I always listened to the one that wasn't so nice. Because it sounded better. To my ears, it sounded more authentic."

"Maybe 'cause that's the way you heard them the first time?"

"But I think it's about how technology doesn't always make things better. People try to fix things that aren't broken. We got a lot right the first time. As a species, we figured a lot of things out a long time ago. And then we just mess them up by trying to make them better. There was nothing wrong with books that aren't on a tiny screen you can carry around with you. The Internet kind of makes things worse more than it makes it better."

"I miss my old record player," I said suddenly. And I said it with the same trembling force in my voice that I would have used to admit how much I miss my dad. Maybe those two things were intertwined somehow. Mixed up together.

He smiled at me. A tender, compassionate smile that isn't the typical emotional currency of two guys who've known each other less than a collective twenty-four hours.

"Let's smoke some more ganja," he said.

He rolled another joint, and I breathed it in greedily. The weed agreed with me. Not because it was especially potent—any medicated bliss lasted no longer than an average Ramones song—but because it reminded me of weed from the eighties and nineties. It was unhealthy-looking and full of seeds and you had to smoke a preposterous amount of it to feel anything approaching stoned. In fact, I wouldn't be surprised if Bob's weed was just as old as all the records in his basement.

I liked that idea. It made me happy. I laughed out loud, till tears started rolling down my cheeks. It was comforting and also stupid— two things that coexist so perfectly together. I could, at that exact moment, be listening to the very same Iggy Pop album I'd bought at Record Swap back in the late eighties, while simultaneously smoking the exact strain of terrible weed, made on the cheap in a closet with a heat lamp, that I'd bought from a guy with a purple Mohawk and the jeans with preshredded knees in the alley behind the Record Swap.

"You feeling anything?" Bob asked, passing the joint back to me.

I was feeling something, all right. Something I thought I'd never feel again.

I felt invincible.

Ten

Mom, be careful, Jesus!"

The table slipped from her hands and dragged against the door-frame with a screeching BREEEEK.

"I've got it," she lied, and reached under the table with purpose, as if she'd just discovered, with absolute certainty, the table's center of gravity.

I held the screen door open with my foot, and looked nervously toward the street. "We need to hurry this up," I said.

She pushed, and grunted like a weight lifter. I fell backward, not doing an especially good job at being the "muscle" in this equation.

"Okay, too fast," I panted.

"We should just call Alan," my mom said. "He'd be happy to help."

"No," I barked at her. "We're fine."

The less Alan knew, the better. Alan was a neighbor—a neighbor from many years ago, from back when we actually lived here. He's one of the people who owned this house, who'd agreed to let me spend an entire day (and most of a night) here. But that was all he'd agreed to. He hadn't said yes to the table or the chairs in the backseat of my mom's car.

There were a few things I'd forgotten to mention.

We managed to shove the table inside, and it took off like a bobsled, carrying us along with it. It slid to a stop just shy of the refrigerator, and we looked up at a room that was much, much smaller than either of us remembered.

"They put in all new cupboards," my mom said.

"Was there a wall there?" I asked.

"I'm pretty sure we had a washer and dryer in there," my mom said. "And a toilet."

"I'm not sure what I feel about this floor," I said.

"Is it new tile?" she asked.

"It feels like new tile. But I'm not sure."

"Maybe they just cleaned it."

"No, it looks new."

"It's so hard to tell. I'd need to see pictures."

We stood there, looking at the kitchen and the kitchen table we'd brought, which we knew for a fact belonged here, which made everything else in here seem like it belonged, even if maybe it didn't.

It'd been a long time since I'd been inside this house. At least since 1983, when my brother and I sat on the kitchen's linoleum floor and watched movers carry boxes full of our stuff past us, grunting under the weight. I remember thinking at the time, "This is it. I'll never see this house again. It's all over." And I wasn't being melodramatic. That was realism. What possible reason would I have for coming back here, to a place that stopped being my home when I was barely a teenager?

"This window was smaller," my mom said, pointing to a window over the sink. "And it was a hurricane window. Does that look like the same refrigerator?"

But I was already out the door, back in the driveway, pulling chairs out of the backseat of her car. The same broken-down wooden chairs that went with the kitchen table, even though they didn't match in any conventional sense, not just with the table but with one another, like they were children in an orphanage, thrown together by circumstance.

My mom came out to help, pulling out chairs and also grabbing a few extra things she'd brought along. Like the afghan blankets my grandmother had sewn for my brother and me when we were kids. I hadn't asked for this, but she insisted, saying it'd make the place "more homey."

"It's gonna look weird though," I said. "Where are we putting them, in the kitchen?"

"No, the living room," she said.

"On the floor?"

"Well . . . okay, I see what you mean." She paused to consider this. "Why don't we bring the couch?"

I couldn't argue that, at least aesthetically, this would be perfect. The couch, like the kitchen table and chairs, had previously existed here, so it would certainly help set the scene, so to speak. But this seemed unnecessarily complicated. And also, why did my mom still own a couch that I remember as lumpy and old back in the seventies?

"No, that's too much," I insisted.

"I want to do it," she said. "It'll be easy. I'll get some helpers."

When I was a kid, any time she used the word *helpers*, she was always referring to Mark and me.

Northport, the town where my family and I lived during most of my childhood, is a small place. And as in any small town, people are nosy. The last thing I needed was for somebody to make a few calls, let the real owners know what we were doing in their house. Because they hadn't agreed to all of this. All they'd offered was a twelve-hour window to see the house again, and maybe listen to a few songs within those familiar walls. Nobody had consented to a kitchen set and a couch. And the cereal. And the other guys who'd be joining me soon, at least one of them with a sack full of punk-rock records, which we were intending to play very, very loud.

They weren't the only ones who wanted to come. Not for the music, but to see our old house semidecorated. Several aunts and uncles called, asking if they could "stop by for a peek." I've said no to all of them. This wasn't Lincoln's log cabin. I didn't want to put up velvet rope dividers, so visitors could gawk at my childhood tableaux from a safe distance. I had enough to worry about without hosting any tour groups.

I walked upstairs with the posters, looking for my old room, and Mom followed. I immediately realized that something was wrong.

"Your bedroom," I gasped, turning to her.

It was . . . gone.

The place where a door used to be, which once led into the room where their bed used to be, was conspicuously absent. There was a wall now. We both just stood there, confused, like lost children in a hedge maze. We touched the fresh paint—or maybe old paint, I don't know. It could've been like this since the nineties. It didn't matter. There was a wall! Where there wasn't supposed to be a wall!

I walked down the hall. The carpeting felt weird under my feet. The sound of it made no sense to me. My every memory of this hall-way came with a soundtrack of squeaking. The constant feet scutt-ling across wood floors. It sometimes sounded like the nails were loosening and everything would crumble under us. There was none of that now.

They'd taken all the life out of the house, the ghosts had been whooshed away. And they probably thought it was an improvement too.

I found my room—which, by some miracle, wasn't walled up. It looked about the same as I remembered it, maybe a little smaller. But Mark's room, across the hall, couldn't have been more different.

"Fuck," my mom said, offering a rare curse word to capture her emotions. "This is huge."

Back in the seventies, my brother did have the largest bedroom in the house, as he did in every house we'd ever lived in. But not this big. This room was almost as big as the first apartment I rented after graduating from college. Its ceilings were somehow higher than the rest of the house. The walls, a soft yellow, seemed like they'd been covered in a more expensive brand of paint. And the closet . . .

"It's a walk-in closet!" my mom exclaimed.

"I think it used to be your bedroom," I said.

That's why a wall was blocking access to what had been my parents' marital bedroom. It'd been converted into a walk-in closet for whoever lived in this room.

I'm sure you don't care. Why would you care? Houses are renovated all the time. There is nothing remarkable about this. But for us—okay, maybe just me—it was egregious. An unthinkable atrocity. This room—a room that was now a closet—was where I went when I had nightmares. It's where I crawled into the covers, protected by the impenetrable walls of my parents' bodies. It's where my brother and I would pound on the door or just come charging in on the weekends, at least until that time I accidentally walked in on them having sex, and then I always knocked. It's where my dad would tell ghost stories to Mark and me under the covers, and they always involved dead birds on the beach, because that was my brother's personal phobia, and it was always guaranteed to send shivers up his spine, even if a random dead bird usually didn't make much narrative sense in the story.

At least my brother's room could be restored to its original aesthetics, if only in piecemeal, and temporarily. I opened my messenger bag, filled with rolled-up posters, and pulled out the one with *KISS* written in pencil on the side. I placed it against the back wall of

Mark's old room, right about where I remembered his bed being, and slowly spread it open.

It was a portrait of all four band members, mugging for the camera with their best Kabuki-rock poses. I had spent weeks trying to find this very specific poster, which I only remembered because of an old Polaroid from that era—a curious portrait of my brother looking like somebody who has subsisted entirely on sugar and power chords—which is to say, bloated and weak and unclear of his surroundings. I have no clue why anyone felt "This is a moment that needs to be preserved forever in a photograph." Behind him is the poster, hanging over his bed like a coat of arms.

I had to sift through a lot of KISS merchandise online before finding this exact poster. I learned that it's called a "KISS Destroyer Sparkle Poster."

My mom looked at the poster and decided it was on the wrong wall. "It should be over there," she said, pointing toward the wall next to the door.

"Are you sure?" I said, when she held the poster up to show me. "That doesn't look right."

"I'm sure it was here," she said. "See . . ." She took the Polaroid and placed it against the wall. "There's just enough room here for a single bed."

We taped it up and stepped back for a better look. "I don't know," I said, unconvinced.

"Are you sure that's the right poster?" she said, her eyes darting from the Polaroid to the wall and back again. "It looks so much smaller here."

"It's the right one," I insisted. But now I wasn't so sure.

We tried every wall—a little higher, a little lower, no, no, closer to the window—but everything seemed off. It wasn't exactly how we pictured it in our muddy memories.

"We could bring a bed in here," my mom suggested. "That might give us the frame of ref—"

"No, absolutely not," I shot back. "We're done with furniture."

I finally stopped listening to her, and put it on the wall I'd argued for in the first place.

"Is this where you're going to do it?" she asked.

"Do what?"

"The thing. Whatever you're doing with the records." She laughed. "Mark says you're having a séance."

"Of course he says that. If he bothered to return my calls, I could explain a little better."

I had probably already explained too much. That was the problem. At first, he was excited about seeing the old house, even if he didn't entirely understand why it had to involve listening to a bunch of vinyl records. But sure, if that was the price of admission, he'd pay it. But his enthusiasm wavered with each new e-mail, when I mentioned the furniture, and the guests who would be joining. He was nervous that this was becoming something he didn't want to be involved in, so he stopped responding.

"I'll just call him, tell him to come over now," my mom said, taking out her cell phone.

"It can't be now, we're not ready," I said.

"It's fine," she insisted.

"It's not fine. It has to be perfect."

I didn't know what I meant by that.

She shrugged and put her phone away. And we both sat on the floor of Mark's gigantic empty bedroom and said nothing.

I could feel the panic rising in me again. What the hell was I doing? I hadn't intended any of this. I wanted to keep it simple, like my brother preferred.

It's not like it happened overnight, and I just woke up one morning and said, "Let's take this to a really weird and uncomfortable place." It happened in inches, so I never really saw what it was turning into until it was too late.

Here's a timeline of how I remember it unfolding.

A little over a month ago

During a phone call with my mom, I mentioned that I'd been thinking about visiting the old house, maybe asking the owners if I could bring a record player in there, play a few songs, just for old time's sake. I laughed as I said this. But she liked the idea. She encouraged me.

"You should talk to them," she said.

My father was a pastor, so our home was never technically owned by us. It was and continues to be owned by the church, a United Church of Christ parish with a congregation of about a hundred people. Mom had heard through the grapevine that the current pastor was leaving, and there might be a vacancy before the new pastor moved in.

"Just tell them what you want to do," my mom said. "Don't mention the records, though. Make it sound more normal."

A month ago

I sent a letter to one of our old neighbors, a long-standing church board member with political clout. She replied with an optimistic e-mail, promising that it would be discussed in a church council meeting. Also, she wanted me to know that she'd seen photos of my son on Facebook, and he is adorable.

Three weeks ago

I can't recall if I went looking for it or if I just found it, but I saw an eBay listing for an unopened box of Boo Berry, dated 1978. I was astounded that such a thing existed—that somebody had managed to resist not just the urge to open it up at some point over the last thirty-six years and satiate his brain's self-destructive hunger for delicious chemicals, but the constant nagging sensation that comes with the futility of saving something that has no real value and is almost certainly garbage, and might actually be growing in strength, becoming more powerful and deadly with each passing year, becoming like the man-made aberration of some Japanese monster movie from the fifties, ready to burst from its box and terrorize humanity.

I made the one and only bid, purchasing it for the low price of $6.99. After shipping costs—the seller was based in Oregon—it came to $17.24. Expensive, sure, but if you factor in inflation, I'd probably come out ahead. I did some snooping online and learned that a twelve-ounce box of Kellogg's Corn Flakes cost just fifty-nine cents in 1978. Cereal actually cost less than a dollar during my childhood?

That seems preposterous. But I wouldn't feel comfortable sharing that information with anybody in their twenties, lest I come across sounding like one of those "When I was a kid, movies cost a nickel" grandpas.

I really didn't know why I was buying it. It just seemed like something I should own. An unblemished artifact from my youth. Like a *Star Wars* action figure still in the box. But edible.

Of course I was going to tear open the tabs and release the ghosts inside, let them drift out and float angrily around the room like the dead spirits at the end of *Raiders of the Lost Ark*.

If you have an Ark of the Covenant that contains dextrose, modified corn starch, trisodium phosphate, and red 40, you're insane if you don't open it. It's not a collectible. It was created to be consumed in a sugar-fueled frenzy and then expelled from your angry bowels with extreme prejudice.

Two weeks ago

I received a call from Janet, the church secretary. The council had approved my request. But I had only a forty-eight-hour window to visit the house, between the old pastor moving out and the new pastor moving in, and at some point in that time frame they'd be bringing in carpet cleaners to shampoo the premises, so would I rather visit the house pre- or post-shampooing? Or they could just work around me, if that was easier. What a wonderful trip down memory lane! Also, the entire council wanted me to know that they'd seen photos of my son on Facebook, and he's adorable.

I did not mention the record player.

Twelve days ago

I contacted Mike C., the guy who used to live down the street from us, who during the seventies and early eighties was my, and alternately (and sometimes simultaneously) my brother's, best friend. I had not spoken to him in at least thirty years.

I had absolutely no idea what he was like as an adult.

I called him out of the blue and asked if he wanted to come sit in my old house, without furniture, which may or may not have mushy, recently shampooed carpets, and listen to records from our youth on the floor. Oh, and I have a copy of KISS *Alive II* that may have been the exact same copy that he and several other music enthusiasts in our tiny town had once traded for favors, like cigarettes in a prison yard. Oh, also, I'd be bringing an unopened box of Boo Berry from 1978, which could possibly give us all botulism. See you then!

He said yes. Absolutely yes. Also, his mom had a few records in her crawl space that he could bring. Maybe there were a few things in there that we'd listened to as kids.

Ten days ago

I purchased several more items from eBay, including posters of Farrah Fawcett, KISS, and Kansas City Royals third baseman George Brett. I informed Mike C. of this, and he insisted that I got it wrong, that I should have acquired a poster of Catherine Bach in her Daisy Dukes. I tried to explain to him just how wrong he was, that he was likely thinking of his own bedroom and not my own. I was 100 percent certain that Farrah Fawcett in her red—or burnt orange, my memory is fuzzy on that part—bathing suit, which could barely contain the ballistic missiles that were her erect nipples, had been affixed to my walls, at an optimal vantage to the bed, for the entirety of my preteen years.

I could not tell you a single relevant piece of information that I retained between the fifth and eighth grades of school. Something to do with math, maybe? But I could tell you, without a shadow of a doubt, that the poster of Farrah Fawcett in a red/burnt-orange bathing suit was located at an upper left corner vantage from my bed, at approximately ten o'clock, and maybe five feet off the ground. If the shades were open, the morning sun would create a distracting glare that made it difficult to appreciate the details of her torso. The perfect viewing hours were between four fifteen and six thirty.

Nine days ago

Mike suggested that I contact Darren I., who was several years older than us and was likely the original owner of the KISS *Alive II* record. He was, Mike reminded me, the person responsible for purchasing much of the music that somehow ended up in our possession, despite the fact that it frightened us. Or more specifically, that guys like Darren frightened us. I remembered that Darren had blue hair at one point. Blue hair! That was all the evidence I needed that he was capable of extreme violence and would pull my entrails out of my body like a magician pulling silk handkerchiefs from his wrist.

"You should go visit him," Mike suggested. "He's a mechanic now. Works at a place about a mile from our old school."

Seven days ago

My mom called with a suggestion.

"Remember that table we had in the kitchen?"

"Um," I responded. "I think so. You mean the kitchen table?"

"That's the one! I still have it. So I was thinking, if you're going to do this, you might as well do it right."

I was skeptical, but after twenty minutes of talking about it with her, I got very excited. I saw what she meant. Sitting on the floor of an empty house is kind of silly. How do you get anything meaningful from that experience? Your legs fall asleep, you get charley horses, you're annoyed and uncomfortable.

"We'll bring the chairs too," she said. "There's no reason you have to be nostalgic with leg cramps."

I couldn't argue with that logic.

Six days ago

After some soul-searching, Mike realized that the KISS *Alive II* in question hadn't come from Darren. It really belonged to John J., another former school peer who was now living in Traverse City and, according to my memory, was equally as dangerous.

I barely knew John, but I knew that at some point in the eighties, he'd broken a few laws and spent a little time in jail. Or at least those were the rumors. I had no clue about the details, but it seemed in keeping with his reputation. Although John was two years younger than me, he was ahead of the curve in just about everything. He was the first one at our school to start smoking cigarettes, when the rest of us were still playing with Evel Knievel dolls. He was listening to the Butthole Surfers and Bad Brains albums when I still thought Men at Work were badass. I was in awe of the guy, but he also scared the shit out of me.

"I already talked to him," Mike told me. "He's gonna join us. He's got a lot of records you might be interested in. Also, he's bringing booze."

My stomach got queasy, and my pulse quickened. On the one hand, John was the first guy I'd ever known with an appreciation for punk rock. It's entirely feasible that he's the reason I first encountered the music that still matters to me the most.

But he also has a criminal record. And he'd been invited to a home I didn't own, and he'd be bringing alcohol. And god knows what else.

Five days ago

My mom called again. She found the blankets. The blankets my grandmother had made for my brother and me shortly after our births.

"I'll bring them," she said. "They're a little mildewy, but you'll hardly notice."

"It's really not necessary," I insisted.

"Don't worry about it," she said. "This is fun. I'm enjoying this."

Three days ago

John e-mailed me:

"Hey, Eric . . . wow . . . you are going way back . . . Here is what I remember . . . I did own that KISS album and I do remember rocking out in the church house with Mark and Mike C. . . . I don't recall loaning it out though . . . it's very possible though since I loaned Mike my Richard Pryor *Bicentennial Nigger* album and his mom was so upset that she nearly called the cops on me."

He gave me a complete list of the records in his basement, which included the Dead Kennedys, Elvis Costello, the Gun Club, the Clash, Iggy Pop, Devo, Blondie, and the Ramones. He also asked if we were drinking just beer or also wine. "I'll bring wine too," he offered. "Let's do this right."

Then he closed his e-mail with: "I'll bring over some records. Some greasssssy disks . . . you bring the Lipitor . . . mmmmm Boo Berry . . . laterzzzz."

What have I done?

Two days ago

My brother finally called, responding to my numerous e-mails, which explained exactly what was happening and why he needed to be involved. He wasn't convinced.

"I just want to go on the record saying I think this has gotten way out of hand," Mark said before I even managed to get in a hello. "You've taken things entirely too far, and it's making everybody really uncomfortable. It's just weird, okay? It's weird."

I would have been offended if this wasn't, in some respects, entirely accurate.

"Help me understand what this is," Mark said. "I want to see the house again, but I don't get what else is happening. There's furniture now?"

"Just a kitchen table and some chairs." I coughed nervously. It probably wasn't a good idea to tell him about the KISS poster taped to the wall of his old bedroom.

"And you seriously invited John J.?" he asked.

"What's wrong with John? You haven't seen him in years; you're still judging the guy?"

"Wasn't he arrested?"

"Just once. It wasn't a big deal at all. And it was a long time ago."

I assumed, like I always did in recent years when my brother refused to be cooperative, that our disagreement had something to do with him being superrich.

My brother had some money. Many monies, in fact. By some accounts, his company had assets in the ballpark of $8 billion. How much of that is profit for him? I couldn't begin to tell you. We've never talked about it. There's just never an appropriate time to ask a family member, "No, seriously, how filthy rich are you?"

To be fair, even before he crossed over, Mark and I weren't exactly two halves of the same coin. He was a Republican by age fifteen, with a NIXON FOR PRESIDENT poster on his bedroom wall. I was a Democrat who marched in his first war protest before he was old enough to drink, and threatened to join the Peace Corps just to piss off our parents. Mark's interests included tai chi, the Chicago Board of Trade, and Gustav Mahler. I was into punk bands from the eighties, smoking weed, and not having health insurance.

When he suddenly had more money than Bruce Wayne, we had even less to talk about. He's still my brother, and I adore him, but our lives are fundamentally different. For me, it's still a big deal to buy first-class plane tickets. Meanwhile, he's wondering whether to keep chartering private flights or just buy the damn plane already. During the last election, I felt like I was making a political statement with my Obama bumper sticker. Mark hosted a $2,500-a-plate campaign fund-raiser for Ron Paul at his house.

"You've lost me, bro," Mark said. "It doesn't mean I can't take a joke; you've just lost me. What are you trying to accomplish? What's the end goal here?"

"Why does it have to be something?" I told him. "Why can't it just be listening to records?"

"Well, what do you want to happen?"

"I want to listen to records."

"But what else?"

"Just that! Just that! It's just a couple of guys who grew up together listening to records in a mostly empty house. Why is that strange? Don't make that strange."

One day ago

A voice mail from the church:

"We're so excited that you're doing this. You can pick up the key with me, or we'll just leave the door open. There'll be a few surprises in there for you."

I had still failed to mention the fact that I was bringing a record player. And several very loud albums, including KISS *Alive II*, and whatever John J. had in his basement, and whatever Mike C.'s mom had in her crawl space. Oh, and Mike C. and John J. would be joining me. And maybe not my brother, because he thought this whole thing was kind of insane. And maybe it was. And maybe the church council would think so too, if I'd bothered to tell them everything. Which I hadn't.

I have never been so certain that I was making a mistake, and so reluctant to actually stop that mistake from happening.

One of the things I've noticed, as I've gotten older, is that some changes you're able to accept with grace, or at least a resigned sigh of acceptance. And some things, you just can't let go.

If you grew up someplace and then moved away, and then came back many years later to visit, you're in for at least a little heartbreak. But nothing is going to be exactly as you remember it. Houses will be torn down and replaced with new houses. Stores will have gone out of business, maybe replaced with something else or maybe just a parking lot. That corner store where you used to buy comic books and smoke bombs with your brother? It's a Starbucks now. Your summer camp? Gone. Replaced with condos. The restaurant where you could throw peanut shells on the floor, which gave every grown-up you knew such unmitigated bliss—"You can litter!" they told one another. "You just throw your shells on the ground and they don't care. They want you to do it."—that had closed its doors, been replaced with a children's bookstore, and then a candle shop, and then a craft beer brewery, which was closed almost before anyone had learned it was open.

The sledding hill that hosted so many epic races between you and your peers? Torn down so they could build another wing on the hospital, which of course closed down. Can you believe that? We don't have a hospital anymore. A hospital! We're not talking about a restaurant where you can throw peanut shells on the floor. This is where you go if the bleeding doesn't stop, or if you notice that your spouse is much bluer than usual. The nearest hospital is now an hour to the south, but I'm told you can get medevaced during an emergency. In other words, you better be goddamn sure those chest pains aren't just indigestion, because if you call 911, you're paying for a fucking helicopter.

But these were changes I could live with. I griped about them, and complained bitterly with friends and family who still remembered how things used to be, how they were supposed to be. But in the end, I learned to accept the changes. They just took some getting used to. After the fifth time of passing by the hardware store that's not a hardware store anymore, you stop doing a double take. You just accept how the structure of your world has shifted.

But some memories run deeper, and they don't ever go away.

During the six-hour drive up to Northport from Chicago, I had a lot of time to think. I thought about what could go wrong, as well as how it could just be a monumental waste of time and energy.

The backseat of my car rental looked like the inside of my brain. A record player, protected on all sides by pillows; a duffel bag full of clothes, only a few of which had been washed; and dozens of record sleeves scattered everywhere, flung at every corner of the backseat, like I'd left a window open during a tornado.

About twenty minutes outside of Northport, I drove across a stretch of road that I'd traveled countless times in my life. And like always, I waited for the bump.

But there was no bump.

During my youth, there was always a bump.

A month or so before my trip home, I'd gone to a Record Store Day in Chicago, the annual countrywide celebration of non–chain stores that still sell vinyl records. I'd never participated before, so I was excited to see what was involved. I'd heard about the inexplicable long lines, made up almost entirely of young people born after vinyl ceased to be a dominant medium, all waiting for the chance to buy limited-edition recordings that were utterly worthless outside of social circles where people waited in line on Record Store Day.

I came out, first and foremost, for the lines. I just wanted to see people standing outside of record stores again. The last time I'd seen something like that was in the late eighties, when I waited outside a record store in suburban Chicago to buy U2's *The Joshua Tree*. I actually almost got elbowed in the face by a guy at least twenty years older than me, who I guess was worried that I might get a copy of *The Joshua Tree* with a more desirable serial number.

I know people still wait in lines for things. When some new limited-edition technology comes out, there'll be lines stretching across city blocks. Any time there's a new iPod or smartphone or some new device that can carry more songs than I could even imagine existing when I was eighteen, there are lines. But that's different. It's stupid. We didn't wait in line to buy record players. If people were out there for some new amazing MP3 that they could get only at this store, that I could understand. But an iPod? What fucking moron waits in line for an iPod?

Nobody has ever cried or felt less alone because of an iPod. They've done it because of what was on the iPod.

I picked Dave's Records in Lincoln Park as my first stop on my hometown tour, mostly out of nostalgia. It's where I used to go when I was first dating Kelly. It was right down the street from her apartment. This place—this block, really—had special resonance for me.

"I've got a whole list of shit I want."

The guy in front of me in line, who was wearing a knit cap despite the unseasonably warm weather, was getting snippy with whoever he'd decided to call during our hour-plus wait.

"Well it's my fucking money, I'll spend it on what I want."

All around me was a sea of bleached hair and indie band T-shirts and scarfs. I counted at least two waxed handlebar mustaches, and that was just in my periphery.

There was a palpable anxiety among the gathered dozens standing outside on Clark Street, checking their phones and trying not to look anxious. The air was thick with impatience. No, not impatience exactly. It was that horrible feeling that they might be missing something—that something better could be happening somewhere else.

There's even a word for it now. FOMO. "Fear of missing out." That's what the kids today call it. They created an acronym for an anxiety that every generation of human beings in the history of human existence has experienced. I distinctly remember feeling it in the eighties and nineties. I'm sure my dad and my grandfathers felt it. Young people today are not unique in their FOMO. They're just the first to admit it.

Record Store Day was created to torment your FOMO. You could see it on everybody's face. Maybe they were waiting outside the wrong store, and a few miles across town, Wayne Coyne was at Reckless Records giving away super-rare Flaming Lips Japanese imports to the crowd. What if they had made the wrong choice?

I was certainly in no position to sneer at anybody's obsessive music-hoarding. I was the old pot calling the new kettle rusty. But I wondered if any of the kids, with their detailed lists of limited releases and special box sets and Bulgarian split EPs that they absolutely HAD TO BUY TODAY, would still feel the same way about these records in another ten years. When the Record Store Day–only special editions lost some of their special newness, and started gathering dust on their shelves, and got replaced with something else, something newer and more rare and collectible, would they forget? Or would it still be something they needed, literally needed to stay alive, like oxygen?

If it wasn't, well, then what was the fucking point? It was too early on a weekend, they should go home and crawl back into bed.

A homeless guy strolled past the line, carrying—inexplicably—a twelve-pack of paper towels. Seeing the unexpected crowd, he paused for a moment, stopped right in his tracks, and just stared at us, trying to figure out what we were doing, aimed toward a record store of all places. He looked at the store, and then the crowd, and then back at the store. His face contorted as he tried to make sense of what was happening.

"What are you guys, DJs?" he asked.

Nobody looked at him. They stared at their phones, or at their feet. I smiled, but I don't think he noticed.

"You're all damn fools," he said, getting legitimately upset. "This is not living. This is not living!"

So . . . the bump.

It was on M-22, the only road out of Northport—the town where I grew up—that would take you toward the rest of the world. If you lived up at the tippy-top of Michigan's little finger, and you wanted to get the hell out of there, you had to drive on M-22. And somewhere on the road between Peshawbestown, the Native American settlement, and Suttons Bay, the next big town south of Northport, was a stretch of road with a slight concave, like an asphalt bubble, that if you hit perfectly—going at, say, twenty or so miles over the speed limit—would cause your automobile to become momentarily airborne.

For an adult, with concerns about things like auto suspension and tire pressure and the resale value of your car, this wouldn't be all that fun. But for a kid between the ages of seven and ten, who has decided that *The Dukes of Hazzard* was not just a great television program but also a lifestyle choice, the pavement irregularity was proof, to paraphrase Ben Franklin, that God loves us and wants us to be happy.

Our parents ignored us when we shouted from the backseat, "The bump! The bump! Speed up for the bump!" They did the exact opposite, slowing down so that the car's tires didn't rattle menacingly, and it didn't levitate alarmingly for several seconds before making a hard landing. But sometimes, you might be getting a ride from a friend's older brother, and you'd be squeezed in the back of an old Chevelle—oh man, I can still visualize it so clearly, those leather seats, sticky with cola and sweat, like an adhesive against your bare legs, trapping you like flies on a glue trap—and the brother could be coaxed, with very little chanting, to hit that bump in the road with just the right velocity.

"Faster," we'd yell from the backseat. "Faster! Faster!"

He wouldn't say anything, but we'd hear the growling engine, we'd feel the seats trembling under us. We'd hold on to each other, cling to the little silver ashtrays in the armrests, ready for liftoff. And then he'd hit it, and it was exhilarating. Sometimes we'd float, hovering in the air for lack of any seat belts holding us down, and hit our heads against the soft rooftop.

"Again!" we'd shout through tears of laughter. "Turn around and do it again!"

I don't know when they fixed it. It happened long after my family moved away. When we returned for visits, I didn't notice it at first. But driving on that familiar road, I had an uneasy feeling, something didn't seem right. It wasn't until many years later that I realized what was missing.

I eventually gave up on the Dave's Records line. The homeless guy with the paper towels had made a convincing argument. Having your life choices doubted by a guy without shoes didn't seem to bother any of the other Record Store Day patrons, but it got under my skin. I went looking for a more accessible venue.

Reckless was just as overcrowded. As was Logan Hardware and Laurie's Planet of Sound and Groovin High. I thought I'd enjoy the throngs of people who cared about the same things I did. Like being in the audience of a *Star Wars* sequel on opening night. But it felt more like being on a subway in rush hour.

I took the L to uptown, to the one place I could be reasonably sure wouldn't have much traffic. Shake Rattle & Read, a small storefront located a few doors from the Green Mill, a one-time haunt for Al Capone. (There are still bullet holes in one of the booths.) Not only was there no line, there were only three other people in the store. The only indication that today was special were the six multicolored balloons hanging near the entrance, and a handwritten sign reading 25% OFF ALL RECORD LPs!

Ric Addy was there, the legendary owner who I'd heard about from many a vinyl-loving friend. He was short and plump, with a gray goatee and a weathered leather jacket. He moved around the store, full of busywork, answering questions from customers. One young kid, who looked no older than twenty, asked about some exclusive Record Day Store–only release, and Ric looked at him like he'd just asked for child porn.

"I don't have any of that rare shit," he spat. "You sell maybe ten percent of it, and they won't buy the rest of it back from you. It's a racket. I want no part of it."

I wanted to stay here and live in this store and be around Ric every day and his delicious, wonderful grumpiness.

I started flipping, and it gave me a rush of excitement like I hadn't felt in months. Maybe it was because the front doors were propped open, and the warm spring breezes came rushing in, filling the small store with the sweet smells of a city waking up from winter. Maybe it was because the handful of customers weren't as panicky or pushy as I'd seen everywhere else. They would've been here even if Record Store Day didn't exist. I overheard them say things like, "At two dollars, you can't afford not to buy the Outfield," and I knew this was the only place in the universe I wanted to be.

Somewhere between the Ss and the U-V-Ws, my arm brushed against a guy as we reached for adjoining boxes. I mumbled an apology, but he took it as an excuse to strike up a conversation. He told me, apropos of nothing, that he was trying to replace an entire record collection.

"Say again?" I asked.

"Oh, you know how it is," he said. "Your brother steals all your records, sells 'em for drug money, and you spend the rest of your life trying to replace everything."

"Brother-in-law," a woman standing a few boxes away corrected him.

His wife wandered over to join him. She was carrying a stack of records almost an inch thick, which she dropped next to him with a surprisingly loud thud.

We continued flipping, and they both kept talking, weaving in and out of each other's sentences, telling me all the details that I hadn't actually asked for.

"My brother has light fingers," the wife explained. "He's cheap as hell."

"Of all the things to steal," the guy said, shaking his head. "Who steals records to buy drugs? Why not steal our TV? Or a laptop."

"He's set in his ways," the wife explained. "It's how he did it in the eighties, so it's all he knows."

The man was balding with a silver mustache and a tattoo on his left forearm of a bikini girl. The wife wore a red sweatsuit that made her look like a *Six Million Dollar Man* drag queen. While all three of us stared down at the boxes—our fingers flipping in such perfect symmetry that it almost sounded like crickets chirping—Silver Mustache told me about his regular summer job, as a Lollapalooza medic, which apparently involved mostly hanging out with Willie Nelson's son. His wife, who worked the night shift at a hotel where all the touring musicians stayed, had her own stories of meeting rock royalty.

"I had the Temptations stay with us when Richard Street was still in the band," she said. "I couldn't make the show, so they sang 'My Girl' a cappella to me in the lobby of the hotel."

"Tell him about Night Ranger," Silver Mustache said.

"Total assholes," she said. "Total assholes! The lead singer was, like, 'You have to put me in as a pseudonym.' And I was like, seriously, dude? Nobody is going to call here looking for you, okay? But Debbie Harry, she was a different story. A real sweetheart. Nice as can be."

Every few minutes, one of them would pull out a record and add it to the stack, which was growing into an unsteady mountain, ready to avalanche onto the floor.

"Are those all the records your brother stole?" I asked, pointing to the stack.

"Yep," he said. "I've almost found them all. I didn't have anything too obscure, so it's not that difficult."

"No, I mean the exact ones," I said. "Did you try to find the exact ones he took?"

They both laughed. "How the fuck would I do that?" Silver Mustache asked, sneering at me under his mustache. "Talk to my brother's drug dealer, find out what flea market he sold my records to? What a colossal waste of time."

I shrugged. "I could think of worse things to do."

Silver Mustache narrowed his eyes at me, growing suddenly cold. "You're not one of those first-pressing weirdos, are you?"

"Oh no, no, not at all," I said.

A smile returned to his face. "Good."

"I want the cracks and whistles."

"Yes! The cracks and whistles. That's what it's all about. This guy understands."

I reached over and looked through his pile. I could sense both of them stiffening, uncomfortable with my greedy hands picking through territory they had already claimed. There weren't any major surprises there. A few Springsteens, a few Zeppelins, some Yes and Rush and Deep Purple and Steely Dan and a whole lot of Skynyrd— exactly what you'd expect from a guy with a silver mustache and bikini girl tattoo who grew up in the seventies.

And then I saw it. I recognized it almost immediately. Which is weird, because I'd studied at least two dozen of the same record trying to decide if any of them might be mine. But this time, I just knew. It was like the moment I imagined in my head, of seeing my dad in the crowd at a Mardi Gras parade, with his handlebar mustache and a safari hat. But I know it's him. There's not a question in my mind.

KISS *Alive II*. This was it. This was the one. This was the copy owned by my brother during our youth. The one I'd borrowed too many times, forcing him to deface the front cover with a "HANDS OFF!!!" warning. The message was gone. But there was a smudge at the top, right around the K in KISS, where someone had clearly tried to wipe away an ink stain. They managed only to make it illegible, but not to disappear. Like an old tattoo of an ex-girlfriend's name, some bad decisions can't ever be expunged completely.

"Can I have this?" I asked.

Silver Mustache looked at me, like you might look at a stranger you just discovered standing naked in your living room.

"Why?" he said, his voice now devoid of all friendliness.

"I've just been looking for this for a while, and I'd really like it."

He glanced down at the record and then back at me. His hands dangled at his sides, like he was waiting to draw his gun for a duel.

"Is it rare or something?" he asked.

I tried to appear calm. "No, not rare especially," I said, forcing a laugh. "It's just something I'm nostalgic about, and I've been meaning to buy it, and, you know . . ."

He snatched it out of my hands and placed it back on his stack. "Sorry, man. Can't do it."

"I'll give you a hundred bucks," I said.

Our eyes locked in a showdown. His mustache twitched as he considered my offer.

"I don't know."

"Two hundred."

He looked at his wife, who was wide-eyed and unblinking, staring at me like I'd just pulled a knife on them. His mustache twitched again, and he ran a finger through it.

"Well," he finally said. "I'll tell you what I'll do . . ."

"Three hundred."

So much for not being one of those panicky Record Store Day assholes terrified of losing something rare.

Ric pushed past us with a baseball bat in his hand. He was chasing a homeless man, stinking of urine and booze, who had gotten into the store unnoticed.

"Get the fuck out of here, you fucking piece of shit," Ric screamed, his voice thundering with believable rage.

I didn't move. Didn't stop staring at Silver Mustache. I was not going to let this go.

"You come back in here again," Ric screamed out the front door, swinging the baseball bat like he was swatting flying monkeys out of the sky, "and I will fucking destroy you!"

"Deal," Silver Mustache said.

As I drove alone on that six-hour trip up to Michigan, I would occasionally reach over to the passenger seat and touch the KISS *Alive II*, the most expensive piece of music I've ever bought in my life. Maybe this was cosmic retribution for all the music I've stolen on the Internet in the last few years. But if you itemize it, it wasn't really that bad. There are twenty songs on KISS *Alive II*, so I basically paid fifteen dollars per song. Pricey, sure, but not highway robbery. If you want to be even more precise about it, I wasn't really buying the music at all but the album sleeve. So I paid three hundred dollars for what might be a now-illegible smudged-out threat from my pre-pubescent brother.

So fine, maybe that wasn't the smartest of financial investments. It's not valuable in any practical, real-world sense. But I don't regret anything.

This record is my talisman. It's the thing someone carries around because you think it's protecting you from evil or bad things. The logical part of your brain knows that it's horseshit. It's just a thing. It's not magical. It's not going to save you. But knowing it's there, being able to touch it whenever you feel uneasy, it makes you feel safe. Or at least safer.

It's stupid, and you know it's stupid, but you don't care.

I drove over the spot where the bump used to be. I waited for it, even though I knew it wouldn't come. And I was sad when the car didn't lurch forward, the shocks didn't protest angrily, I didn't feel the car lift into the air. But it was okay. It was less depressing this time.

Because I was bringing some bumps home again.

"Is he bleeding from his mouth?" my mom asked.

We were still sitting on the floor of Mark's bedroom, gazing up at the KISS poster. And I think she finally started to see it. How many years had she walked past it, or glanced up while tucking my brother in at night, and she'd never really noticed it? She got the general gist of it, but never paid attention to the details.

"He's always bleeding, Mom. That's kind of his thing."

"Well, I don't know." She shrugged. "You boys never explained this stuff to me."

"And you're only asking these questions now?"

"We didn't know!" she protested. "You convinced us they were nice guys."

"KISS?"

"Yeah. You were probably lying through your teeth. They were probably all on the LSD. It was such a racket. Every time you played those records, your father and I took a walk. It shook the whole house."

"You could have taken the records away from us," I said.

"We didn't want to be those kinds of parents," she said. "It's just music, it's not going to kill anybody."

We sat and looked at the poster again, and I wondered if it would be a good or bad idea to bring her downstairs right now and force her to listen to KISS *Alive II*. Really listen to it.

The front doorbell rang. It echoed through the empty house like a cavalry trumpet. My body stiffened. I wanted to hide somewhere, crawl into Mark's walk-in closet and turn out the lights.

"Do you think that's Mark?" my mom asked, beaming.

I didn't. I knew exactly who was waiting outside, bringing trouble to my doorstep.

Eleven

I know the right way to hold a record. You're supposed to cup it by the outer edges or center label. The less you actually touch, the better. All that oil on your hands is like acid to vinyl.

But the record I was currently holding—K-Tel's *Night Flight*—it really didn't matter what I was doing with my hands. Because the damage had already been done. There were fingerprints spanning three decades, from fingers crossing several generations—more than a few of them mine—and, from what I could tell, at least one paw print. They were like muddy footprints, roaming in every direction, crisscrossing, and sometimes getting into kicking brawls.

But surprisingly, there were no scratches. None that were visible anyway. If I took it out to the back lawn, gave it a prison bath with a garden hose, it would be as good as new. Of course, I wasn't going to do that. Those fingerprints were precious. There was a lot of history on one piece of synthetic plastic.

I knew this was my record. There wasn't a doubt in my mind. I didn't need to send it to a forensics lab, get the fingerprints analyzed. It had come from the crawl space in the home of Mike C.'s mother, who lived just a block away. It's been in there, fermenting, with all the other records that circulated around the neighborhood during those early years.

They're all here, splayed out on the very same kitchen table of my youth, in the same kitchen I haven't set foot in since I was just getting comfortable with the idea of having pubic hair.

I still hadn't decided if this was awesome or just really, really confusing.

There was more undeniable proof that this was indeed the same K-Tel's *Night Flight* I'd bought in 1982 at a Meijer in Traverse City, about thirty miles away from this kitchen: it had no sleeve. It was sleeveless! Not even a white inner sleeve. Which is exactly as I'd left it.

I'd bought the record first and foremost for "The Theme from *The Greatest American Hero* (Believe It or Not)." Side two, track one. By Joey Scarbury. I don't know if I actually would have liked the song if it wasn't for *The Greatest American Hero*, which at the time was my favorite thing on TV. The best thing to happen to television since Lee Majors got bionics.

At first, I only listened to the Scarbury song. Over and over and over again. It was my anthem. But sometimes, I wasn't so quick to scramble back to the record player when the "believe it or nots" started to fade away. I just let it keep playing. And I ended up getting an introduction to Al Jarreau and the Four Tops and Quincy Jones.

The exact opposite of every type of music I'd been programmed to love. But there was a sort of Stockholm syndrome that developed from hearing those songs so many times by circumstance. I've got a punk-rock heart, but I know all the lyrics to Juice Newton's "Angel of the Morning," and I can and will sing it loudly and passionately if the melody happens to drift into my ears.

Like all the records in our neighborhood, it became part of the communal lending library. It was everybody's property. My brother, or Mike, or any kids who had access to our home (which was never locked) could just come in and help themselves to our collection. And return the borrowed records, well, maybe never. A record could get passed on to another kid, and another kid, until you lost all track of who had it. Maybe you'd get it back in the rotation eventually, but that was always fleeting. Because you never knew when somebody was going to be like, "Ah, yeah, the *Greatest American Hero* song! I'm gonna borrow this for a few days, 'kay?"

So I got rid of the sleeve. It was too recognizable, with *Night Flight* in a 3-D silver font, like it was being shot at you with lasers. I ripped it up, threw it away. And then I hid the record in other, less desirable record sleeves. I bought a Lawrence Welk record, *Music for Polka Lovers*, at a yard sale, specifically to use as a disguise. I threw out the polka record and hid the *Night Flight* record inside.

They found it. Like they always did. No matter where I hid it, they found it. I had to chase it through the neighborhood, until I finally gave up or lost interest in *The Greatest American Hero*, whichever came first. (Probably the latter.)

Our neighborhood communal record lending library wasn't chaos. There were rules, which every member followed and respected. They were never written down, or explicitly stated out loud, but we all understood them. If my memory is to be believed, they were as follows:

Rule #1. Take as Many Records as You Can Haul Away, but Be Cool About It

This was not like the local library, where you were compelled to check out only as many books as you reasonably expected to read. If you could carry them out of the house without assistance, they were yours (at least temporarily).

When it came to records, it wasn't always the quality that mattered but the quantity. If you'd had a shitty week at school, or your parents were being asshats, or that girl you were briefly convinced might be the love of your life had made unnecessarily public proclamations that she found you repugnant, sometimes the only thing that would make it better was sitting alone in a dark bedroom and listening to every Lou Reed album sequentially. Or not. Maybe you just wanted to listen to *Transformer* over and over again, while looking at that creepy-ass cover—what was up with the Nosferatu whiteface?—and feeling sorry for yourself while bobbing your head along to romantic songs about urban blight that couldn't have had less to do with growing up in a town with the population of about six hundred, where the main export was cherries.

The point is, you took the records you thought you might need, not the records you knew you'd need.

If, however, you came to a person's home with a bag or suitcase, you were clearly being a greedy fuck, and possibly a thief. You took what you could carry, and nothing more. Ideally, you carried the records out of the previous owner's house like you were shoplifting—the goods perched between an arm and your side ribs, your hands casually hooked into your pockets, so it almost didn't appear like you were leaving with anything.

The trick was to act like you were stealing, despite the fact that you weren't stealing. You were taking what was legally yours to take, but you didn't want to be too obvious about it.

Rule #2. There Are No Firm Return Dates

Again, this wasn't a library. Nobody was stamping the record with a due date. There were no borrowing periods or return policies. The record or records stayed in your possession for as long as you needed them, or until somebody noticed that you had them and claimed them for himself.

That said, no attempts could be made to conceal your ownership of a record. It could not be hidden from view, either in a closet or under a bed, or anywhere you might otherwise keep pornographic contraband from discovery by your parents. If the record in question had a cover that could feasibly get you into trouble—like Black Sabbath's *Born Again*, with the devil baby, or Black Flag's *Family Man*, with the suicidal dad, or *Sticky Fingers*, with the obvious gigantic cock—it was acceptable to hide the record, as long as the other members of your loaning community were aware of this arrangement (e.g., "My mom still hasn't found that Dead Kennedys record, thank god").

Rule #3. Possession of Record Immediately Negates All Expectations of Reasonable Privacy

By taking a record home, you made yourself and your property, or your parents' property, entirely accessible to the entire record-sharing community. If, for instance, one of your peers decided that he really, really needed to hear that ABBA record *Super Trouper*, and he was well aware that it was in your bedroom, he could, without written or verbal consent, walk into your house, at any hour, and claim it.

This, in theory, was a fine idea. Unless you happened to be engaged in a private matter, involving you and . . . well, just you. There would be no warning knock. The door would simply swing open, and while you struggled to cover yourself and the intimate act you were in the middle of performing on yourself, your friend would simply stride in, pick up the ABBA record in question, and say, "Sorry, man. I've had 'The Winner Takes It All' in my head all day, and I had to hear it. Catch you later!"

It happened. And all you could do was pretend not to be mortified. If you wanted total autonomy over your possessions, you shouldn't have entered into a communal-living, hippie co-op, vinyl-sharing situation.

Rule #4. You Cannot Claim Sole Ownership of a Record, or Claim Political Asylum for an Album

Records were owned by the community, not by the individual. Suddenly deciding "I'm going to hang on to this for a while," or worse, insisting that it now belonged to you exclusively, was unacceptable and egregious, and would result in swift punishment and immediate excommunication from the record-sharing community.

Even if you personally paid for, say, *The Harder They Come* soundtrack or Springsteen's *Born to Run*, you didn't own it anymore. It was part of the collective. It belonged to everybody now. If you loved a record, then you had to set it free. You'd get to hear it again. It just didn't live with you anymore. It was a train hobo, and it traveled from town to town, only staying as long as it needed to, before jumping on the next boxcar, on its way to wherever. You can't domesticate a train hobo. You can't ask him to hang up his bindle and settle down for a life in one bedroom. What were you even thinking? Let it go, man. Let it go.

Rule #5. All Items Left in a Record Become the Property of the New Owner

Let's say, hypothetically, that you acquired (i.e., stole) a single card from a deck of nude playing cards— each featuring a different topless model—from the older brother of one of your peers. You stole this particular card because the woman on the back was breathtakingly beautiful, with breasts that you—okay fine, I—literally couldn't stop thinking about. Everything about them: the size, the areolas, the nipples. I mean seriously, those nipples. What was even happening with those nipples? They were each as big as my little toe, and looked like they had their own unique personalities. It was insane! I remember everything about her—she was brunette, she smiled without showing her teeth, and she represented the eight of clubs. As an adult, every time I play cards with somebody, and the eight of clubs comes up, I still think of those aesthetically exquisite nipples.

But I left her in a record. I remember the exact one. Because I left it there as part of an imagined game of cat and mouse with my parents. Like they cared. Like the moment I left the house, they were scouring every inch of my bedroom for nude paraphernalia. But I overthought it, went too deep into the psychology of where my parents would expect to uncover pseudo-porn. I imagined my dad throwing a record against a wall in frustration, shouting, "Dammit, I was sure it'd be in Blondie's *Parallel Lines*!"

If he'd just thought about it more analytically, he would have figured it out. Blondie? Like I'd be that stupid! Obviously, I hid it in Bob Dylan's *Blood on the Tracks*. Because that naked playing card wasn't about sex. It was about yearning. That's what my father had missed. It wasn't just the nipples. It was what the nipples, and the rest of her, represented. She was an idea of femininity that felt achingly unattainable to me. When I looked at that playing card, the lyric in my head wasn't "I'm gonna get ya, get ya, get ya, get ya." It was Dylan singing, "I'm going out of my mind / With a pain that stops and starts / Like a corkscrew to my heart."

But just because your parents don't find it doesn't mean somebody else won't. Like the next person who gets that copy of *Blood on the Tracks*. You don't realize it till it's gone, and by the time you catch up with the record, that nude playing card is long gone. And nobody's saying anything. "I didn't see any card," they'll tell you with exaggerated shrugs. You have no legal recourse. You left it there. Finders keepers. The same law that protects a previous owner from all culpability if a record sleeve should happen to contain pubes or an old Band-Aid also protects the new owner from liability if he's accused of absconding with whatever treasures are discovered in said album sleeve while in his possession.

The law is the law.

"You might want to be careful with it," Mike C. told me, point-ing to the *Night Flight* I was gripping a bit too intensely. "It may have a little hantavirus on it."

I looked up from the record at Mike. I was still amazed to see him—not just in this kitchen, but at all. I hadn't set eyes on him since puberty. Now here he was in his forties, with a goatee, nicotine-stained fingers, and a smoky baritone voice. It was surreal.

"Are you serious?" I asked.

"No, I'm kidding," he said. "But it probably does though. When we pulled it out of the crawl space, it had a lot of dust on it, and what looked like rat feces."

I took a quick whiff of one of my hands. Yep, that was rat poop all right. Ah well, there are worse ways to die.

"We might be out of luck, boys." Mike pulled the record player's plug from yet another outlet. "Either this thing doesn't work any-more, or somebody turned off the power."

I tried to mask my concern, but I was a little freaked out. I hadn't brought a backup. I'd left the Crosley at home. Bob had scared me straight with all his talk of "the right record player," and how you needed to listen to those old records on something cheap and plas-tic, like we did when we were younger. So I went searching for some-thing that looked like the record player that had been in my family for the first two decades of my life—the sole record player we could afford, and one that was shared with everybody. I studied photos on eBay and tried to find something that looked even vaguely familiar.

I finally tracked it down. It wasn't a Fisher-Price or Tele-tone at all. It was a 1974 General Electric V638h three-speed automatic rec-ord player. I confirmed it with my brother, who responded in an e-mail with far more exclamation points than I've ever seen him use. Everything about it made our collective hearts beat a little faster—

the way it wasn't quite big enough to comfortably fit a normal-size LP, or how it folded into a beige suitcase, in case you wanted to bring your music to a picnic or a hootenanny, or the various knobs on the side, including one mysteriously labeled REJ, which neither my brother or I touched in eighteen years, just in case it did something terrible.

I paid twenty-five dollars for it on eBay. And I hadn't bothered to give it a test run before driving up here. What was the worst that could happen?

"I don't know, man," John J. said, looking up from the KISS *Alive II* he'd been studying for the last ten minutes. "You sure this is ours?"

I was annoyed by his insistence on calling it "ours," even though I was well aware that technically it was more his than anybody's. It had originated from him and eventually became community property, as all our records did, but in my memory, it was always in Mark's bedroom or mine. When Mark had written "HANDS OFF!!!" he was referring to me. Not everybody in our music-sharing community. Specifically me. I felt very territorial about this, and the issue was not open for discussion.

Also, holy shit, John J. was in our house.

Well, what used to be our house. But he was here, sitting right across from me. The last time he was between these walls, we were both preteens. He was wearing a Misfits T-shirt and combat boots, he already had a criminal record, and he asked if he could smoke a cigarette in my bedroom.

At forty, he wasn't all that different from how I imagined he'd be as an adult. He was wearing an Iron Maiden T-shirt and combat boots, he was divorced with kids, and he showed up with a six-pack of beer. He was also completely gray, and from what I gathered during our brief conversation thus far, he worked for a slot machine company.

I leaned over the table and pointed to the inky smudge on the KISS *Alive II* cover. "Right there," I said. "That's where my brother wrote on it."

John wasn't convinced. "You sure?" he asked. "That's not really legible."

"But that's where it was," I insisted.

"Yeah. But it doesn't look like anything. How do you know it was Mark? Maybe somebody else wrote on it."

"On that exact spot?"

"That's not possible?"

I huffed loudly. "I've been doing this for a while. I've seen a lot of KISS *Alive II*s. I haven't come across a single copy with writing over that specific spot on the K. You show me another KISS *Alive II* where somebody has written over the *K*, and I'll concede that maybe I'm not right about this."

Oh fuck, I totally threw away three hundred dollars, didn't I?

"Got it!" Mike announced. The GE record player slowly whirred to life, creaky as an old carousel.

"Nice," John said, raising a beer in salute. "What'd you do?"

"It wasn't on," Mike said.

"So where do we start?" John asked, looking at the records in front of us.

I had no idea. And not because I wanted to hear it all. I did, of course. But that wasn't the difficult part. What we had in front of us, essentially, were a bunch of records that contained two perfectly separate worlds: music that represented who we wanted to be, and music that maybe represented what we kinda actually were.

On one side, we had Iggy Pop, and the Clash, and the New York Dolls, and the Replacements, and the Ramones, and the Dead Kennedys, and Devo, and Blondie, and Social Distortion, and Elvis Costello. On the other side, we had the Bangles, and Mr. Mister, and

Rick Springfield, and Gordon Lightfoot, and ABBA, and Captain & Tennille, and Kenny Rogers, and Barry Manilow, and a K-Tel collection featuring a song from a TV show about a clumsy superhero.

I loved all of it. But only some of it I'd admit to.

I looked down at the record in my hands, I'm holding the K-Tel so tightly, my thumbs are leaving little craters in the vinyl. I know what I want to hear. I want to hear the "Believe It or Not" song. I want to play that shit loud. Really belt out the "Should have been somebody eeeeeelse" part, with a little bit of Zack de la Rocha venom. That would be pretty awesome right about now.

But the other part of me, the part that wanted to be cool, knew that it was a much better idea to say, "Let's play the fucking Misfits." Because that's what you say to the cool guy in the combat boots who wants to smoke in your house. Because he's going to snarl-smile at you and say, "Fuck yeah!" And you'll feel cool by association.

"Let's play the fucking Misfits," I said.

John snarl-smiled and saluted me with rock horns. "Fuck yeah." Told you.

Before John, there was no music. Oh sure, we had the occasional ABBA album. Or the Jim Croce or Fleetwood Mac records we borrowed from our parents' bedroom. But nothing that was uniquely ours. That made you feel like you were listening to something that could change your DNA in some fundamental way.

Mike told the story again, about how he'd gone over to John's house to play his Atari 2600, because he was the only kid in the entire state (as far as we knew) who owned an Atari 2600. Mike noticed the KISS *Alive II* album on John's bedroom floor, and he was like, "Cool bloody guy," about the photo of Gene Simmons drooling blood in the rain. John insisted that Mike borrow and listen to the record, although Mike had no interest. But he pretended to like KISS, so John would continue to let him use his Atari 2600.

"You wanted to play the Atari games, you had to pretend to like KISS," Mike said.

"That's true," John said. "That was part of the deal."

Mike dropped the needle on the Misfits' *Beware* EP. And almost immediately, I wanted it to stop. Not just that, I wanted to take the record out into the backyard and bury it. Make sure it couldn't find us anymore. Because Glenn Danzig, holy crap, what was he going on about? I understood about as much as I did when I first heard it in the early eighties, and the most I could figure out is that all of Danzig's mirrors are black, and he really, really wanted to stab me. I wasn't comfortable with any of this information.

When John first loaned this record to me, when I was barely thirteen, I listened to the entire thing in one sitting, and decided it was the single most terrifying thing I'd ever heard. I took it down to the basement in our house and left it there. I knew I couldn't throw it out, because John would be wanting it back at some point. But I didn't want it near me. I sure as hell didn't want it in the same room where I slept. Just having the physical object that contained these songs anywhere near my sleeping body seemed like a terrible idea.

"There was this record player in first grade," John said, nodding his head along to the music. "And Mike and your brother used to bring in ABBA. Which the teacher thought was pretty terrific."

"She was into it," Mike agreed.

"But then I brought in my sister's Ted Nugent *Double Live Gonzo!* and played it. And that is not a good record for school. He started dropping the f-bomb. And the teacher just went off."

"I think she wasn't a fan of 'Wang Dang Sweet Poontang.'" Mike laughed.

"Yeah, my mom got a call on that one. I had no idea. I just brought it in 'cause it looked cool. The album looked cool."

The more we talked, I almost forgot that the Misfits were scary.

They became a perfect soundtrack to talking about how John became our musical black sheep, the perfect fall guy for our every attempt to dip our toe in unfamiliar water. Every time we got caught with something we shouldn't have—a record with profanity, some *Mad* magazines, a deck of playing cards with nude women on the backs—it was always easier to blame John than take accountability. He already had a bad reputation, it's not like we were smearing his good name. It was like pinning another murder on a serial killer with an already double-digit body count.

"So are we going to eat some Boo Berry or what?" John said, leaping out of his seat and toward the refrigerator.

My stomach lurched. I'd been planning on this all along, but now that it was actually happening, I was having second thoughts.

"It's got high fructose corn syrup," Mike said, reading the box's label.

"This is good for you, dude," John said, sliding a finger under the cardboard top and slowly breaking open the seal. "It's probably better for you than the cereal they make today. There was nothing genetically modified back then."

"I'm feeling nervous about this," I admitted.

"Don't be silly," John scoffed. "If you had a bottle of wine from 1978, wouldn't you drink it?"

"Well . . ."

"Of course you'd drink it."

He tilted the box toward a chipped Pottery Barn blue bowl, and the little blue clumps, like cerulean rat turds, tumbled out, hitting the porcelain with a surprisingly metallic thud. It sounded like pennies dumped into an aluminum trash can.

We stared as John poured two more identical bowls, and then passed the carton of milk, which he'd purchased just a few hours earlier from a gas station.

The first thing I noticed was the smell. I could feel the microscopic particles hit my nostrils, little jagged asteroids of crystal happiness. I recognized it like I recognized the Old Spice cologne on my dad's old ties. It brought me back to when we were nine years old, and Boo Berry was our crystal meth. Our heroin chic.

I remember once, Mark and Mike and I went camping. Not in the forest just a half mile from our home. In the backyard. It felt like a bold step toward manhood and independence. Among our supplies, we brought a box of Boo Berry, and ate the entire thing in one sitting. We didn't even need milk, we just passed it around and ate handfuls dry, straight from the box. Our little bodies weren't accustomed to sugar—our moms didn't even allow us to drink soda except on special occasions—so we went a touch crazy. Our eyes got as big as saucers, and our heartbeats pounded like a drum circle. We talked without pauses, excited about everything and laughing hysterically at the slightest hint of humor.

At some point, and this may've been the sugar talking, somebody had the bright idea that we should go streaking. Being particularly suggestible, our brains stained as blue as our tongues, we immediately ripped off our clothes and went running through the forest, howling at the moon like we were something to be feared. We felt huge and indestructible.

The next day, Mike got a call from the elderly widow who lived down the block. I don't even remember her name anymore. I don't think I ever exchanged more than a nod with her. She was the house everyone avoided on Halloween just out of instinct. Even from a distance, it smelled like rheumatism ointment. So Mike was understandably rattled even before she explained the reason for her call. She told him that she'd seen us last night. Not when we were gorging on Boo Berry. The other part. Apparently the darkness hadn't shaded our nudity quite as well as we'd hoped. Mike tried to apologize, but she assured him that we had nothing to worry about. She had no intention of telling our parents. In fact, if we ever decided to go streaking again, she welcomed us to do so a little closer to her house, maybe even in the backyard, where we'd have more privacy.

"It'd be our secret," she told him.

I poured milk into my bowl and submerged a spoon. I had to do this. This was communion. One little bite wouldn't kill me, right?

It tasted . . . dusty.

We sat quietly and crunched. Somebody had put on a Stooges record, and Iggy was bemoaning how "There's nothing in my dreams / Just some ugly memories," which seemed like an entirely appropriate serenade for this late afternoon brunch.

"Isn't your brother coming?" John asked, his jaw moving in odd ways, like he was trying to swallow a tiny squirrel that wanted very much to escape.

"Yeah, he'll be here," I said, swallowing hard, trying not to think about what I was ingesting. The distraction of eating thirty-six-year-old cereal made it easier to conceal my disappointment about my brother. I was pretty sure Mark wouldn't be showing up.

"It's like a blueberry White Russian," John said, now on his third spoonful.

"It tastes exactly the same," Mike said, his teeth already bright blue.

"No, no, it tastes better," John said. "I feel like it's making me stronger."

Maybe my brother wasn't coming because he already knew something that hadn't sunk in for me until I had a mouthful of mealy cereal. I was a fool. This wasn't harmless nostalgia. I was an old man spinning his wheels. Quite suddenly, I was acutely aware that everything I'd done over the past year had been a colossal waste of time.

"What are you trying to accomplish?" Mark had yelled at me just a few hours earlier. "What's the end goal here?"

I had no fucking clue. All I really had to show for it was some bloody cuticles and a bunch of antiques, some of which I might have owned when I was a teenager. It's a fucking miracle that I found any of it. But so what? How was I not just chasing shadows, or worse, a dog chasing its tail? A mangy, chewed-up tail that wouldn't be all that satisfying even if he ever managed to catch it.

I wanted to burst into tears, but I was pretty sure it'd just come out a sugary dark blue.

"This is good," John said, looking down at his bowl. "I really needed this."

"Old cereal?" Mike asked.

"No, the whole thing. The records, being in this house, hanging out with you guys again. It's been a rough couple of days."

He told us about his uncle—a man who'd been closer to him than his own dad, who'd supported John through some of the roughest periods of his life—and now he was dead, after a long battle with cancer. His body just gave up, John told us. "The chemo did him in. If he hadn't done the chemo, he might've had three good years instead of two horrible years with his body pumped full of chemicals."

It all came gushing out, like John had stepped into a confessional after holding on to these bad thoughts for too long. Any echoes of the punk kid I remembered had evaporated in an instant, and he suddenly seemed very fragile, very human.

"He reminded me of your dad," John said, as he replaced the Stooges with some Blondie.

"Really?" I said. I wasn't sure yet if that was supposed to be a good thing.

"Your dad was a great guy," John said. "He was really kind to me when things went south."

"Yeah," Mike agreed. "Such a smart, funny, radical dude."

"Radical?" This was fascinating and entirely new information. "Radical how?"

They told me stories about my dad that didn't seem real. They were like medieval folk tales, something shirtless gladiators would brag about after a few flagons of mead. My dad, if their stories were to be believed, was a badass in a clerical collar, somebody willing to get into philosophical smackdowns with sneering atheists, and leave them just enough to chew on to give them a 3:00 a.m. sit-up-in-bed existential crisis. Also, if you were young and confused and angry, he invariably knew the exact thing to say to make you think twice about your self-hatred.

Stories of my dad evolved into stories about Mike's dad, who'd died a few years earlier. I'd only ever known his father as a volunteer fireman and Boy Scout leader, and apparently those were the first things mentioned in his obituary. And then we talked of John's real dad, a highway patrolman in California—like Erik Estrada in *CHiPS!*—who John had lived with briefly after his parents' divorce, which is where he discovered punk music, which he brought back to us in our sleepy little northern Michigan town.

Between the three of us, we had zero fathers or father figures. They were all dead or gone. We could feel the crispness of their absence all over again, like they'd only just disappeared and we were still grappling with the idea that they wouldn't be coming back.

I still hadn't really accepted it. And the way Mike and John talked about their dads, it was obvious they hadn't either. We all knew our dads were supposed to die someday, but that was supposed to happen in the future, when we were old. Well, older. Older than this. It was too soon. We needed more time. Life was happening too fast. We needed everything to slow the fuck down for a minute.

Sometimes life feels like I'm one of those goddamn millennials grazing on YouTube videos. It's always, "Next, next, next, okay what's next? That was funny. Next video!" Calm the hell down, junior! What is the rush? Can't we all just take a deep breath and not be in such a hurry to get into the next thing?

We talked about our dead dads over the course of a Dinosaur Jr. record (*You're Living all over Me*), a U2 record (*Achtung Baby*), two songs into a Dead Kennedys record (*Frankenchrist*—until we realized it wasn't really conducive to conversation), and the first side of David Bowie's *Heroes*. It wasn't maudlin. Maybe it was the music, which was too loud and forced us to talk even louder to be heard over it. It never occurred to us to turn it down. Bowie was ostensibly singing about lovers in Berlin, but we were only hearing what we wanted to hear. To our ears, it was about three guys in their forties, sitting around a mostly empty kitchen, eating Boo Berry.

"We're nothing," Bowie wailed. "And nothing will help us."

Amen.

And then the phone rang.

Not our cell phones, which were sitting on the kitchen table. No, the ringing was coming from the wall-mounted rotary phone, in jaundice white, with its well-worn finger wheel, helpful sets of letters next to each number, and a self-identifying phone number, written in faded typewriter ink on the middle faceplate and protected under plastic.

The phone was just out of reach, in the empty space between the table and the door leading out into the dining room and the rest of the house. It was exactly where it'd always been—the only thing here that was entirely unchanged since we left. It was even the same model 554 phone—the one both sets of my grandparents had owned, and my parents owned during the entirety of my childhood.

The record ended, but nobody got up to change it. We let the needle tread water, stuck in the dead wax, grumbling static about being ignored. We were too transfixed by the phone, which kept ringing, and ringing. It rang so hard, it rattled the house. I don't remember it being that loud, but I suppose it must've been. Before we all started carrying miniature phones around with us, there was just the one phone in the kitchen—the command center for all outside communication. It had to be loud enough to get the attention of anyone in a four-bedroom, three-story house. If you were doing laundry down in the basement or taking a shit in the upstairs bathroom, it had to find you, and let you know, SOMEBODY WANTS TO TALK TO YOU! COME HERE, COME HERE BEFORE THEY GO AWAY!

We stared at the phone as it kept ringing, practically shouting at us, and we steadfastly refused to answer it. We didn't need to discuss it. We were on the same page. If you're in an empty house, with no legal occupants or furniture (other than what you dragged in with you), and you've consumed two six-packs of beer while talking about your respective dead dads and how much you'd like to hear their voices again, and a phone that shouldn't still be connected—is by all accounts a useless piece of antique machinery that has been abandoned and rendered incapable of achieving a dial tone—starts ringing out of the blue, under no circumstance is it a good idea to pick up that receiver.

Unless, you know, you want to pee yourself.

So we waited. And the phone kept ringing, and we scrunched up our faces in that way you would if you were thinking, "Please stop ringing. Please stop ringing. This is freaking me out. Please stop. Just stop. I'm begging you to stop. One more ring, and I'm running out of here screaming."

It finally stopped. And then there was just the silence, and the gentle crackling of a stylus waiting to be plucked from vinyl purgatory.

Nobody knew what to do next.

And then John figured it out.

"Holy shit, man, is this *Night Flight*?"

I looked over, and John was holding the greasy black K-Tel disk.

"It is," I told him. "But I think we lost the cover somewhere."

"Did that record ever even have a cover?" Mike asked.

"You know what's weird?" John said. "I remember borrowing records from you guys, or borrowing back my own records, and every now and then this thing would be inside."

"What?" I said, trying to appear like this was new information to me. "That's crazy."

"I used to get so pissed off. But then I was like, 'All right, fine, let's listen to it.' And it kind of rocks."

"You want to listen to it now?" I asked.

"*Greatest American Hero*?" Mike said.

"Hell to the yes," John shouted.

Maybe my brother had been right after all when he'd flippantly suggested that I was hosting a séance. It hadn't started out that way, but it was now abundantly clear to all of us that there were ghosts in this kitchen. The ringing phantom phone just drove that point home. And it was kind of spooky at first. But now that they'd given up trying to make a long-distance call from the afterlife and seemed content with just hanging out and being chill, we could all enjoy ourselves again.

> Look at what's happened to me
> I can't believe it myself

I could see the goose bumps on John's arms. They were the size of silver dollars. But I'm not sure if it's because he thought his dead uncle was here—that he could practically feel his uncle's breath in the air, warm and alive and present—or because singing along to "Believe

It or Not" at the top of your lungs while making rock horns is way more satisfying than pretending not to be terrified by the Misfits.

Mark arrived, with his wife, Amy, in tow, right around the time we'd finished our second bowl of Boo Berry. At first, they just stood at the door, peeking inside but not fully committing to actually coming inside.

John and Mike jumped up to greet them, and exchanged stiff handshakes with Mark.

"You're looking good, man," John said.

"Yeah, yeah, you too," Mark responded.

Their eyes darted across each other, trying to decide if this was what they'd expected. Did Mark look like a billionaire? And did John embody everything Mark had anticipated from a convicted criminal? In both cases, they seemed disappointed. Shouldn't Mark have been wearing a monocle and top hat? And John, shockingly, had neither a cat burglar mask nor a burlap sack.

Mark and Amy finally felt safe enough to venture inside, and I gave them a tour of the old house. We went from room to room, trying to trace the furniture with our fingers, debating where end tables had been located, and the color of vases that now only existed in our memories. Mark reminded me that the guest room—which I remembered as Dad's office—was intended for a baby Cambodian girl that our parents had intended on adopting but for whatever reason never did.

With the others trailing behind us, Mark and I scoured the house for evidence of us. We'd find scratches on doorframes and baseboards that had somehow escaped the revisionist history of paint, and we'd lean in for a closer look. We'd trace our fingers around the edges, like anthropologists trying to piece together the clues of an ancient civilization. And then we'd debate its origins, sometimes fiercely. Were those ragged holes on my bedroom door from the sliding bolt lock I'd installed to keep my brother out? I thought the placement was all off, but Mark was convinced. We gave every battle scar a rich backstory, assigning them more narrative weight than they probably deserved.

I showed Mark his bedroom, and waited for him to be delighted by the KISS poster—the exact KISS poster he'd slept under for most of his prepubescence. But it didn't even get a smile out of him. He acknowledged that it was the right poster, but was unconvinced with the placement.

"I think it was on the other wall," he said, his arms crossed tightly.

"No, no, you're confused. It wouldn't make any sense over there. It was right above your bed's headboard."

"Yes, which was over there."

He was far more interested in the record player, the General Electric V638h that was our introduction to music, the "cheap piece of shit" (Mark's words) that helped us learn all the words to Bob McGrath songs, and gave us chills every time those trumpets blared the opening on the *Star Wars* soundtrack, and made us believe that grown men in Kabuki makeup and codpieces singing about important topics—rocking all night, partying every day, and Detroit being a city in which both of those activities could be voraciously enjoyed—had access to information about life that would be useful to us, so we better listen up.

I carried the record player up to the second floor and put it in the hallway between our two bedrooms, right where we had always kept it. When Mark caught a glimpse of it, his entire face lit up. All of that cynicism and reluctance, it just instantly disappeared, or at least got momentarily shoved into a dark corner.

He dropped to the floor and started examining the GE, feeling his way across the familiar knobs and switches.

"How have these knobs not broken off?" he asked. "They couldn't be made of cheaper plastic."

"Well, I guess whoever owned this never actually used it."

"It's just terrible," Mark said, with a huge smile. "It's amazingly bad craftsmanship. How did we keep ours for so long?"

"I think it was taped together near the end," I said. "Also, I don't think we had a choice."

Mark looked at it, unblinking and amazed, laughing at its stone-age technology, but still showing very real tenderness for it. This was a man worth millions. And here he was on all fours in an empty house, transfixed by a plastic record player barely worth twenty-five bucks on eBay.

While Mark and I huddled around the record player on the floor, Amy stood patiently by the stairs, and the other guys wandered in and out of rooms, discussing what they remembered, and how the current dimensions of the house betrayed those memories.

"How'd you fit the drum set in here?" John asked from my old bedroom.

John was perplexed. The room wasn't big enough for all the things he remembered being in there. Like the drum set, which I never actually owned. Or the two desks I'd apparently lined up like the wrap-around command console on the starship *Enterprise*—which, again, wasn't true.

"Are you thinking of somebody else?" I asked him.

"No, no, you had drums in here, I'm sure of it," he insisted.

"I really didn't."

"You absolutely did! Don't tell me you didn't have drums."

"I didn't have drums."

"Come on! I remember you were always beating us up, roughing up the younger kids. And then you'd come back here and start drumming. It always sounded like 'Moby Dick' coming from your room."

Nothing about this was accurate.

It was curious hearing John's many misconceptions about me, especially given all of my misconceptions about him. As we listened to records and talked, the details of his criminal history eventually came out. His crimes were directly related to his addictions, which involved obsessive playing of video games like *Ms. Pac-Man*, *Asteroids*, and *Pole Position*.

"I remember sneaking into the bars," John told us. "And finally my mom would come in and pull me by my hair and say, 'You are not supposed to be in here!'"

To pay for his habit, he broke into a Laundromat in search of quarters. "I was maybe ten years old," he said. "Teddy B. and I, we hit the same Laundromat three times. That's how we got busted."

"You got arrested for stealing quarters to play *Ms. Pac-Man*?" I asked.

"I'd do all sorts of crazy shit to get my arcade money. Remember when there was a pizzeria downtown, in the Pier 1 building? They used to keep stacks and stacks of soda. And the place was run by teenagers who'd always be in the back, goofing off. So, Teddy and I would walk in and take off with six or seven cases of pop. We were just pouring the pop into the lake. We couldn't drink it all, but we needed the empty cans to get the recycling deposit."

I'd paid too much credence to the whispered warnings from our parents. I imagined switchblades and bathtubs full of heroin and cash stuffed into tube socks, not a ten-year-old emptying stolen soda into Lake Michigan so he could play *Asteroids*.

We played more music, and more secrets started to spill out. We listened to the Smiths' *Meat Is Murder*, and John told us about his divorce, and then his second divorce, and how he's been drunk and depressed for a few years, but now he was doing much better and had a great relationship with his thirteen-year-old twin daughters. We listened to *Led Zeppelin III*, and Mike told us about how he'd been a professional carpenter for a few years, but then he'd been involved in a major accident in which he almost died—he showed us the scars to prove it—and now he's focusing on photography, which is what he really wants to do with his life. And then we talked about how we used to listen to the Smiths and Led Zeppelin without ever noticing that they existed in starkly different fictional sexual universes. On one side you had "My dick is like a gladiator sword," and on the other it was, "But no one will ever love me!" It was a miracle these records didn't make us bipolar.

We listened to the *Star Wars* soundtrack, which as always immediately got less interesting after the first three minutes. But then Amy, Mark's wife, made us listen to "Attack of the Sand People" because she'd done a *Star Wars*–themed dance recital when she was seven and this was her song.

"I was a dancing Tusken Raider," she said. "I had shredded fringes on my arms, and a costume with lots of bandages."

"How does a Sand Person dance?" I asked.

"There was a lot of sashaying."

We asked her for an impromptu "Attack of the Sand People" dance recital. She agreed, and it was one of the greatest things I've ever seen another human being do. There was much laughing and applauding.

At some point, I passed KISS *Alive II*—the double LP that had cost me three hundred dollars—over to Mark. "This look familiar?" I asked.

He looked at it blankly. "Yeah," he said.

"See that handwriting in the corner?" I said, pointing toward the smudge over the *K*. "Ringing any bells?"

"Nope."

"Well then, let's give it a listen and see if it does anything for you," I said, letting one of the black disks slide out of the gatefold into my hand. I flipped it around with my fingers, twisting it like a magician doing a card trick, and let it slide weightlessly onto the turntable.

I'd been practicing for that moment. I'd rehearsed it a few times. This was a big deal. It was my chance to share something with Mark, something that we'd lost, that I'd found and brought back to us. It wasn't just an old record. There was something in these grooves—these specific grooves—that was part of who we were. And by playing it again, I don't know . . . something would happen.

The ways in which we'd drifted apart, the years that had turned us into different people, without any common ground, that wouldn't matter anymore. That distance between us would just disappear. In just a few songs, everything would change, and we'd be back to the way we were, when we weren't strangers, when he was my pain-in-the-ass little brother who lived across the hall from me, and I knew everything about him.

"Holy crap, is that ABBA?"

I had barely dropped the needle when he'd stopped paying attention altogether and moved on to something else.

Mark had uncovered ABBA's *Greatest Hits*. Not the more well-known *Gold*, from 1992. The 1976 *Greatest Hits* from Atlantic. With the cover art of both couples sitting on park benches, Benny and Frida making out like horny teenagers, and Björn and Agnetha trapped in a loveless marriage (and yes, I seriously remember their names).

"We have to listen to this," Mark insisted.

There was no point in arguing. I put on the record, and as it played, we passed around the sleeve so everybody could offer their analysis.

"What's remarkable is that the band didn't fall apart," John remarked. "They clearly hate each other, but they're like, 'We can't break up ABBA.'"

"They're professionals," Mike offered.

"They're running a business," Mark said.

"But they're honest," Mike added. "So their honesty comes through in their art."

We were as full of shit in our forties as we were in our preteens.

The music didn't do anything for me. But the album cover, that was a different matter. When it was passed to me, I looked at it and felt an instant calm wash over me. Our parents never got divorced, but they'd come close. There were arguments, and whispered threats, and that constant anxiety that hung in the air that everything was falling apart, and you were never really sure if it was happening or if it was all in your imagination. After overhearing things I wasn't supposed to overhear, I'd come up to my bedroom and look at the ABBA *Greatest Hits* album and feel a little more normal.

"This is ours," Mark proclaimed, somewhere around the middle of "Ring Ring."

"Totally," John agreed.

"No, I mean this record. This one. This one here." He held up the gatefold and shook it for emphasis.

"There's a good chance," John said.

"I'm convinced of it! I'm convinced!"

"I'm agreeing with you."

Mark turned to the rest of us, daring us with his eyes to challenge him. "This is it," he said.

It was enough. It wasn't the KISS epiphany I'd been hoping for, but it was enough. To see Mark get so passionate, so vehemently certain that he'd found a record from our past. Maybe it was, maybe it wasn't. Like John said, there was a good chance, since it'd come from the crawl space/rat lavatory just a block away. Hearing the songs on that specific record, from the crappy speakers of a crappy GE record player exactly like the one we'd grown up with, had set off a chain reaction in his brain. It awakened something in him. And suddenly the guy who thought this whole thing was insane, who never really understood why I'd want to listen to old records in an empty house, was ready to get into a fistfight with anybody who didn't believe he was hearing something authentic.

We kept listening to records for at least another few hours. Some of it I hated; some of it I loved. Sometimes I wasn't even listening. It was enough just to be in the same room with these people, with the records as our anchor. There were no earth-shattering moments. There were just a lot of stories, and a few crazy theories. Like Mike's insistence that there was an exposed nipple on the inner sleeve of *The Magic of ABBA*. He showed it to us, explained how Agnetha's nipple was on full display if we just looked closely enough.

"Don't question me on this," Mike said. "I've studied it from every possible angle. I spent almost my entire childhood looking at it. That's a nipple."

"It's way too high on her chest to be a nipple," Mark protested. "Unless you think it's a superfluous nipple."

"That's a nip. Dude! Dude! That's exactly where a nipple would be."

"No, no, no," I shouted back at him. "You know nothing about nipple placement!" I lifted up my shirt, showing him where nipples should be. "A nipple is down here."

"That doesn't count," Mike scoffed. "You're a guy."

"Amy, will you back me up on this?" I handed her the record. "There's no way that's a nipple, right?"

"That could be a nipple." Amy laughed.

Something about this felt familiar. Not the specific topics of conversation—although it was hardly the first (and maybe not the last) time this gathering of people would be discussing nipples. No, what was familiar was the tenor of our laughter. The way it all felt so natural, and so unforced. The ease of it reminded me of what I missed so much about smoking cigarettes. It's not the nicotine necessarily. What I really miss is the community that comes with smoking. The gathering of outcasts looking for a shared safe place for a cigarette, and you're there with people you know, or just as likely people you've just met, and you start talking to them, because what the hell else are you going to do, other than stare at the burning ember. Over the span of that cigarette, you learn things about them that you don't take the time to learn with anyone else. Smokers have a bond that nonsmokers could never understand. It's why, to this day, when I'm out driving and I see a bunch of smokers huddled outside a building, puffing away in the cold and laughing at some private joke, I look at them and think, "Those are my people." Even if I never touch another cigarette for the rest of my life, those will always be my people.

This was it. This was that feeling again. We'd created a little bubble of intimacy, something larger than just family or old friendships. It'd be done the moment the record was over. But right here, right now, these were my people.

Twelve

I lay on the floor, because there was no place else to sit.

The chairs and the table had been taken away, carted off by my mom and her husband like they were stagehands. John and Mike had left too, and taken with them a trash bag full of the afternoon's props—the crushed beer cans and empty wine bottles and surprisingly foraged box of Boo Berry. We'd taken down the posters up in the otherwise empty bedrooms, even chipped away the Scotch tape remnants with our fingernails, and made sure we'd removed every last piece of evidence that we'd been here.

The only thing they left were the records. Everything Mike had dug out of his mom's crawl space, and the records John had found in his basement, they told me to keep it all.

"We'll get it back the next time we see you," they said.

Those were 1978 rules. It was a system that worked much better when we all lived a few blocks away from each other. It would prove to be a little more difficult to orchestrate a vinyl lending library when all the members lived in different states. But I didn't protest. I thanked them for their generosity, and promised to take good care of their records until I returned them, which we both knew wouldn't be happening. We'd had our fun with this trip down memory lane, but if I didn't call dibs on these musty records, they'd be going straight back to being rat urinals.

When everybody had gone, it was just me and the records and the beige GE record player, which was now hot to the touch from almost six hours of constant use (clearly not something it was designed for). I took everything into the living room and made a little campsite, spread out the records like they were rose petals on a honeymoon suite bed. And then just let my limbs flail.

I reached out blindly, grabbing the first record I could get my fingers around, and pulled it up to my face.

Paul's Boutique. Okay then, let's do some Beasties.

I put the needle down on "Shake Your Rump." Because that's the song I needed to hear. It reminded me of one of my favorite formative experiences as a music listener: not having the faintest idea what the lyrics in a song were, and yet singing along anyway.

Like a pen I'm pimpin', Lab-ra-dor eatin' shrimp in
Well you bustin' my bank, you're pissin' for a living

No?

I remembered when Adam Yauch died, and it happened to fall on my mom's birthday. I called her, and she could tell I was sad, and when I explained why, she was even more confused.

"I didn't know you listened to rap," she said.

"Well no, not all the time," I told her. "But the Beastie Boys were different."

"Because they're white?"

"No, no, no!" I barked a little too defensively. "They're from Brooklyn," I reminded her, like that somehow canceled out their whiteness. "And they're Jewish."

I don't know where I was going with that.

I rehashed every cliché I'd read in countless magazine and online obituaries and tributes. The Beasties represented a New York City that didn't exist anymore. A New York that, coincidentally, I never actually experienced firsthand. The closest I got to the eighties New York rap and hard-core scene was walking around Lincoln Mall in the south suburbs of Chicago listening to "Shake Your Rump" on a Walkman. I didn't feel stupid about this. My nostalgia for things that had nothing to do with me is pretty common. I'm not the only one who owns a CBGB T-shirt despite never having set foot in CBGB.

"They don't make records like that anymore," I told my mom. Which isn't even an original observation. I'm sure every living person on the entire planet—all seven billion of them—has thought the same thing (or will when they reach a certain age). The only thing more common to the human experience than "they don't make records like that anymore" is "I don't want to die" and "I've never loved somebody as much as I loved (person they haven't seen naked in twenty years)."

I wasn't suggesting that music should sound exactly like it did in 1989. That would be insane. They don't make medicine or fingerless gloves like they did in 1989 either, and our world is better for it. When I said, "They don't make records like that anymore," what I was really saying is "I'm not twenty like I was when I was twenty anymore."

Thinking about Adam Yauch made me remember that I'm also going to die someday. Which isn't something I like to be reminded of. Yauch died when he was forty-seven, and I'm rapidly approaching that age. And Yauch took considerably better care of himself. He had a pretty nice BMI, an active lifestyle, and he was into meditation. Me, I spend a good deal of time sitting and drinking and feeling anxious.

I lay there and listened to my heartbeat, and wondered if the heart attack I always knew was coming would happen now, while I was lying on this floor, listening to a Beastie Boys record. Is this how it'd end? Is this how they'd find me? I wonder if that would be comforting for my family—that I'd died surrounded by things I loved, rather than in some office under fluorescent lights, angry at how I'd gotten there. Or would Charlie obsess over it? Would he hold on to this *Paul's Boutique* and listen to it too many times, wondering what his dad had been thinking at the end, why these particular songs made his heart finally stop?

You think about these things. My dad died while eating an egg salad sandwich, and I've dissected that sandwich more times than I care to admit. It became a metaphor for loss. And an egg salad sandwich doesn't even come with lyrics! There are no lines to read between, no musical themes to deconstruct, to ponder what they meant in your father's final minutes. It's just an egg salad sandwich! If I died here, I'd be setting up my son for a lifetime of overanalyzing the Beastie Boys, trying to understand why he'd been robbed of his dad.

And then there's the funeral to consider. What music will they be playing? Given the circumstances, they'll probably choose from among the records I died with. And there are a lot of great choices here. The Replacements, Lou Reed, the Stooges, any of them would make for an amazing funeral soundtrack. But there were also a few Kenny Rogers records in there. And some ABBA. Jesus Christ, what if my mom put on ABBA? Well, of course she would. She'd take one look at the blood-splattered *Let It Be*, like something Jackson Pollock had painted with his own plasma, and say, "Oh no, we can't play this. We have guests coming from out of town. Let's pick something everybody can enjoy." And that's how I'd leave this mortal coil rocking out to "Fernando."

Side one of *Paul's Boutique* was over. The needle waited for me to do something, purring for attention. But I ignored it.

I closed my eyes and listened to the house. It was still vibrating. I could still hear the music echoing through the halls. My mom liked the carpeting. She thought it was an improvement. "So much warmer," she said. Warmer? Maybe the temperature was warmer, but the character was gone. It was like people who thought a FLAC file was superior to an old vinyl forty-five that'd been gathering dust in the attic of a rarely visited record store. Only a fool would think this. Art is not more meaningful when it's shinier.

But the carpeting could only cover up so much. The floorboards still creaked if you listened hard enough. You could still hear echoes in the walls. You could hear music still pulsating through the house's old beams like a tuning fork. You could hear tiny footsteps running down the hall, giggles reverberating as someone small and fast runs closer and closer . . .

Wait, what?

My son burst into the room, jumped into the air like David Lee Roth being excited about Panama. His hair was long, messy, and blond, his clothes like something from a Brooklyn thrift store, and he smiled in the big, unironic way I'd forgotten how to do anymore. He was simultaneously the coolest person I knew and the happiest, which were two things I didn't realize could coexist so easily.

"Daddy," he shouted, running over to me and doing a belly flop into my arms. "Are you still listening to records?"

"I am," I told him, pulling him into a bear hug. "I'm glad you're here."

"Everybody left?" Kelly asked, peeking into the room.

I knew they were coming. She told me they'd be driving up later, joining me after I did what I needed to do. But seeing her face, holding my son in my arms, it was still a relief. Like coming up for air in the ocean.

"They left a while ago," I said. "Come on in, sit down, make yourself at home."

She tiptoed inside, looking around like there was something to see besides empty walls and high ceilings. "This is bigger than I imagined," she said.

"Well, there's no furniture," I said. "Shove a couch in here and it's a little different."

She brushed some records aside with her foot, clearing a spot, and sat down next to me. Charlie had already gotten up and was running around the room, leaping from record to record like he was hopping on rocks to cross a river.

"Charlie, don't, those are very special to Daddy," Kelly said.

"No, it's okay," I whispered to her. "Charlie, it's fine. If you see anything in there you want to listen to, let me know."

I went looking through the pile nearest me, flipping through to find the perfect soundtrack for this reunion.

"It's okay, we don't need any music," she said.

"Of course we need music," I insisted. "Blondie? Kenny Rogers? Lady's choice."

"Can you just leave it alone for a minute? You've been listening to music all day. How about we just have a quiet moment together?"

This was a long-standing disagreement between us. I felt that every room feels empty without music. I instinctively want to fill it with sound. But my wife likes music only occasionally, like when she wants to actively listen to it. She'll say things like, "Can we turn that down so we can finish this conversation without yelling?" Or "I can't hear myself think, can we please turn that off?" That's always seemed weird to me. I can't hear myself think without music.

"Talking Heads! That's what we need."

I dropped the needle onto side two of *Remain in Light*, letting "Once in a Lifetime" put everything we were feeling into perfect context.

*And you may find yourself in a beautiful house, with a
        beautiful wife*
And you may ask yourself, Well, how did I get here?

Charlie started dancing, as he always does when we put on music. And he instinctively went into the David-Byrne-in-a-huge-suit moves. Despite never having seen the video, he just knew. He felt the rhythmic shrugging in his bones.

"So how did it go?" she asked.

I just smiled. "It went well," I said.

Actually, it had gone considerably better than "well." My ears were still ringing from the glorious racket of familiar melodies. My stomach was aching from laughing with my brother, harder than we ever had since prepubescence. I actually cried out of ecstatic joy. I didn't think that was possible. I cried like I guess people do at soul churches, when they're clutching Bibles and praising Jesus.

But I went with "well," because explaining all of that would have taken too many adjectives, and would have sounded like hyperbole. Like so many of life's meaningful moments—the ones you still talk about years later and you feel amazed and grateful that they actually happened to you—you'll never be able to capture exactly what it felt like to be there.

"That's nice," Kelly said, squeezing my hand. "So why do you still seem so sad?"

I pretended to be surprised. "I'm not sad," I insisted.

"You look sad."

"No, I'm just tired," I said. "The day took it out of me."

We lay on the floor and stared up at the ceiling. Somewhere upstairs, Charlie was exploring, his feet pitter-pattering across the floors like a mouse.

She was right, of course. Like she's usually right. I was sad. Because there was a finality to this. Already the day was fading in my memory, becoming past tense. I'd have to leave the house eventually, take the records and the record player and leave the key on the kitchen floor, like I'd promised. And then tomorrow, another family would move in, and they'd bring all their stuff with them. They'd shove couches and mattresses into rooms, and put things on the walls that weren't KISS posters, and start acting like they owned the joint.

Kelly and Charlie and I, we'd drive back to Chicago in the morning. Back to an apartment that needed to be packed. Because we were moving soon too. I'd said yes to the *Men's Health* job. In another month, we'd be living in Pennsylvania. In a town called Macungie, which sounded like the medical name for a skin abscess. I'd be getting up every morning, putting on slacks and a tie and a sensible shirt with buttons, and I'd go to an office that paid me an adult salary. On my commute to work, I'd sing along to Harry Chapin's "Cat's in the Cradle" and try not to cry.

It would get easier with time. Of course it would. Eventually, what felt foreign and weird would just be the way our lives were now. And we'd have a house with a basement and a garage and a yard that Charlie could run in. That's not a bad trade for having to show up at an office and wear pants occasionally.

Life was changing. It was a good thing. A step forward. I just wasn't ready for it yet.

I wanted to stay here. Or keep looking for records. But it was over. I knew it. I was done. At the end of the line. There were no more record stores to scour. No more basements to dig through, or old friends to track down, or milk crates trapped in crawl spaces to be uncovered.

I mean sure, there were a few leads I hadn't explored. An old high school buddy who I'd exchanged records with (and also porn mags) during our teens was now living in Hawaii, on a military base, with his wife and two teenage sons. There was a .00001 percent chance he still had my copy of *Exile on Main St.*, which I'd lent him in 1987 and never got back. But he was a born-again Christian and a devout Republican and gun advocate. I'm not sure I wanted to slog through that conversation in the off chance that maybe he'd let me go through the boxes in his garage.

Besides, I had found enough. I'd started a quest in which coming up empty-handed was a foregone conclusion. But somehow, inexplicably, I'd found some old treasures. I had a Bon Jovi *Slippery When Wet* covered in dried swamp mud, a stolen *Let it Bleed* with a boot footprint on the vinyl, a KISS *Alive II* that cost me three hundred dollars, a box of my dad's old country records that smelled like mothballs and mildew, a Guns N' Roses *Appetite for Destruction* with my (alleged) initials written on the front, and a Replacements *Let It Be* splattered with my own blood.

Kelly was sitting next to the record player, gently turning over *Remain in Light* like it was something pristine and fragile, and not just an unloved antique that'd spent the last three decades smooshed into a box with some old shoes and *TV Guide*s. She dropped the needle onto the first track, and waited for those first familiar notes.

A smile crept over her face, and she closed her eyes and breathed in, like the record had released something fragrant into the air.

Charlie bounded down the stairs, laughing wildly, and leaped into the room like a clumsy ballerina. He wasn't wearing clothes. Just his Batman underwear.

"Charlie, where are your pants?" Kelly asked.

He gestured toward the ceiling. "Somewhere up there." Then, his shoulders began to move, slowly at first and then increasing in speed, a rhythmic shrug, his head bobbing along to the music.

"Daddy, what is this?"

"Talking Heads," I said.

"I love it!"

These types of emotional proclamations weren't uncommon for him. He made up his mind fast and decisively. If he loved something, he'd know it more or less immediately. And the same for the things he hated. (Lettuce had never had a fighting chance.)

He burst into a joyful dance, moving his body in every direction at once. I've always adored the way he dances, without any self-consciousness and with total abandon. He dances like Michael Jackson would have if he'd had too many wine coolers and completely forgot his choreography.

"This is my favorite!" he shouted, diving between us as he attempted another complicated move. "This is my jam!"

"I thought Elvis Costello was your jam."

His brow furrowed. "No, that's not my jam anymore. This is my jam!"

"Okay," I said, laughing. "Duly noted. This is your jam."

"It's my jam and I love it and it's the only thing I want to hear forever and ever!" he shouted.

Kelly got up to dance with him, but I sat there, watching the two people I love more than anything else dance in my childhood living room, while listening to music that I'd never paid all that much attention to in the eighties with fresh ears.

The feeling returns whenever we close our eyes
Lifting my head, looking around inside

Charlie's smile was so big, and so perfect and so pure, I wanted to capture it and wrap it up and hide it somewhere, so it couldn't ever be ruined by the cynical, sneering world. But I probably wouldn't have done it even if I could. Because nothing good in this world ever stays in mint condition. And if it does, you're doing it wrong.

A few scratches—deep, irrevocable scratches that stay there forever—aren't a bad thing.

When we got home, I was going to take Charlie to a record store. And I was going to pay attention to him this time. We'd buy everything they had by Talking Heads. Because that was his new jam, and a dude's new jam has to be respected. But I'd also coax him into wandering the aisles, let him pull out some records and see if anything caught his eye. If he ended up with a pile of Roxy Music, I wouldn't be like, "Yeah, don't be fooled by the arty covers." That was not my decision to make for him. He needed to make his own mistakes, take his own chances, choose his own jams.

And what the hell, as long as I was there, maybe I'd take a chance on something new. Pick out a record based on nothing but the coolness of a band's name and some trippy album art. It's been a long time since I jumped into the abyss and hoped for the best.

I think I'm finally ready to see what that feels like again.

Acknowledgments

This book wouldn't exist without two people. First, there's Mike Ayers, my former editor at MTV Hive—may it rest in Internet peace—who pushed me to write new things every week even when I wasn't in the mood, which resulted in a lot of questionable stories—including, if memory serves, columns about plaster cast vaginas and an interview with seven David Bowie impersonators—but eventually caused me to come up with the concept for this book. I'm forever indebted to you, Mike. Also, I think MTV Hive still owes me three hundred dollars. Would you mind looking into that?

The other reason this book exists is because of my editor, Becky Cole, who believed in it from the beginning, when there wasn't much there but a really insane premise. She's guided me through several incarnations, shaping and molding this story with a gentle but surgical precision. I've worked with a lot of editors in my time, but rarely have I felt this protected and challenged, which are two things that rarely coexist peacefully. I remember being in her office in New York, going over the first round of edits and having a picnic on her desk with sandwiches she'd bought from some deli down the street, and thinking, "This woman is my Gandalf."

I owe a debt of gratitude to Dan Mandel, my agent for almost two decades, who has continued to believe and fight for me even when there was no compelling reason to do so. I hope I live to ninety, just so I can write his obituary for *The New York Times*, and be one of those writers who waxes nostalgic about how Dan changed my life.

I'm endlessly grateful for my mom—who has supported and encouraged me long after when most parents would've said, "You're on your own, kid"—and my brother, Mark, who is legitimately one of the funniest people I've ever known. There are few things in this life as satisfying as making him laugh. Mark is the only person who's ever knocked out one of my teeth with one punch, and the only guy who made me feel fearless about my writing when I needed it the most. And I'm not just saying that because he can have me "disappeared" and sent to a Turkish prison with the cash he has in his wallet at any given moment.

Thanks to the Wednesday night Edgewater Lounge drinking collective—Ryan, Jeff, Mike, ET, Brad, Carl, and Jeremy—who were my sounding board back when this idea was just a vague, stupid notion. We spent many an evening discussing this book, long before it became a book, over way too many beers, at a bar we never realized didn't actually have a liquor license. The Edgewater Lounge is dead; long live the Edgewater Lounge!

Thanks to the people I dragged to record stores—T. J. Shanoff, Brian and Liz, and I'm sure others I'm not remembering—who tolerated and sometimes encouraged my worst vinyl instincts. Thanks to my many magazine editors, who shaped me like a literary Frankenstein's monster. Without Stephen Randall, Jon Kelly, Michael Hogan, Julian Sancton, Frank DiGiacomo, Adam Campbell, Paul Schrodt, Bill Phillips, Peter Moore, and Willy Staley, I would be a formless, shapeless, word-vomiting blob.

Thanks to the buildings where I wrote most of this book—like Metropolis Coffee Company in Chicago, in which I'm two card punches away from getting a free coffee; my family's cottage in Omena, Michigan; and the Sayre Mansion in Bethlehem, Pennsylvania, which I'm pretty sure is haunted. Seriously, I'm like 99 percent sure I was in a haunted room while finishing the last chapter of this book. I distinctly heard the giggling of a girl under my bed, which I later learned was probably a ghost from the nineteenth century who, according to one of the innkeepers, was known to tickle the toes of visitors. That did not happen to me, thankfully, because I would have literally crapped my pants in fear.

Thanks to Questlove, who put me on this journey, even if it was unintentional. Thanks to Bob Diener, Rob Harless, Heather Godbout, and Alan Hunter, who were in many ways the backbone of this book. And thanks to my old friend John Swanson, who always reminded me to "Keep typing, Dorothy." Thanks for the motivation, John. Now go fuck yourself.

Above all, thanks to Kelly and Charlie, my wife and son, who sacrificed so much so that I could write this thing. There were too many nights and weekends (and months, if we're being honest) when I had to disappear because of this book, and you both never wavered in your support. Except for that one time Charlie told me, teary-eyed, "I hate Daddy's book!" Which I completely understood. I kind of hated my book at that point too. I would have much rather been playing dinosaur-robots with you, like I'd promised. But I did this instead. You've both been more patient with me than I probably deserved, and unconditionally supportive in ways I can't begin to repay you for. If this book doesn't suck, it's because of you. Everything that I am, everything that I'm trying to be, is because of you.